International Dimensions of

Human Resource Management

SECOND EDITION

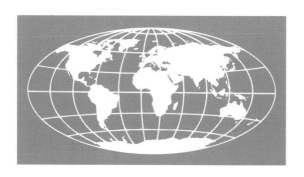

Peter J. Dowling
University of Tasmania, Austr

Randall S. Schuler
New York University

Denice E. Welch
Monash University, Australia

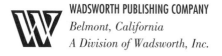

D1051595

THE WADSWORTH INTERNATIONAL DIMENSIONS OF BUSINESS SERIES
David A. Ricks—*Series Consulting Editor*

WADSWORTH PUBLISHING COMPANY
Belmont, California
A Division of Wadsworth, Inc.

Business Publisher: Larry Alexander
Editorial Assistant: Joan Paterson
Production Editor: Anne Draus, Scratchgravel Publishing Services
Print Buyer: Randy Hurst
Permissions Editor: Peggy Meehan
Cover/Interior Designer: Julie Gecha
Copy Editor: Stephanie Prescott
Compositor: Scratchgravel Publishing Services
Printer: Edwards Brothers

International Thomson Publishing
The trademark ITP is used under license.

Printed in the United States of America
5 6 7 8 9 10—98 97

Library of Congress Cataloging-in-Publication Data

Dowling, Peter.
    International dimensions of human resource management. — 2nd ed.
 / Peter J. Dowling, Randall S. Schuler, Denice E. Welch.
     p. cm.
    Includes bibliographical references and index.
    ISBN 0-534-21366-9
    1.   International business enterprises—Personnel management.
I. Schuler, Randall S. II. Welch, Denice E. III. Title.
IV. Title: Human resource management.
HF5549.D627   1993
658.3—dc20   93-11499

International Dimensions of

Human Resource Management

Series Foreword

Prior to World War II, the number of firms involved in foreign direct investment was relatively small. Although several U.S. companies were obtaining raw materials from other countries, most firms were interested only in the U.S. market. This situation changed, however, during the 1950s—especially after the creation of the European Economic Community. Since that time, there has been a rapid expansion in international business activity.

The majority of the world's large corporations now perform an increasing proportion of their business activities outside their home countries. For many of these companies, international business returns over one-half of their profits, and it is becoming more and more common for a typical corporation to earn at least one-fourth of its profits through international business involvement. In fact, it is now rather rare for any large firm not to be a participant in the world of international business.

International business is of great importance in most countries, and that importance continues to grow. To meet the demand for increased knowledge in this area, business schools are attempting to add international dimensions to their curricula. Faculty members are becoming more interested in teaching a greater variety of international business courses and are striving to add international dimensions to other courses. Students, aware of the increasing probability that they will be employed by firms engaged in international business activities, are seeking knowledge of the problem-solving techniques unique to international business. As the American Assembly of Collegiate Schools of Business has observed, however, there is a shortage of available information. Most business textbooks do not adequately consider the international dimensions of business, and much of the supplemental material is disjointed, overly narrow, or otherwise inadequate in the classroom.

This series has been developed to overcome such problems. The books are written by some of the most respected authors in the various areas of international business. Each author is extremely well known in the Academy of International Business and in his or her other professional academies. They possess an outstanding knowledge of their own subject matter and a talent for explaining it.

These books, in which the authors have identified the most important international aspects of their fields, have been written in a format that facilitates their use as supplemental material in business school courses. For the most part, the material is presented by topic in approximately the same order and manner as it is covered in basic business textbooks. Therefore, as each topic is covered in the course, material is easily supplemented with the corresponding chapter in the series book.

The Wadsworth International Dimensions of Business Series offers a unique and much needed opportunity to bring international dimensions of business into the classroom. The series has been developed by leaders in the field after years of discussion and careful consideration, and the timely encouragement and support provided by the Wadsworth staff on this project. I am proud to be associated with this series and highly recommend it to you.

David A. Ricks
Consulting Editor to the Wadsworth
    International Dimensions of Business Series
Vice President, Academic Affairs,
    American Graduate School of International
    Management

Preface

The globalization of business is having a significant impact on human resource management. The integration of European markets and of North American markets, along with the rapid growth of the Asia-Pacific region, is heightening this impact tremendously. It is more imperative than ever for organizations to engage in human resource management on an international scale. Decisions have to be made concerning (1) the numbers and proportions of host-country nationals, third-country nationals, and expatriates in staffing plants and offices all over the world; (2) where and how to recruit these individuals and how to compensate them for their performance; and (3) whether human resource practices will be uniform across all locations or will be tailored to each location. While sometimes these decisions are partially answered by the strategy and structure decisions made by the organization, there still remains a great deal of latitude in the design of the final package of international human resource management practices.

This second edition of *International Dimensions of Human Resource Management* touches upon human resource practices in many of the countries of the world. The primary focus of the book, however, is on the choices of international human resource management practices that confront multinational enterprises and some factors to consider in making those choices.

The book has been organized into eight chapters, one appendix, and a glossary. Chapter 1 begins with a description of international human resource management and what differentiates it from domestic human resource management. Chapter 2 examines the organizational context of international HRM, including the impact of the strategy and structure of multinational enterprises (MNEs) on those aspects. Recruitment and selection of international employees is the focus of Chapter 3, with particular attention given to expatriates and the process of repatriation. Chapter 4 identifies the issues and choices in international performance appraisal, and Chapter 5 discusses the dimensions of international training and development. Chapter 6 covers the many issues and dimensions of international compensation and includes numerous comparisons of pay practices across nations. Chapter 7 reveals the complexities and differences in labor relations when operating as an MNE. Chapter 8 examines future directions and theoretical developments in international HRM. The appendix raises a number of thorny and challenging research issues in international human resource management, while the extensive glossary presents and defines approximately 250 terms that are unique to this evolving field.

The chapters vary in length and depth of coverage. To a large extent, this variation is a reflection of the progress made in some areas in the three years between editions. Chapter 3, especially, on selection and recruitment, reflects such progress. Readers who are familiar with the first edition will recognize that Chapter 8 is entirely new, indicating the rapid developments in the international HRM field, in both management practices and theoretical approaches.

AACSB and Course Design

This book can be used in a variety of ways:

- As the main text in a course in international HRM. We would recommend *Readings and Cases in International Human Resource Management* by Mark Mendenhall and Gary Oddou as an excellent supplement.

- As one of several texts in a comparative management or international management course, in combination, for example, with *International Dimensions of Organizational Behavior* by Nancy Adler and/or *International Dimensions of Management* by Arvind Phatak.

- As a supplement to a traditional introductory HRM course to bring an international dimension into the course and satisfy AACSB requirements.

Acknowledgments

Because our intent was to prepare a book that is useful for students and practitioners alike, we sought the input of both managers practicing international human resource management and academics teaching and researching international human resource management. We are grateful for the assistance of Patti Digh and several members of the International Institute of the Society for Human Resource Management. Patrick Morgan, the 1989 president of the International Institute of the Society for Human Resource Management, Dan Kendall of The Associated Group, and Marcus Moore of New York University were particularly helpful in the preparation of a survey questionnaire that we sent out to the SHRM/I membership. The responses to this questionnaire proved to be invaluable in offering insights into and providing examples of international human resource management choices and dimensions. Patrick Morgan prepared the glossary that appears at the end of this book, which he developed in order to facilitate communication about the new and different ideas and concepts in international human resource management.

We have been assisted in the preparation of both the first and second editions by various colleagues around the world. Their comments, suggestions, and general feedback have been helpful to us in adding, deleting, and refining sections and chapters of the book. Colleagues include: Hugh Scullion of the University of Newcastle; Paul Sparrow and Cary Cooper of the Manchester Business School; Lynda Gratton and Nigel Nicholson at the London Business School; Chris Brewster and Shaun Tyson at the Cranfield Management School; Michael Poole at the Cardiff Business School; Paul Stonham at the European School of Management, Oxford; Jan Krulis-Randa and Bruno Staffelbach at the University of Zurich; Albert Stahli and Cornel Wietlisbach at the GSBA in Zurich; Shimon Dolan at the University of Montreal; Per Jenster and Jean Marie Hiltrop at IMD; Susan Schneider and Paul Evans at INSEAD; Jason Sedine at ISA/HEC; Stewart Black and David Ricks at Thunderbird; Mark Mendenhall at the University of Tennessee, Chattanooga; Helen De Cieri, Monash University; Yoram Zeira of Tel-Aviv University; Dan Ondrack, the University of Toronto; Cal Reynolds, ORC; Vladimir Pucik, Cornell University; Gary Florkowski, University of Pittsburgh; Moshe Banai, Baruch College; Steve Kobrin, Wharton School; Steve Barnett, York University; Stuart Youngblood, Texas Christian University; Christian Scholz, University of Saarlandes; Pat Joynt; Henley Management College; Reijo Luostarinen, Helsinki School of Economics & Business Administration; Mickey Kavanagh, SUNY, Albany; Wayne Cascio, University of Colorado, Denver; and Ricky Griffin, Texas A & M University.

We also gratefully acknowledge the support and encouragement of Bernard Barry, director of the Graduate School of Management at Monash

University. The capable secretarial assistance of Lillian Murphy at Monash University is also acknowledged and appreciated.

We thank Larry Alexander and Peggy Meehan at Wadsworth Publishing Company, Stephanie Prescott, and Anne Draus at Scratchgravel Publishing Services for working with us and getting the book into its final form. They did a great job with the book. We also owe our thanks to David Ricks for letting us be a part of the excellent series he has assembled with and for Wadsworth.

Finally, we wish to thank Fiona Dowling, Susan Jackson, and Lawrence Welch for their help and encouragement throughout this project.

Peter J. Dowling
Randall S. Schuler
Denice E. Welch

About the Authors

Peter J. Dowling (Ph.D., The Flinders University of South Australia) is Professor of Management at The Business School, University of Tasmania at Launceston. Previous teaching appointments include the University of Melbourne, Cornell University, and Monash University. He has also worked for the Postmaster-General's Department and the Australian Air Force. His current research interests are concerned with the cross-national transferability of HRM practices and the HR implications of European integration. Professor Dowling has co-authored two books (*Human Resource Management in Australia,* with Randall Schuler, John Smart, and Vandra Huber; and *People in Organizations: An Introduction to Organizational Behavior in Australia,* with Terence Mitchell, Boris Kabanoff, and James Larson). He has also written or co-authored over twenty-five journal articles and book chapters. He serves on the editorial board of *Human Resource Planning* and *International Journal of Human Resource Management* and is the editor of *Asia Pacific Journal of Human Resources.* He is a member of the Institute for International Human Resources of the Society for Human Resource Management, the Academy of Management, the Australian and New Zealand Academy of Management, the Academy of International Business, and the International Industrial Relations Association. Currently he is a vice president of the Australian Human Resources Institute.

Randall S. Schuler (Ph.D., Michigan State University) is Professor, Stern School of Business, New York University. His interests are international human resource management, personnel and human resource management, and the interface of competitive strategy and human resource management. He has authored and edited thirty books, has contributed over twenty chapters to reading books, and has published over eighty articles in professional journals and academic proceedings. His current research interests are concerned with studying how companies align their human resource practices with strategy. Presently, he is on the editorial boards of *International Journal of Human Resource Management, Human Resource Management, Academy of Management Review,* and several other journals. He is a fellow of the American Psychological Association. Professor Schuler has been on the faculties of the University of Maryland, Ohio State University, Pennsylvania State University, and Cleveland State University. He has also worked at the U. S. Office of Personnel Management in Washington, D.C., and has done extensive consulting and management development work in North America, Europe, and Australia.

Denice E. Welch (Ph.D., Monash University) is a Senior Lecturer in the Graduate School of Management at Monash University where she teaches International Business and International Strategic Management. She has also taught cross-cultural management and international HRM courses at the Norwegian School of Management, Oslo, Norway, and the Helsinki School of Economics and Business Administration, Finland, for a number of years. Her research interests include international HRM, cross-cultural management, and international strategic management. Dr. Welch's publications have appeared in a number of international journals and conference proceedings and have been concentrated in the area of international HRM and its strategic implications. She is a member of the Academy of International Business, the European International Business Association, and the Australian Human Resources Institute.

Contents

Chapter **FOUR**

Performance Appraisal   102

Chapter **FIVE**

Training and Development   121

International Dimensions of

Human Resource Management

Chapter ONE

Introduction and Overview

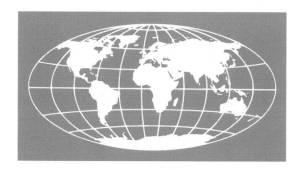

As more firms move outside their domestic borders into the dynamic world of international business, the globalization of world markets appears to be gaining momentum. The last two decades, in particular, have seen dramatic changes in international trade and business. Once-safe markets are now fierce battlegrounds where firms aggressively fight for market share against foreign and domestic competitors. It is, therefore, not surprising to find that a large proportion of the workforce in an increasing number of firms, regardless of their national origin, is located in other countries. For example,

- The Ford Motor Company has half its employees outside the United States.
- Philips has three-fourths of its employees working outside the Netherlands.

- More than half of Matsushita Electric's employees are outside Japan.
- Just over half of Ericsson's staff work outside Sweden.[1]

These trends are likely to continue throughout the 1990s as "employers will increasingly reach across borders to find the skills they need."[2] The multicultural workforce is beginning to slowly percolate to the top echelons of the management of multinationals: For example, Unilever headquarters staff includes 30 different nationalities, and DuPont appointed its first non-American president in 1991.

The globalization of business is forcing managers to grapple with complex issues as they seek to gain or sustain a competitive advantage. Faced with unprecedented levels of foreign competition at home and abroad, firms are beginning to recognize not only that international business is high on the list of priorities for top management but that finding and nurturing the human resources required to implement an international or global strategy is of critical importance. The effective management of human resources is essential, especially perhaps for small and medium firms, where international expansion places extra stress on limited resources, particularly people. As Duerr[3] points out,

> Virtually any type of international problem, in the final analysis, is either created by people or must be solved by people. Hence, having the right people in the right place at the right time emerges as the key to a company's international growth. If we are successful in solving that problem, I am confident we can cope with all others.

The objective of this book is to explore the implications that the process of internationalization has on the activities and policies of human resource management (HRM). In this first chapter, we shall define international HRM and examine the similarities and differences between domestic and international HRM.

DEFINING INTERNATIONAL HRM

Before we can offer a definition of international HRM, we should first define the general field of HRM. Typically, HRM refers to those functions undertaken by an organization to effectively utilize its human resources. These functions would include at least the following:

- Human resource planning
- Staffing

- Performance evaluation
- Training and development
- Compensation
- Labor relations
- Benefits and in-house communications

We can now consider the question of which functions change when HRM goes international. A paper by Morgan[4] on the development of international HRM is helpful in considering this question. He presents a model of international HRM (shown in Figure 1-1) that consists of three dimensions:

1. The three broad human resource functions of procurement, allocation, and utilization.

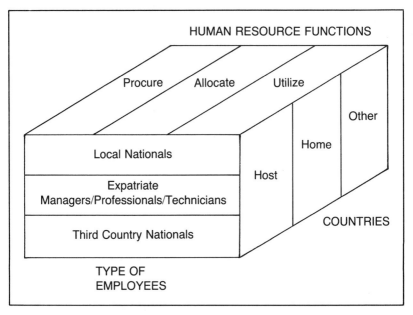

FIGURE 1-1   Model of International HRM

Source: P. V. Morgan, "International Human Resource Management: Fact or Fiction," *Personnel Administrator,* Vol. 31, No. 9 (1986), p. 44. Reprinted with permission from the Sept. 1986 issue of *Personnel Administrator* © 1986, The American Society for Personnel Administration, Alexandria, VA.

2. The three national or country categories involved in international HRM activities: (1) the host country where a subsidiary may be located, (2) the home country where an international company is headquartered, and (3) "other" countries that may be the source of labor or finance.

3. The three types of employees of an international enterprise: (1) local/host-country nationals (HCNs), (2) expatriates/parent-country nationals (PCNs), and (3) third-country nationals (TCNs). Thus, for example, IBM employs Australian residents (HCNs) in its Australian operations, often sends U.S. employees (PCNs) to Australia on assignment, and may send some of its Australian employees on an assignment to its Japanese operations (as TCNs).

Morgan defines international HRM as the interplay among these three dimensions—human resource functions, types of employees, and countries of operation. We can see that in broad terms international HRM involves the same functions as domestic HRM (the three broad functions listed by Morgan can be easily expanded into the six HR functions listed above). Domestic HRM, however, is involved with employees within only one national boundary.

The complexities of operating in different countries and employing different national categories of workers are the main factors that differentiate domestic and international HRM, rather than any major differences between the HRM functions performed. Many companies underestimate the complexities involved in international operations, and there is some evidence to suggest that business failures in the international arena may often be linked to poor management of human resources. Desatnick and Bennett[5] conducted a detailed case study of a large U.S. multinational company and concluded:

> The primary causes of failure in multinational ventures stem from a lack of understanding of the essential differences in managing human resources, at all levels, in foreign environments. Certain management philosophies and techniques have proved successful in the domestic environment: their application in a foreign environment too often leads to frustration, failure and underachievement. These "human" considerations are as important as the financial and marketing criteria upon which so many decisions to undertake multinational ventures depend.

Increasingly, domestic HRM is taking on some of the flavor of international HRM as it deals more and more with a multicultural workforce. Thus, some of the current focus of domestic HRM on issues of managing workforce diversity may prove to be beneficial to the practice of international HRM.

It is worthwhile examining in detail what is meant by the statement that international HRM is more complex than domestic HRM. Dowling[6] summarized the literature on similarities and differences between international and domestic HRM. He concluded that the factors that differentiated international from domestic HRM were:

- More functions and activities
- Broader perspective
- More involvement in employees' personal lives
- Changes in emphasis as the workforce mix of expatriates and locals varies
- Risk exposure
- More external influences

Each of these factors is discussed in detail on the following pages to illustrate its characteristics.

More Functions and Activities

To operate in an international environment, a human resources department must engage in a number of activities that would not be necessary in a domestic environment: *international taxation, international relocation and orientation, administrative services for expatriates, host government relations,* and *language translation services.*

- Expatriates are subject *international taxation,* and typically have both domestic and host-country tax liabilities. Therefore, tax equalization policies must be designed to ensure that there is no tax incentive or disincentive associated with any particular international assignment.[7] The administration of tax equalization policies is complicated by the wide variations in tax laws across host countries and by the possible time lag between the completion of an expatriate assignment and the settlement of domestic and international tax liabilities. In recognition of these difficulties, most large international companies retain the services of a major accounting firm for international taxation advice.

- *International relocation and orientation* involves arranging for predeparture training; providing immigration and travel details; providing housing, shopping, medical care, recreation, and schooling information; and finalizing compensation details such as delivery of salary overseas, determination of various overseas allowances, and taxation treatment. Many of these factors may be a source of anxiety for the expatriate and require considerable time and attention to successfully resolve potential problems—certainly much more time than would be involved in a domestic transfer/relocation.

- An international company also needs to provide *administrative services* for expatriates in the host countries in which it operates. Commenting on the need for these services for expatriates, a consultant in the area of international HRM has noted that "anyone who has ever been responsible for an administrative service such as company-provided housing knows the importance of this activity, where both employees and spouses often 'help' the human resource manager by clarifying a policy and procedure."[8] Providing administrative services can often be a time-consuming and complex activity because policies and procedures are not always clear cut and may conflict with local conditions. For example, ethical questions can arise when a practice that is legal and accepted in the host country may be at best unethical and at worst illegal in the parent country. A situation may arise in which a host country requires an AIDS test for a work permit for an employee whose parent company is headquartered in California, where employment-related AIDS testing is illegal. How does the HR manager deal with the employee who refuses an assignment and the overseas affiliate that issues the assignment? These issues add to the complexity of providing administrative services to expatriates.

- *Host-government relations* represent an important activity for a HR department, particularly in developing countries where work permits and other important certificates are often more easily obtained when a personal relationship exists between the relevant government officials and multinational enterprise (MNE) managers. Maintaining such relationships helps resolve potential problems that can be caused by ambiguous eligibility and/or compliance criteria for documentation such as work permits. American MNEs, however, must be careful in how they deal with relevant government officials. Payment or payment-in-kind such as lunches, dinners, and gifts may violate the Foreign Corrupt Practices Act.

- Provision of *language translation services* for internal and external personnel correspondence is an additional activity for an international HR department. Morgan[9] notes that if the HR department is the major user of language translation services, the role of this translation group is often expanded to provide translation services to all foreign operation departments within the company.

Broader Perspective

Domestic HR managers generally administer programs for a single national group of employees who are covered by a uniform compensation policy and taxed by one national government. Because international HR managers face the problem of designing and administering programs for more than one national group of employees (for example, PCN, HCN, and TCN employees who may work together at the regional headquarters of an overseas subsidiary), they need to take a more global view of issues. For example, a broader, more international perspective on expatriate benefits would endorse the view that all expatriate employees, regardless of nationality, should receive a foreign service or expatriate premium. Yet some international companies that routinely pay such premiums to their expatriate employees on overseas assignment (even if the assignments are to desirable locations) do not pay premiums to foreign nationals assigned to the home country of the company. Such a policy confirms HCN and TCN employees' belief that expatriate employees are given preferential treatment.[10] Complex equity issues arise when employees of various nationalities work together, and the resolution of these issues remains one of the major challenges in the international HRM field. (Equity issues with regard to compensation are discussed in Chapter 6.)

More Involvement in Employees' Lives

A greater degree of involvement in employees' personal lives is necessary for the selection, training, and effective management of expatriate employees and TCNs. The international HR department needs to ensure that the expatriate employee understands housing arrangements, health care, and all aspects of the compensation package provided for the assignment (cost-of-living allowances, premiums, taxes, and so on). Many international companies have an international personnel services branch that coordinates administration of the above programs and provides services for expatriate employees and TCNs such as handling their banking, investments, and home rental while on assignment and coordinating home visits and final repatriation.

In the domestic setting, the HR department's involvement with an employee's family is limited. It may, for example, provide company insurance programs. Or, if a domestic transfer is involved, the HR department may provide some assistance in relocating the employee and family. In the international setting, however, the HR department must be much more involved in order to provide the level of support required and will need to know more about the employee's personal life. For example, some governments require the presentation of a marriage certificate before granting a visa to an accompanying spouse. Thus, marital status can become an aspect of the selection process. As will be discussed in Chapter 3, the family situation may be included as a selection criterion, and family members may be included in predeparture training activities—especially cultural awareness programs—to improve chances of expatriate success. Apart from providing suitable housing and schooling in the assignment location, the HR department may also need to assist children left behind at boarding schools in the home country. In more remote or less hospitable assignment locations, the HR department may be required to develop, and even run, recreational programs. For a domestic assignment, most of these matters either would not arise or would be primarily the responsibility of the employee rather than the HR department.

Changes in Emphasis as the Workforce Mix of PCNs and HCNs Varies

As foreign operations mature, the emphases put on various human resource functions change. For example, as the need for expatriates declines and more trained locals become available, resources previously allocated to areas such as expatriate taxation, relocation, and orientation are transferred to activities such as local staff selection, training, and development. The last activity may require establishment of a program to bring high-potential local staff to corporate headquarters for developmental assignments. This need to change emphasis in personnel operations as a foreign subsidiary matures is clearly a factor that would broaden the responsibilities of functions such as human resource planning, staffing, compensation, and training and development.

Risk Exposure

Frequently, the human and financial consequences of failure in the international arena are more severe than in domestic business. For example, expatriate failure (the premature return of an expatriate from an international assignment) is a persistent, high-cost problem for international companies.[11] Direct costs (salary, training costs, and travel and relocation expenses) per failure to the parent company may be as high as three times the domestic salary plus relocation expenses, depending on currency exchange rates and location of assignment.[12] Indirect costs such as loss of market share and damage to overseas customer relationships may be considerable.[13] The topic of expatriate failure rates is discussed in more detail in Chapter 3.

Another aspect of risk exposure that is relevant to international HRM is terrorism. Most major multinational companies must now consider this factor when planning international meetings and assignments. It is estimated that MNEs spend 1 to 2 percent of their revenues on protection against terrorism. Terrorism has also clearly had an effect on the way in which employees assess potential international assignment locations.[14] The HR department may also need to devise emergency evacuation procedures for highly volatile assignment locations. The invasion of Kuwait and the ensuing Gulf War in 1991 is an example of a recent situation in which employees were at risk.

More External Influences

The major external factors that influence international HRM are the type of government, the state of the economy, and the generally accepted practices of doing business in each of the various host countries in which the business enterprise operates. A host government can, for example, dictate hiring procedures, as was the case in the late 1970s in Malaysia. The government introduced a requirement that foreign firms comply with what became known as the "30:30:30 Rule," which required that 30 percent of employees be indigenous Malay, 30 percent Chinese Malays, and 30 percent Indian Malays, at all levels of the organization. Monthly statistics had to be forwarded to the relevant government department.

In developed countries, labor is more expensive and better organized than in less-developed countries, and governments require compliance with guidelines on issues such as labor relations, taxation, and health and safety. These factors shape the activities of the international

HR manager to a considerable extent. In less-developed countries, labor tends to be cheaper and less organized, and government regulation is less pervasive, so these factors take less time. The HR manager must spend more time, however, learning and interpreting the local ways of doing business and the general code of conduct regarding activities such as bribery and gift giving. The HR manager may also become more involved in administering company-provided or -financed housing, education, and other facilities not readily available in the local economy.

VARIABLES THAT MODERATE DIFFERENCES BETWEEN DOMESTIC AND INTERNATIONAL HRM

In our discussion so far, we have argued that the complexity involved in operating in different countries and employing different national categories of employees is the main factor that differentiates domestic and international HRM, rather than any major differences between the HRM functions performed. In addition to complexity, there are three other variables that moderate (that is, either diminish or accentuate) differences between domestic and international HRM. These variables are the cultural environment, the industry with which a company is involved, and the attitudes of senior management.

The Cultural Environment

There are many definitions of *culture,* but the term is usually used to describe a shaping process. That is, members of a group or society share a distinct way of life with common values, attitudes, and behaviors that are transmitted over time in a gradual, yet dynamic, process. As Phatak[15] explains:

> A person is not born with a given culture: rather she or he acquires it through the socialization process that begins at birth: an American is not born with a liking for hot dogs, or a German with a natural preference for beer: these behavioral attributes are culturally transmitted.

An important characteristic of culture is that it is so subtle a process that one is not always conscious of its effect on values, attitudes, and behaviors. One usually has to be confronted with a different culture in order to fully appreciate this effect. Anyone traveling abroad, either as a tourist or businessperson, experiences situations that demonstrate cultural differences in language, food, dress, hygiene, and attitude to time. While the traveler can perceive these differences as novel, even enjoyable, for people required to live and work in a new country, such differences can prove difficult. They experience *culture shock*—a phenomenon experienced by people who move across cultures. The new environment requires many adjustments in a relatively short period of time, challenging the person's frame of reference to such an extent that his or her sense of self, especially in terms of nationality, comes into question. The person, in effect, experiences a shock reaction to new cultural experiences that cause psychological disorientation because he or she misunderstands or does not recognize the cues. Culture shock can lead to negative feelings about the host country and its people and a longing to return home.[16]

Because international business involves the interaction and movement of people across national boundaries, an appreciation of cultural differences and when these differences are important is essential. Research into these aspects has assisted in furthering our understanding of the cultural environment as a key variable that moderates differences between domestic and international HRM. However, while cross-cultural and comparative research attempts to explore and explain similarities and differences, there are problems associated with such research. A major problem is that there is little agreement on either an exact definition of culture or on the operationalization of this concept. For many researchers, culture has become an omnibus variable, representing a range of social, historic, economic, and political factors that are invoked post hoc to explain similarity or dissimilarity in the results of a study. As Bhagat and McQuaid[17] have noted, "*Culture* has often served simply as a synonym for nation without any further conceptual grounding. In effect, national differences found in the characteristics of organizations or their members have been interpreted as cultural differences." To reduce these difficulties, researchers must specify their definition of culture a priori rather than post hoc and be careful not to assume that national differences necessarily represent cultural differences.

Another methodological issue concerns the *emic-etic* distinction.[18] Emic refers to culture-specific aspects of concepts or behavior, and etic refers to culture-common aspects. These terms have been borrowed from linguistics: A phon*emic* system documents meaningful sounds specific to a given language, and a phon*etic* system organizes all sounds that have meaning in any language.[19]

Both the emic and etic approaches are legitimate research orientations. A major problem may arise, however, if a researcher imposes an etic approach (that is, assumes universality across cultures) when there is little or no evidence for doing so. A well-known example of an imposed etic approach is the convergence hypothesis that dominated much of U.S. and European management research in the 1950s and 1960s. This approach was based on two key assumptions.[20] The first assumption was that there were principles of sound management that held regardless of national environments. Thus, the existence of local or national practices that deviated from these principles simply indicated a need to change these local practices. The second assumption said that the universality of sound management practices would lead to societies becoming more and more alike in the future. Given that the United States was the leading industrial economy, the point of convergence would be toward the U.S. model.

Adoption of the convergence hypothesis has led to some rather poor predictions of future performance. For example, writing in the late 1950s, Harbison[21] concluded the following with regard to the Japanese managerial system: "Unless basic rather than trivial or technical changes in the broad philosophy of organization building are forthcoming, Japan is destined to fall behind in the ranks of modern industrialized nations."

To use Kuhn's[22] terminology, the convergence hypothesis became an established paradigm that many researchers found difficult to give up, despite a growing body of evidence supporting a divergence hypothesis. In an important paper reviewing the convergence/divergence debate, Child[23] made the point that there is evidence for both convergence and divergence. The majority of the convergence studies, however, focus on macrolevel variables (for example, structure and technology used by organizations across cultures), and the majority of the divergence studies focus on microlevel variables (for example, the behavior of people within organizations). His conclusion was that although organizations in different countries are becoming more alike (an etic or convergence approach), the behavior of individuals within these organizations is maintaining its cultural specificity (an emic or divergence approach). As noted above, both emic and etic approaches are legitimate research orientations, but methodological difficulties may arise if the distinction between these two approaches is ignored or if unwarranted universality assumptions are made.

The Importance of Cultural Awareness

Despite the methodological concerns about cross-cultural research, it is now generally recognized that culturally insensitive attitudes and behaviors stemming from ignorance or from misguided beliefs ("my way is best," or "what works at home will work here") not only are inappropriate but often cause international business failure. Therefore, an awareness of cultural differences is essential for the HR manager. Activities such as hiring, promoting, rewarding, and dismissal will be determined by the practices of the host country and often are based on a value system peculiar to that country's culture. A firm may decide to head up a new overseas operation with an expatriate general manager but appoint as the HR department manager a local, a person who is familiar with the host country's HR practices. This practice can cause problems, though, for the expatriate general manager, as happened to an Australian who was in charge of a new mining venture in Indonesia. The local responsible for recruitment could not understand why the Australian was upset to find that he had hired most of his extended family rather than staff with the required technical competence. The Indonesian was simply ensuring that his duty to his family was fulfilled—since he was in a position to employ most of them, he was obligated to do so. The Australian, however, interpreted the Indonesian's actions as nepotism, a negative practice according to his own value system.[24]

Wyatt[25] recounts a good example of the fallacy of assuming "what works at home will work here" when dealing with work situations in another culture. Personnel department staff of a large organization in Papua New Guinea were concerned over a number of accidents involving operators of very large, expensive, earth-moving vehicles. The expatriate managers investigating the accidents found that local drivers involved in the accidents were chewing betel nut, a common habit for most of the coastal peoples of Papua New Guinea and other Pacific islands. Associating the betel nut with depressants such as alcohol, the expatriate managers banned the chewing of betel nut during work hours. In another move to reduce the number of accidents, free coffee was provided at loading points, and drivers were forced to, at the least, alight from their vehicles at these locations. What the managers did not realize was that betel nut, like their culturally acceptable coffee, is, in fact, a stimulant, though some of the drivers were chewing it to cover up the fact that they had a few beers before commencing work. As Wyatt points out, many indigenous workers used betel nut as a pick-me-up in much the same way as the expatriates used coffee.

As will be further discussed in Chapters 3 and 4, adjusting to a new cultural environment can cause problems for both the expatriate employee and the accompanying spouse and family members. Coping with cultural differences, and recognizing how and when these differences are relevant, is a constant challenge for the international manager. Helping to prepare expatriates and their families for the cultural environment has now become a key activity for HR departments in those international firms that appreciate (or have been forced, through experience, to appreciate) the impact that the cultural environment can have on staff performance and well-being.

Industry Type

Recent work by Porter[26] suggests that the industry (or industries if the organization is a conglomerate) in which a firm is involved is of considerable importance because patterns of international competition vary widely from one industry to another. At one end of the continuum of international competition is the *multidomestic industry*, one in which competition in each country is essentially independent of competition in other countries. Traditional examples include retailing, distribution, and insurance. The other end of the continuum is the *global industry*, one in which a firm's competitive position in one country is significantly influenced by its position in other countries. Examples include commercial aircraft, semiconductors, and copiers. The key distinction between a multidomestic industry and a global industry is described by Porter as follows:

> The global industry is not merely a collection of domestic industries but a series of linked domestic industries in which the rivals compete against each other on a truly worldwide basis. . . . In a multidomestic industry, then, international strategy collapses to a series of domestic strategies. The issues that are uniquely international revolve around how to do business abroad, how to select good countries in which to compete (or assess country risk), and mechanisms to achieve the one-time transfer of know-how. These are questions that are relatively well-developed in the literature. In a global industry, however, managing international activities like a portfolio will undermine the possibility of achieving competitive advantage. In a global industry, a firm must in some way integrate its activities on a worldwide basis to capture the linkages among countries.

The important implications for the role of the HRM function in multidomestic and global industries can be analyzed using Porter's value-chain model[27] shown in Figure 1-2. In Porter's model, HRM is seen as one of four support activities for the five primary activities of the firm. Since human resources are involved in each of the primary and support activities, the HRM function is seen as cutting across the entire

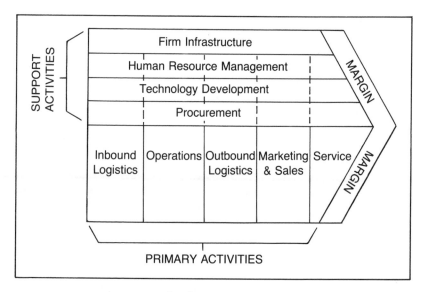

FIGURE 1-2 The Generic Value Chain

Source: Reprinted with permission of The Free Press, a division of Macmillan, Inc. from *Competitive Advantage: Creating and Sustaining Superior Performance* by Michael E. Porter, p. 37. Copyright © 1985 by Michael E. Porter.

value chain of a firm. If the firm is in a multidomestic industry, the role of the HR department will most likely be more domestic in structure and orientation. At times there may be considerable demand for international services from the HRM function (for example, when a new plant or office is established in a foreign location and the need for expatriate employees arises), but these activities would not be pivotal—indeed, many of these services may be provided via consultants and/or temporary employees. The main role for the HRM function would be to support the primary activities of the firm in each domestic market to achieve a competitive advantage through either cost/efficiency or product/service differentiation.[28] If the firm is in a global industry, however, the "imperative for coordination" described by Porter would require a HRM function structured to deliver the international support required by the primary activities of the firm.

The need to develop coordination raises complex problems for any international firm. As Laurent[29] has noted,

In order to build, maintain, and develop their corporate identity, multinational organizations need to strive for consistency in their ways of managing people on a worldwide basis. Yet, and in order to be effective locally, they also need to adapt those ways to the specific cultural requirements of different societies. While the global nature of the business may call for increased consistency, the variety of cultural environments may be calling for differentiation.

There is no easy solution to such a fundamental issue, and both Porter and Laurent recognize the complexities involved. In discussing possible solutions, Porter is the more circumspect and general: He notes that the ability to coordinate globally through the value chain is increasing because of modern technology, and he argues that a study of Japanese multinationals would be worthwhile, as "Japanese firms enjoy an organizational style that is supportive of coordination and a strong commitment to introducing new technologies such as information systems that facilitate it."[30]

Laurent is more specifically concerned with the HRM function and proposes that a truly international conception of human resource management would require the following steps:

1. An explicit recognition by the parent organization that its own peculiar ways of managing human resources reflect some assumptions and values of its home culture.

2. An explicit recognition by the parent organization that its peculiar ways are neither universally better nor worse than others but are different and likely to exhibit strengths and weaknesses, particularly abroad.

3. An explicit recognition by the parent organization that its foreign subsidiaries may have other preferred ways of managing people that are neither intrinsically better nor worse, but could possibly be more effective locally.

4. A willingness from headquarters to not only acknowledge cultural differences, but also to take active steps in order to make them discussable and therefore usable.

5. The building of a genuine belief by all parties involved that more creative and effective ways of managing people could be developed as a result of cross-cultural learning.

Laurent acknowledges that these are difficult steps that few organizations have taken: "They have more to do with states of mind and mindsets than with behaviors. As such, these processes can only be facilitated and this may represent a primary mission for, executives in charge of international human resource management."[31]

Implicit in Laurent's analysis is the idea that by taking the steps he describes, an organization attempting to implement a global strategy via coordination of activities would be better able to work through the difficulties and complex trade-offs inherent in such a strategy. To date there is a dearth of research that investigates how organizations overcome the problems of coordination, but the ideas of Porter and Laurent are a valuable contribution to the emerging literature on the role of international HRM.

Attitudes of Senior Management to International Operations

The point made by Laurent that some of the changes required to truly internationalize the HR function "have more to do with states of mind and mindsets than with behaviors" illustrates the importance of a final variable that may moderate differences between international and domestic HRM: the attitudes of senior management to international operations.

It is likely that if senior management does not have a strong international orientation, the importance of international operations may be underemphasized (or possibly even ignored) in terms of corporate goals and objectives. In such situations, managers may tend to focus on domestic issues and minimize differences between international and domestic environments. They may assume that there is a great deal of transferability between domestic and international HRM practices. This failure to recognize differences in managing human resources in foreign environments—regardless of whether it is because of ethnocentrism, inadequate information, or a lack of international perspective—frequently results in major difficulties in international operations.[32] The challenge for the HR manager is to work with top management in fostering the desired "global mindset." This goal requires, of course, a HR manager who is able to think globally and to formulate and implement HR policies that facilitate the development of globally oriented staff. This book attempts to demonstrate the ways in which an appreciation of the international dimensions of HRM can assist in this process.

SUMMARY

The purpose of this chapter has been to provide an overview of the field of international HRM. We did this by discussing a model and definition of international HRM and examining how this differed from domestic

HRM. We concluded that the complexity involved in operating in different countries and employing different national categories of employees is the main factor differentiating domestic and international HRM, rather than any major differences between the HRM functions performed. This complexity may be moderated by the cultural environment, the nature of the industry structure in which the company is engaged (for example, global vs. multidomestic), and the attitudes of senior management in the company to international operations.

In our discussion of the international dimensions of HRM in this book, we shall be drawing on the HRM literature. Subsequent chapters will examine the international dimensions of the major functional areas of HRM: human resource planning, recruitment and selection, performance evaluation, compensation, training and development, and labor relations. We will provide comparative data on HRM practices in different countries, but our major emphasis is on the international dimensions of HRM confronting MNEs, particularly those dealing with expatriate employees.[33]

QUESTIONS

1. What are the main similarities and differences between domestic and international HRM?

2. Define these terms: PCN, HCN, and TCN.

3. Discuss two HR activities in which a MNE must engage that would not be required in a domestic environment.

4. Why is a greater degree of involvement in employees' personal lives inevitable in many international HRM activities?

5. Discuss the variables that moderate differences between domestic and international HR practices.

FURTHER READING

1. P. J. Dowling, "Human Resource Issues in International Business," *Syracuse Journal of International Law and Commerce*, Vol. 13, No. 2 (1986) pp. 255–271.

2. ———. "International HRM," in *Human Resource Management: Evolving Roles and Responsibilities*, Volume 1, ed. L. Dyer. ASPA/BNA Handbook of Human Resource Management series. Washington, D.C.: BNA, 1988.

3. *Human Resource Management*, Vol. 25, No. 1 (1986). Symposium on international human resource management issue.

4. *Human Resource Management,* Vol. 27, No. 1 (1988). Symposium on human resource management in the multinational corporation issue.

5. J. Main, "B-Schools Get a Global Vision," *Fortune,* July 17, 1989, pp. 78–86.

6. C. Vance and M. Sailer, "Human Resource Management Issues in Europe," in *Readings and Cases in International Human Resource Management,* ed. M Mendenhall and G. Oddou (Boston: PWS-KENT Publishing Co., 1991).

NOTES

1. S. Ronen, *Comparative and Multinational Management* (New York: John Wiley, 1986); and K. Barham and M. Devine, *The Quest for the International Manager: A Survey of Global Human Resource Management,* Special Report No. 2098 (The Economist Intelligence Unit, Ashridge, United Kingdom: 1990).

2. W. B. Johnston, "Global Workforce 2000: The New World Labor Market," in *Harvard Business Review,* March–April 1991, pp. 115–116.

3. M. G. Duerr, "International Business Management: Its Four Tasks," *Conference Board Record,* October 1986, p. 43.

4. P. V. Morgan, "International Human Resource Management: Fact or Fiction," *Personnel Administrator,* Vol. 31, No. 9 (1986) pp. 43–47.

5. R. L. Desatnick and M. L. Bennett, *Human Resource Management in the Multinational Company* (New York: Nichols, 1978).

6. P. J. Dowling, "International and Domestic Personnel/Human Resource Management: Similarities and Differences," in *Readings in Personnel and Human Resource Management* (3rd ed.), ed. R. S. Schuler, S. A. Youngblood, and V. L. Huber (St. Paul, Minn.: West Publishing Co., 1988).

7. See D. L. Pinney, "Structuring an Expatriate Tax Reimbursement Program," *Personnel Administrator,* Vol. 27, No. 7 (1982) pp. 19–25; and M. Gajek and M. M. Sabo, "The Bottom Line: What HR Managers Need to Know About the New Expatriate Regulations," *Personnel Administrator,* Vol. 31, No. 2 (1986) pp. 87–92.

8. F. Acuff, "International and Domestic Human Resources Functions," in Organization Resources Counselors, *Innovations in International Compensation* (New York, 1984).

9. Morgan, "International Human Resource Management."

10. R. D. Robinson, *International Business Management: A Guide to Decision Making,* 2nd. ed. (Hinsdale, Ill.: Dryden, 1978).

11. R. L. Tung, "Selection and Training of Personnel for Overseas Assignments," *Columbia Journal of World Business,* Vol. 16, No. 1 (1981) pp. 68–78.

12. M. Mendenhall and G. Oddou, "The Dimensions of Expatriate Acculturation: A Review," *Academy of Management Review*, Vol. 10 (1985) pp. 39–47; M. G. Harvey, "The Multinational Corporation's Expatriate Problem: An Application of Murphy's Law," *Business Horizons*, Vol. 26, No. 1 (1983) pp. 71–78.

13. Y. Zeira and M. Banai, "Present and Desired Methods of Selecting Expatriate Managers for International Assignments," *Personnel Review*, Vol. 13, No. 3 (1984) pp. 29–35.

14. "How U.S. Executives Dodge Terrorism Abroad," *Business Week*, May 12, 1986, p. 41; and "Terrorism," Chapter 4 in T. M. Gladwin and I. Walter, *Multinationals Under Fire: Lessons in the Management of Conflict* (New York: John Wiley, 1980).

15. A. V. Phatak, *International Dimensions of Management*, 2nd ed. (Boston: PWS-KENT, 1989).

16. P. R. Harris and R. T. Moran, *Managing Cultural Differences* (Houston: Gulf, 1979).

17. R. S. Bhagat and S. J. McQuaid, "Role of Subjective Culture in Organizations: A Review and Directions for Future Research," *Journal of Applied Psychology*, Vol. 67 (1982) pp. 653–685.

18. J. W. Berry, "Introduction to Methodology," in *Handbook of Cross-Cultural Psychology*, Vol. 2: *Methodology*, ed. H. C. Triandis and J. W. Berry (Boston: Allyn & Bacon, 1980).

19. See Triandis and Brislin, "Cross-Cultural Psychology," *American Psychologist*, Vol. 39 (1984) pp. 1006–1016.

20. See G. Hofstede, "The Cultural Relativity of Organizational Practices and Theories," *Journal of International Business Studies*, Vol. 14, No. 2 (1983) pp. 75–89.

21. F. Harbison, "Management in Japan," in *Management in the Industrial World: An International Analysis*, ed. F. Harbison and C. A. Myers (New York: McGraw-Hill, 1959), p. 254.

22. T. S. Kuhn, *The Structure of Scientific Revolution*, 2nd ed. (Chicago, Ill.: University of Chicago Press, 1962).

23. J. D. Child, "Culture, Contingency and Capitalism in the Cross-National Study of Organizations," in *Research in Organizational Behavior*, Vol. 3, ed. L. L. Cummings and B. M. Staw (Greenwich, Conn.: JAI Publishers, 1981).

24. P. J. Dowling, D. E. Welch, and H. De Cieri, "International Joint Ventures: A New Challenge for Human Resource Management," in *Proceedings of the Fifteenth Conference of the European International Business Association*, ed. R. Luostarinen, Helsinki (December, 1989).

25. T. Wyatt, "Understanding Unfamiliar Personnel Problems in Cross-Cultural Work Encounters," *Asia Pacific HRM*, Vol. 27, No. 4 (1989) pp. 5–18.

26. M. E. Porter, "Changing Patterns of International Competition," *California Management Review*, Vol. 28, No. 2 (1986) pp. 9–40.

27. M. E. Porter, *Competitive Advantage: Creating and Sustaining Superior Performance* (New York: The Free Press, 1985).

28. See R. S. Schuler, and I. C. MacMillan, "Gaining Competitive Advantage Through Human Resource Management Practices," *Human Resource Management*, Vol. 23, No. 3 (1984) pp. 241–255, for a discussion of these strategies.

29. A. Laurent, "The Cross-Cultural Puzzle of International Human Resource Management," *Human Resource Management*, Vol. 25 (1986) pp. 91–102.

30. Porter, "Changing Patterns," p. 37.

31. Laurent, "The Cross-Cultural Puzzle," p. 100.

32. Desatnick and Bennett, *Human Resource Management in the Multinational Company.*

33. For an excellent example of a comparative HRM study, see N. K. Napier and R. B. Peterson, *An International Perspective on Personnel Management* (Neutral Bay Junction, Australia: World Federation of Personnel Management Associations, 1989).

Chapter T W O

The Organizational Context

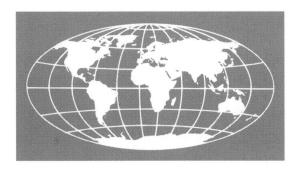

Before we can examine the functions and activities of international HRM in greater depth, it is important to understand the interrelationships between the HR function and other areas of the organization. The HR function does not operate in a vacuum. The activities described in Chapter 1 are determined by various organizational factors, such as the number of countries in which the firm operates, its approach to staffing, and the importance of the overseas operations to overall profitability. Like other areas of the organization, the HR function is expected to respond to the changes necessitated by the shift from a domestic focus to a global operation. These demands on HRM and its responses, discussed in chapters to follow, can be more fully understood if we first look at international HRM in its organizational context and explore its interrelationships.

INTERNATIONAL GROWTH STRATEGIES AND STRUCTURAL RESPONSES

Any international firm's strategy and structure influences and is influenced by international human resource management practices. To understand these various practices, it is necessary to understand first the choices international firms have when deciding on their overall structure and strategy. The organizational strategy and structure define the tasks of individuals and business units within the firm and the processes that result from the intertwined tasks. They also identify how the organization is divided up (differentiated) and how it is united (integrated). Ultimately, the effectiveness of the individuals and units and, therefore, the survival of the firm are influenced by its structure and strategy.

Another variable influencing strategy and structure is the growth and development of the organization.[1] Most firms traditionally pass through several stages of organizational development as the nature and size of their international activities alter. As they go through these evolutionary stages, their organizational structures change. Typically, the strain imposed by the spread into new foreign markets threatens the organizational structure. Thus, growth, coupled with international environmental factors (such as host-government regulations regarding equity and labor) and the need for coordination across business units, influences the strategy/structure response.

A decision to move into a different development stage, although not always rational or methodical, can be regarded as a decision of strategy. The choice of structure evolves to correspond with the changes in the firm's strategy.[2] Decisions regarding HRM practices generally emerge as a result of these two decisions. Therefore, the firm's strategy and structure have significant implications for international human resource management. As human resource management effectiveness depends on its fit with the firm's stage of development,[3] it is important to examine the path a multinational firm takes as it grows and develops and the HRM responses required at each stage.

The Path to Multinational Status

Multinationals are not born overnight; the evolution from a domestic to a truly global organization may involve a long and somewhat tortuous process with many and diverse steps.[4] Most firms do not last the distance.

Although research into internationalization[5] has revealed a common process, it must be stressed that this process is not exactly the same for all firms. Some firms go through the various steps rapidly while others evolve slowly over many years, although recent studies have identified a speeding up of the process. For example, some firms are able to accelerate the process through acquisitions, thus leapfrogging over intermediate steps.[6] Nor do all firms follow the same sequence of stages as they internationalize—some firms can be driven by external factors such as host-government action or an offer to buy a company. In other words, the number of steps, or stages, along the path to multinational status varies from firm to firm, as does the time frame involved. However, the concept of an evolutionary process is useful in illustrating the organizational adjustments required of a firm moving along the path to multinational status. As we have said, linked to this evolutionary process are structural responses, control mechanisms, and HRM policies, as Exhibit 2-1 illustrates. This section now examines the typical path from domestic to global organization and draws out key HRM implications.

Export

This initial stage rarely involves much organizational response until the level of export sales reaches a critical point. Exporting tends to be handled by a middle person (for example, an export agent or foreign distributor). As export sales increase, an export manager may be appointed to control foreign sales and actively seek new markets. Further growth in exporting usually sees the establishment of an export department at the same level as the domestic sales department. This reflects a major commitment to the export activity.[7] At this stage, domestic staff are utilized to control exporting from the domestic-based home office, with the export manager paying frequent visits to the foreign markets. The HRM department (if one formally exists) handles any administrative, selection, and compensation tasks as an adjunct to the domestic activities.

Sales Subsidiary

As the organization develops expertise in foreign markets, agents and distributors are often replaced by direct sales with the establishment of sales subsidiaries or branch offices in the foreign market countries. This stage may be prompted by problems with foreign agents, more confidence in the international sales activity, the desire to have greater control, and/or the decision to give greater support to the exporting activity, usually due to its increasing importance to the overall success of the organization. At this point, the organization must make a decision regarding staffing. If it wishes to maintain control of the sales subsidiary, it usually opts to staff the subsidiary from its headquarters (PCNs). If it regards country-specific factors—knowledge of the foreign market, language, sensitivity to host-country needs, and so on—as important, it may staff the subsidiary with host-country nationals (HCNs).

If the organization decides to use PCNs, the role of the corporate HRM department is limited to supervising the selection and compensation of staff for the export department and sales subsidiary. As Exhibit 2-1 shows, most firms opt for HCNs at this stage.

International Division

For some firms, it is a short step from the establishment of a sales subsidiary to foreign production. This step may be considered small if the firm is already assembling the product abroad (to take advantage of cheap labor or to save shipping costs or tariffs, for example). Alternatively, the firm may have a well-established export and marketing program that enables it to take advantage of host-government incentives or counter host-government controls on foreign imports by establishing a foreign production facility. Other firms find the transition to foreign investment a large, sometimes prohibitive, step. For example, an Australian firm that was successfully exporting mining equipment to Canada began to experience problems with after-sales servicing and delivery schedules. The establishment of its own production facility was considered too great a step, so the firm entered into a licensing agreement with a Canadian manufacturer.[8]

The structural response to foreign production tends to be the creation of a separate international division in which all international activities are grouped (see Figure 2-1) and managed by a senior executive at the corporate headquarters.[9] Most organizations at this stage of internationalization place great emphasis on control mechanisms and staff the foreign facility with PCNs, particularly as the organization expands its foreign production activities into several countries.

According to Stopford and Wells,[10] most U.S. manufacturing firms stumbled into manufacturing abroad without much design. Conscious strategy for growth on a global scale emerged later. Early investments in foreign production facilities were often defensive reactions against the

EXHIBIT 2-1   Evolution and Growth of International Business and Corresponding Changes

Evolution and Growth of International Business	A. Evolution of Organizational Structure	B. Other Structural Characteristics	C. Ownership Policies	D. Control Strategies	E. Staffing Policies
I. Initial stage	Export dept.	Loose, formal relationships	Minority HQ* equity	Indirect, loose coupling	Host-country nationals in charge
II. Early production stage	Export dept./international division	More formalized relationships between HQ* and sub†	Minority or 50–50 equity	Indirect control through technical personnel	Home-country nationals in charge
III. Standardization of production process—mature stage; few products	International division	Increased formalized relationships	Majority or 100% equity in subsidiary operation	Direct control, tight coupling	Host-country nationals in charge
IV. Product innovations and growth through diversification	Product/area bases for structuring of organization	Increased formalization	Minority or 50–50 equity	Indirect control through personnel	Home-country or third-country nationals in charge
V. Quest for global rationalization	Product/area bases for structuring matrix type organization	Increased formalization	Majority or 100% equity in subsidiary	Direct control	Host-country nationals in charge

*HQ: Headquarters   †Sub: Subsidiaries

Source: A. R. Negandhi, *International Management* (Boston: Allyn & Bacon, 1987), p. 23.

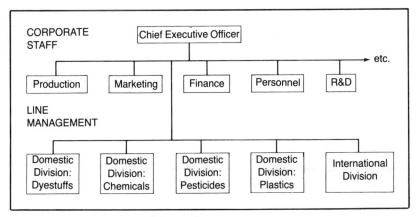

F I G U R E   2 - 1   International Division Structure

Source: A. V. Phatak, *International Dimensions of Management*, 2nd ed. (Boston: PWS-KENT Publishing Co., 1989), p. 84. Reprinted with permission.

threat of losing markets that in the first place had been acquired almost accidentally. The structure and control mechanisms of early foreign production reflect this step to becoming a multinational without having had an explicit plan for doing so. Consequently, the international division is typically considered an independent part of the enterprise and not subject to the same strategic planning that guides domestic activities.[11]

European MNEs have tended to take a different structural path than U.S. MNEs. Franko's study of seventy European MNEs revealed that European firms moved directly from a functional "mother-daughter" structure to a divisionalized global structure (with world-wide product or area divisions) or matrix organization without the transitional stage of an international division.[12] Human resource management practices, changing to serve the needs of the new structure, adjusted accordingly. Swedish MNEs have traditionally adopted the mother-daughter structure, but research by Hedlund[13] reveals that this is changing. These MNEs tend to adopt a mixture of elements of the mother-daughter structure and elements of the product division.

Japanese MNEs are evolving along similar lines to their U.S. counterparts. Export divisions have become international divisions but, according to Ronen,[14] the rate of change is slower. The characteristics of Japanese organizational culture (such as the control and reporting mechanisms and decision-making systems), the role of trading companies, and the systems of management appear to contribute to the slow evolution of the international division. These characteristics also inhibit the transition to the next stage of internationalization.

For firms at the international division stage, the international HRM activity is primarily concerned with PCN management, selection, and compensation. The emphasis is on identifying employees who can direct the daily operations of the foreign subsidiaries, supervising transfer of managerial and technical know-how, communicating corporate policies, and keeping corporate HQ informed.[15]

Global Product/Area Division

At this point, the organization is usually moving from the early foreign production stage into a phase of growth through production standardization and diversification. In the process, the international division becomes overstretched. The strain of sheer size can create problems of effective communication and efficiency of operation. Typically, tensions stem from the need for national responsiveness at the subsidiary unit and global integration at the parent headquarters. The demand for national responsiveness at the subsidiary unit develops because of factors such as differences in market structures, distribution channels, customer needs, local culture, and pressure from the host government. The need for more centralized global integration by the headquarters comes from having multinational customers, global competitors, and increasingly rapid flow of information and technology and from needing large volume for economies of scale. Resulting from this situation is the need for MNEs to grapple with two major issues of structure:

- the extent or degree to which key decisions are to be made at parent headquarters or at the subsidiary units (centralization vs. decentralization), and
- the type or form of control exerted by the parent over the subsidiary unit.[16]

The structural response can be either a product-based global structure (if the growth strategy is through product diversification) or an area-based structure (if the growth strategy is through geographical expansion); see Figure 2-2.[17] One could say that, by this stage, the organization has "come of age" as a multinational. Strategic planning now is carried out on a consistent and worldwide basis (though not all MNEs are equally successful in doing so). This stage marks the really decisive point in the transition to global organization: Top managers recognize that strategic planning and major policy decisions must be made in the

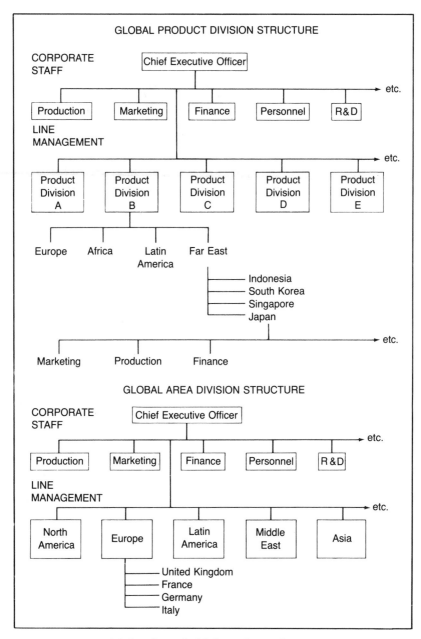

F I G U R E 2 - 2   Global Product and Global Area Division Structures
Source: A. V. Phatak, *International Dimensions of Management*, 2nd ed. (Boston: PWS-KENT Publishing Co., 1989), p. 90, p. 93. Reprinted with permission.

central HQ so that a worldwide perspective on the interests of the total enterprise can be maintained.[18]

This transformation into a full-fledged multinational not only changes the focus of the HRM international activities, but alters the organization of the HRM function as well.[19] As we have seen, at the international division stage the international HRM policies are designed primarily to fit the domestic operations. Gradually, as the MNE strives to adapt its HRM activities to each host country's specific requirements, the HRM function changes. The PCN workforce remains under the control of the corporate HRM department, but local employees become the responsibility of each subsidiary. Corporate HRM staff perform a monitoring role and intervene in local affairs only in extreme circumstances. For example, Ford Australia has a ceiling on its HRM decisions, and those that involve an amount above that ceiling must be referred to regional HQ for corporate approval. This HRM monitoring role reflects management's desire for central control of strategic planning.

The HRM planning process becomes more complex as the organization develops. The coordination of activities and the formation of strategies for worldwide markets develop into independent managerial functions requiring specialized expertise. The growth in foreign exposure combined with changes in the organizational structure of international operations results in an increase in the number of managerial-class employees needed to oversee the contracts between the parent firm and its foreign affiliates. Within the human resource function, the development of managers able to operate in international environments becomes a new imperative.[20]

Global Organization Structures

As the multinational grows and the trend toward a global perspective accelerates, it is confronted with the "think global, act local"[21] paradox. The increasingly complex international environment—characterized by global competitors, global customers, universal products, rapid technological change, and world-scale factories—push the multinational toward global integration while, at the same time, host governments push for local responsiveness. To facilitate the challenge of meeting these conflicting demands, the multinational will typically need to consider a more appropriate structure. At this stage, the following are identified: the matrix; the mixed structure; the transnational; the heterarchy; and the multinational network.

1. The Matrix

As shown in Figure 2-3, in the matrix structure, the international or geographical division and the product division share joint authority. This type of organization violates Fayol's principle of unity of command and brings into the management system a philosophy of matching the structure to the decision-making process. Conflicts of interest are brought out into the open, and each issue that has priority in the decision making has an executive champion to ensure it is not neglected. Therefore, managers with functional, geographical, and product group responsibilities have similar status to those in foreign subsidiaries. Here, the multinational is attempting to integrate its operations across more than one dimension.

Organizations that have adopted the matrix structure have met with mixed success. One reason is that it is an expensive method of organization that requires careful implementation and commitment on the part of top management to be successful. Galbraith and Kazanjian[22] argue that the matrix "continues to be the only organizational form which fits the

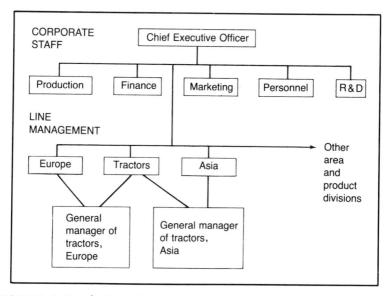

FIGURE 2-3   The Matrix Structure

Source: A. V. Phatak, *International Dimensions of Management,* 2nd. ed. (Boston: PWS-KENT Publishing Co., 1989), p. 100. Reprinted with permission.

strategy of simultaneous pursuit of multiple business dimensions, with each given equal priority. . . . [T]he structural form succeeds because it fits the situation. Thus matrix can work when it evolves, not when it is installed."

One supporter of the matrix organization is Barnevik, the chief executive officer of Asea Brown Boveri (ABB), the European electrical systems and equipment manufacturer. In discussing his organization's approach, Barnevik[23] explains:

> ABB is an organization with three internal contradictions. We want to be global and local, big and small, radically decentralized with centralized reporting and control. If we resolve those contradictions, we create real organization advantage. That is where the matrix comes in. The matrix is the framework through which we organize our activities. It allows us to optimize our businesses globally *and* maximize performance in every country in which we operate. Some people resist it. They say that the matrix is too rigid, too simplistic. But what choice do you have? To say you don't like a matrix is like saying you don't like factories or you don't like breathing. It is a fact of life. If you deny the formal matrix, you wind up with an informal one—and that is much harder to reckon with. As we learn to master the matrix, we get a truly multidomestic organization.

It is in the attempt to master the matrix that many organizations have floundered. Bartlett and Ghoshal[24] comment that, in practice, particularly in the international context, the matrix has proven to be all but unmanageable. They isolate four contributing factors:

1. The dual reporting, which leads to conflict and confusion.

2. The proliferation of channels, which creates informational logjams.

3. Overlapping responsibilities, which produce turf battles and a loss of accountability.

4. The barriers of distance, language, time, and culture, which make it virtually impossible for managers to resolve conflicts and to clarify the confusion.

Bartlett and Ghoshal conclude that the most successful companies today focus less on searching for the ideal structure and more on developing the abilities, behavior, and performance of individual managers; on creating "a matrix in the minds of managers," where individual capabilities are captured and the entire organization is motivated to respond cooperatively to a complicated and dynamic environment. However, if the multinational opts for a matrix structure, particular care must be taken with staffing. As Ronen[25] notes,

> It requires managers who know the business in general, who have good interpersonal skills, and who can deal with the ambiguities of responsibility and authority inherent in the matrix system. Training in such skills as planning procedures, the kinds of interpersonal skills necessary for the matrix, and the kind of analysis and orderly presentation of ideas essential to planning within a group is most important for supporting the matrix approach. Moreover, management development and human resource planning are even more necessary in the volatile environment of the matrix than in the traditional organizations.

2. Mixed Structure

In an attempt to manage the growth of diverse operations, or perhaps because attempts to implement a matrix structure have been unsuccessful, some firms have opted for what can only be described as a mixed form. In a survey conducted by Dowling,[26] more than one-third of the firms indicated that they had mixed forms. Of all the firms with international operations, the types of structures represented included:

- International operations organized into national   11.8%
  subsidiaries with local coordination or production/
  services, marketing, personnel, etc.

- International division structure with senior   14.7%
  management reporting to president or CEO of
  company.

- One or more regional headquarters used to coordinate   20.6%
  production/services, marketing, and personnel among
  national operations.

- World-product or world-matrix structure used for   17.6%
  coordination of international operations.

- Mixed forms of structure.   35.3%

Galbraith and Kazanjian[27] also identify mixed structures that seem to have emerged in response to global pressures and trade-offs:

> For example, organizations that pursued area structures kept these geographical profit centers, but added worldwide product managers. Colgate-Palmolive has always had strong country managers. But, as

they doubled the funding for product research, and as Colgate Dental Creme became a universal product, product managers were added at the corporate office to direct the R & D funding and coordinate marketing programs worldwide.

Similarly, the product-divisionalized firms have been reintroducing the international division. At Motorola, the product groups had worldwide responsibility for their product lines. As they compete with the Japanese in Japan, an international group has been introduced to help coordinate across product lines.

Although all structural forms that result from the evolutionary development of international business are complex and difficult to manage effectively, given an organization's developing capabilities and experience at each new stage, mixed structures appear even more complex and harder to explain and implement, as well as control. Thus, as our discussion of the matrix structure emphasized, it is important that people throughout the global organization understand the mixed framework and that attention is also given to informal control mechanisms, such as corporate identity, interpersonal relationships, and management attitudes.

3. The Transnational

Some writers are identifying a new stage of organization development that builds on the global product/area and matrix structures. It is characterized by an interdependence of resources and responsibilities across all business units regardless of national boundaries. In addition, a set of strong cross-unit integrating devices, a strong corporate identity, and a well-developed worldwide management perspective are present. The term *transnational* has been coined to describe this new form. In their study Bartlett and Ghoshal[28] noted:

> Among the companies we studied, there were several that were in the process of developing such organizational capabilities. They had surpassed the classic capabilities of the *multinational* company that operates as decentralized federations of units able to sense and respond to diverse international needs and opportunities; and they had evolved beyond the abilities of the global company with its facility for managing operations on a tightly controlled worldwide basis through its centralized hub structure. They had developed what we termed *transnational* capabilities—the ability to manage across national boundaries, retaining local flexibility while achieving global integration. More than anything else this involved the ability to link local op-

erations to each other and to the center in a flexible way, and in so doing, to leverage those local and central capabilities.

4. The Heterarchy

A related description of this post-multinational stage is the *heterarchy*, a structural form proposed by Hedlund,[29] in which the multinational has a number of different kinds of centers. Hedlund argues that competitive advantage does not have to reside in any one country (the parent country, for example), but in many, and that each subsidiary center may be simultaneously a center and a global coordinator of discrete activities, thus performing a strategic role not just for itself, but for the MNE as a whole. In a heterarchical MNE, control is less reliant on the top-bottom mechanisms of previous hierarchical modes and more on normative mechanisms, such as the corporate culture and a widely shared awareness of central goals and strategies.

From a HRM perspective, this type of structure is interesting in that its success appears to rest solely on the ability of the organization to formulate, implement, and reinforce the required human resource elements. Hedlund recognizes that this form demands skillful and experienced personnel as well as sophisticated reward and punishment systems in order to develop the normative control mechanisms. In fact, in all three of the maturing multinational's structural responses discussed so far—the matrix, the transnational, and the heterarchy—the common theme is the human resource factor. Therefore, developing transnational managers or global leaders who can think and act across national and subsidiary boundaries emerges as an important task for the management of these complex organizational forms. The use of staff as an informal control mechanism is also a factor here, one which we shall explore later in this chapter.

5. The Multinational as a Network

Recent studies, based primarily on the concepts of social exchange theory and interaction between actors in a network, have looked at the large multinational as a complex system of multiple linkages. Early studies of headquarter-subsidiary relationships tended to stress the flows from headquarters to subsidiary, examining these relationships mainly in the context of control and coordination. The linkages were described formally via the organization's structure and standardized procedures and informally through interpersonal contact and socialization.[30] It is now recognized that this approach can be somewhat limiting in certain cases, that for relatively internationalized firms, "the former periphery of subsidiaries has developed into significant centers for investments, activities, and influence."[31] In fact, the interaction between headquarters and each subsidiary is likely to be dyadic, taking place between various actors at many different organizational levels and covering different exchanges, the outcome of which will be important for effective global performance. It is more realistic to regard such MNEs as loosely coupled political systems rather than tightly bonded, homogeneous, hierarchically controlled systems.[32] Taking account of this trend, Ghoshal and Barlett[33] have expanded their concept of the transnational; they now see the MNE as an interorganizational system—a network of exchange relationships among different organizational units, including the headquarters and the national subsidiaries, as well as external organizations, such as host governments, customers, suppliers, and competitors, with which the different units of the multinational must interact.

The management of such a multicentered structure is complex. Apart from the intraorganizational network (comprising headquarters and the numerous subsidiaries) each subsidiary also has a range of external relationships (involving local suppliers, customers, competitors, host governments, and alliance partners). The management of both the intraorganizational and interorganizational spheres, and of the total integrated network, is crucial to global corporate performance. Human resource management plays a key role here. Since network relationships are built and maintained through personal contact, staffing decisions are crucial to the effective management of the linkages that the various subsidiaries have established. Nevertheless, staffing decisions may be made, and often are, without regard to their effect on network relationships.[34]

Interfirm Linkages

To add to the complexities of multinational management, a firm may enter into an alliance with an external party (or parties) such as a competitor, a key supplier, or an affiliated firm in order to compete more effectively in the global marketplace.[35] Since these partnerships come in all shapes and sizes,[36] the term *alliance* has come to mean different things to different people: strategic alliance, cooperative venture, collaborative agreement, or corporate linkage, of which one form may be a joint venture.[37] For the purpose of this discussion, we will use a broad definition: "A corporate alliance is a formal and mutually agreed commercial collaboration between companies. The partners pool, exchange, or integrate specified business resources for mutual gain. Yet the partners remain separate businesses."[38] The key point is that an alliance is a form of business relationship that involves some measure of interfirm integration that goes beyond the traditional buyer-seller relationship but stops short of a full merger or acquisition, though some alliances can develop into mergers or takeovers at a later date.[39] The particular type of venture that emerges is a function of the strategic importance of the venture to the parent company and the extent to which the parent seeks control over the resources allocated to the venture.

There was a marked growth in alliance formation in the 1980s.[40] Alliances can now be found in such diverse industries as telecommunications, aerospace, automobiles, electronics, and transportation equipment. Shared activities can include research and development, production, and marketing. An alliance can involve arrangements such as licensing agreements, marketing or distribution partnerships, and consortia.

Regardless of the motive for entering into such an arrangement, the resultant partnership adds another dimension to an organization's strategy and structure mix. In order to meet the objectives of the collaborative partnership within the context of broader corporate strategy, the organization needs to integrate or link the partnership venture to its own existing activities and functions and to devise a method of monitoring its performance. The way the partnership is interlinked naturally depends on the form that the collaboration takes.

As we have seen with other forms of structuring arrangements, the various forms of interfirm linkages affect HRM in different ways, depending upon the type of alliance involved. For example, in an international joint venture, a new entity that brings together managers from two or more firms, the managers must become accustomed to working with a foreign partner (or partners). "Staffing the joint venture with managers who are flexible in terms of different management styles and philosophies is probably the single most important task facing the human resource function at this critical time."[41] Indeed, Lorange links success to a match between the form of cooperative venture and human resource components, maintaining that "the human resource function is particularly critical to successful implementation of such cooperative ventures."[42] In their analysis of strategic alliances, Cascio and Serapio[43] classify these collaborative forms of business relationships according to the extent of interaction required among people from the collaborating companies; they point out, for example, that a joint venture involves more interaction than does a marketing or distribution partnership.

While the specific nature of joint ventures, including management issues and the HR implications, will be further explored in Chapter 8, it is important to note here that HR factors play a crucial role in this type of relationship.

Fashion or Fit?

The above discussion has traced the evolution of the organization from a domestic-oriented to a global-oriented firm. A note of caution should be added. Growth in the firm's international business activity does require structural responses, but the evolutionary process will differ across multinationals. As pointed out earlier, U.S., European, Swedish, and Japanese multinationals have different structural responses to growth. Other variables—size of organization, pattern of internationalization, management policies, and so on—also play a part in the strategy-structure mix. Researchers have identified the pattern described here, but the danger is to treat the stages as normative rather than descriptive. To quote Bartlett:[44]

> For some [MNEs] it seemed that organizational structure followed fashion as much as it related to strategy. Reorganizations from international divisions to global product or area organizations, or from global structures to matrix forms, became widespread. This, after all, was the classic organizational sequence described in the "stages theories."
>
> Yet many companies that had expected such changes to provide them with the strategy-structure "fit" to meet the new pressures were disappointed. Developing a multidimensional decision-making process that was able to balance the conflicting global and national needs was a subtle and time-consuming process not necessarily achieved by redrawing the lines on a chart. Examples of failed or abandoned multinational organizations abound.

Because firms vary from one another as they go through the stages of international development, we find a wide variety of matches between human resource approach and organizational structure. Almost half the firms surveyed by Dowling reported that the operations of the human resource function were unrelated to the nature of the firms' international operations.[45] Exhibit 2-2 details Dowling's survey results.

It is also important to remember that strategy and structure influence international HRM planning and policy. For this reason, we have tried to draw out the HRM implications at each stage of the organization's development. The role of HRM is crucial, as the ability to develop a flexible

EXHIBIT 2-2   Structure of Human Resources Function

Question

Is the Human Resources function structured in a similar way to the company's international operations?

Answer	n	%
Yes.	19	55.9
No, the structure of the HR function is different.	14	44.1

If your answer is No, please describe the structure of your HR function:

n	Response
4	Consulting arrangements from central company; international organization is very small, so HR support provided from U.S.; all offshore HR people report to U.S. headquarters; centralized
2	Corporate HR philosophy developed at world HQ and implemented regionally, considering each region's needs
2	International personnel organization with responsibilities for all personnel activities outside the U.S.
1	Small corporate group of HR professionals; professionals in each strategic business unit and at locations
1	Separate corporate, group, and division int. HR functions; all work closely together on a dotted-line basis, although each area has core responsibilities unique to that level
1	Decentralized HR function; HR unit in each operating unit and in world area regional HQ
1	Depending on size of operation, there may be a local HR function; all expatriates and TCNs on head office payroll handled by group HR
1	HR support to international division is provided through corporate functions
1	Separate personnel departments in each company plus a central/functional personnel group

Source: P. J. Dowling, "Hot Issues Overseas," *Personnel Administrator*, Vol. 34, No. 1 (1989), p. 70.

global organization that is centrally integrated and coordinated yet locally responsive requires effective strategic management. Therefore, the multinational must have appropriate HRM policies for staff selection, performance appraisal, rewards, and training that will enhance its overall performance and competitive advantage strategies. Human resource managers should be involved directly in the formulation of strategy as well as in the implementation of that strategy.

INTERNATIONAL HUMAN RESOURCE MANAGEMENT APPROACHES

The HRM literature uses four terms to describe MNE approaches to managing and staffing their subsidiaries, and these approaches are determined to a large extent by the attitudes of top management at headquarters and the strategy-structure mix. Although these approaches will be examined in detail in the next chapter, it is important to define them here, as they have a bearing on international HRM strategy. The four approaches are:[46]

1. *Ethnocentric:* Few foreign subsidiaries have any autonomy, strategic decisions are made at headquarters, and key jobs at both domestic and foreign operations are held by headquarters management personnel. Subsidiaries, in other words, are managed by expatriates from the home country (PCNs).

2. *Polycentric*: The MNE treats each subsidiary as a distinct national entity with some decision-making autonomy. Subsidiaries are usually managed by local nationals (HCNs) who are seldom promoted to positions at headquarters.

3. *Geocentric*: The organization ignores nationality in favor of ability. This approach to staffing without regard to nationality must be accompanied by a worldwide integrated business strategy to be successful.

4. *Regiocentric*: Reflects the geographic strategy and structure of the MNE. Like the geocentric approach, it utilizes a wider pool of managers but in a limited way (personnel may move outside their countries but only within the particular geographic region). Regional managers may not be promoted to headquarters positions but enjoy a degree of regional autonomy in decision making.

Which approach should be used when developing a strategy for international HRM? The answer—"it all depends!"—should come as no surprise. Factors such as strategy, structure, size, availability of staff, headquarters attitudes, and government regulations determine the approach. As Evans states:[47]

> The choice of a global geocentric or polycentric approach to human resource management is not dictated by product-market or industry logic; each approach represents a different way of coping with the different socio-cultural environments of a multinational company. . . . Thus firms in worldwide industries where divisions and subsidiaries are interdependent would be advised to adopt global human resource strategies; the costs of such strategies would be outweighed by the potentially enormous returns of a successful global strategy. Firms where divisions and business elements can be discreetly and independently defined would be advised to adopt cheaper polycentric human resource strategies. Some of the disadvantages of either extreme position can be counteracted by the use of subtle management processes.

Organizational structure and strategy influence the approach to international HRM. For example, the global firm manages its global workforce in a centralized or at least coordinated way. Corporate policy on human resource management is relatively specific and influential. There are numerous guidelines, policies, principles, and guiding corporate values; desired personnel practices are often prescribed. Specific examples are worldwide policies on open-door grievance procedure, single status, and stance toward unions; a uniform procedure of performance evaluation or global compensation policies; monitoring of human resource management through opinion surveys that compare the performance of business units and divisions; and a code of corporate values that guide the indoctrination of new recruits. As we will see in Chapter 3, international transfers of staff are used for management development and socialization to foster commitment to the global organization. Well-known global enterprises include IBM, Hewlett-Packard, Procter & Gamble, Shell, and Unilever.[48]

However, a key assumption underlying the geocentric staffing philosophy is that the multinational has sufficient numbers of high-caliber staff constantly available for transfer anywhere, whenever global management needs dictate.[49] In practice, it is not easy to find or nurture the required numbers of high-quality staff. The HRM activities discussed in the remainder of this textbook play an important role in the development of the effective policies required to sustain a geocentric approach to staffing.

The polycentric firm, on the other hand, decentralizes the management of human resources to the level of business operations in each foreign country location. Corporate coordination, if it exists, is loose and informal. There are few corporate guidelines, vague policies, and no specification of desired practice. All this is left to the foreign subsidiary's general manager and his or her personnel staff, who adapt not only to local product-market conditions but also to local sociocultural circumstances. The role of the headquarters staff is limited to high-potential identification and development (ensuring a supply of appropriate general managers to run decentralized companies) and the organization of occasional meetings of subsidiary executives to exchange the lessons of experience. Examples of polycentric enterprises are Schlumberger, Holderbank (the Swiss enterprise that is the world leader in the cement industry), American Express, GEC in Britain, the Swedish gas firm AGA, and Nestlé.[50]

The ethnocentric firm tends to be at the early stages of internationalization. Because the firm needs to tightly control its foreign business activity, it relies on the use of expatriate managers and technical staff to transfer operational and reporting systems. Once the foreign subsidiary is well established, the expatriates may be replaced by HCNs.

The regiocentric firm devolves control to its managers, but the control is limited to specific regions of the world. This approach allows the MNE to tailor its policies and practices to specific areas yet limit the number of unique policies and procedures. Discussion of this approach to MNE staffing has been limited, although a recent study by Morrison et al. redresses the balance somewhat. These authors conclude that regionalization is being viewed as a stepping-stone to more effective global competition:[51]

> Under a regional strategy, companies extend home-country loyalties to the entire region. Local markets are intentionally linked within the region where competitive strategies are formulated. It is within the region that top managers determine investment locations, product mix, competitive positioning, and performance appraisals. Managers are given the opportunity to solve regional challenges regionally.

They add that such an approach helps avoid the staffing, communication, and motivational problems of the global MNE.

In some cases a MNE may use a combination of approaches. For example, it may operate its European interests in a regiocentric manner and its Southeast Asian interests in an ethnocentric way until there is greater comfort in operating in that region of the world. Also, the unique characteristics of a subsidiary, or its host-country environment, needs to be taken into account when determining its staffing requirements.[52]

THE EXPANDING ROLE OF HRM

Recent literature has focused increasingly on links between HRM and strategic issues.[53] Indeed, Lorange asserts that HRM is a critical dimension of strategic management that should be managed in a proactive manner. "Without the growth of human resources as a strategic resource within a corporation," he argues, "it will be difficult to secure the long-term strategic future of the corporation, even though financial resources might be adequate."[54] This argument holds true for the MNE.

Just as international HRM is a field in its infancy, so too is the role of international HRM in strategic planning. The limited empirical research focuses on human resource managers' involvement in formulating and implementing intended strategy. Some writers place the international HRM role in the context of control. For example, Doz and Prahalad[55] advocate a strong HRM process to ensure the planned development of a large enough pool of young executives to allow staffing flexibility, to provide checks and balances in the complex matrix structure, and to allow an explicit linkage of strategic control configurations with executive appointments.

In a survey by Schuler and Dowling,[56] the major challenges for the international HRM function in strategic planning included:

- Identifying top management potential early.
- Identifying critical success factors for the future international manager.
- Providing developmental opportunities.
- Tracking and maintaining commitments to individuals in international career paths.
- Tying strategic business planning to human resource planning and vice versa.
- Dealing with the organizational dynamics and multiple (decentralized) business units while attempting to achieve global- and regional- (for example, Europe-) focused strategies.
- Providing meaningful assignments at the right time to ensure adequate international and domestic human resources.

Bhatt et al.[57] examined the role of human resource staff and executives in the strategic planning of multinational firms. The study assessed whether and how the human resource department and staff were involved in planning at the corporate and strategic business unit (SBU) levels. The study concluded that human resources involvement at the corporate level tended to be informal, limited in scope, and heavily dependent upon the competence and personal characteristics of the senior human resource executive. The human resource executive thus played a major role separate from the department or functional area. Staffing was the main area in which the human resource executive was involved in strategy formulation; other traditional human resource areas (for example, compensation and evaluation of manager performance) were viewed as general top management concerns and not primarily human resources related. At the SBU level, the human resources department staff was much more involved in strategic planning; its role was more established and the emphasis was on how the human resources staff could help implement a strategy.

The repositioning of the HR function to include strategy formulation, rather than being confined to strategy implementation, is particularly important in the international context. As we have seen through our discussion of the multinational's evolutionary path, each stage of growth has HRM implications, particularly where staffing is concerned. A shift in strategic direction requires HRM responses, and these will be proactive and effective only if HRM implications are included in the strategy-formulation stage. As Doz and Prahalad[58] point out, a HRM system can be strong only if it receives extensive support and involvement from top management. Related to the call for the HR function to become involved in corporate strategic issues of the MNE is the need for HR staff to become internationally, some say globally, oriented. It is difficult to advocate international HRM (IHRM) policies if one is not fully appreciative of the importance of the organization's international operations to its overall profitability and competitiveness, and aware as well of the special demands placed on human resources by the complex global environment. A global perspective, through a broader view of issues, enables the development of more effective corporate policies.[59]

The need for a global perspective applies to both the individual HR manager and the HR department. To accomplish this goal, Reynolds [60] suggests that HR managers be transferred from headquarters to overseas operations, not into subsidiary HR departments but into other line positions that will broaden their perspectives. Moving HR staff from the subsidiaries into headquarters is another way of encouraging headquarter HR staff to appreciate the international operations of the MNE and to develop the policies and activities to support staff throughout the entire global network. However, as Brandt[61] points out, "How fast and how far an individual HR manager can move toward globalizing his or her function often depends on a company's size, the nature of its operations, and its degree of centralization or decentralization." Smaller firms with limited resources that may find it impossible to finance staff transfers for development purposes only can find other ways to globally orientate HR staff, for example, a yearly visit to key overseas subsidiaries. Larger MNEs schedule frequent meetings of corporate and subsidiary HR managers as a way to foster corporate identity and to ensure greater consistency in global HR practices.[62]

Despite these gains, Reynolds's[63] recent survey of thirty-five major U.S. multinationals shows that internationalizing the HR function has some way to go. He found that HR professionals with experience in international human resources were typically narrowly focused on expatriate compensation. By examining the time allocation of IHRM staff in the companies surveyed, Reynolds determined that 54 percent of their time is devoted to expatriate compensation and only 10 percent to international HR strategy. As we shall discuss in Chapter 6, compensation is a complex issue for MNEs, and as Reynolds rightly points out, the focus should not be denigrated, but in order to continue the movement towards globalization, the MNE requires staff whose perspective of the international dimensions of HRM takes in more than expatriate compensation.

SUMMARY

We have, through this discussion, been able to demonstrate that there is an interconnection between international HRM and the organizational context and that structural and strategic imperatives change according to management philosophy and the international business focus of the MNE. International HR managers have a crucial role in effective strategic management. In order to perform this role, they should understand the variations in their firm's development toward a global (even transnational) status. Each growth stage offers new organizational challenges that international HR planning can influence significantly. Anticipating changes in hiring practices, taking a long-term perspective to developing international managers, collecting data, participating in career-path planning, and recognizing potential parent-subsidiary conflict all have implications for both HR planning and policies. The challenges are to be proactive and to create an integrated approach to international HRM that encourages flexibility and local responsiveness.

QUESTIONS

1. What are the stages an international business typically goes through before its final development into a transnational company?

2. Once a MNE reaches the global developmental stage, what tensions develop between headquarters and subsidiaries?

3. What are some of the problems associated with a matrix structure?

4. What are the different practices associated with ethnocentric, polycentric, geocentric, and regiocentric human resource management approaches?

5. What role can international HRM play in strategic corporate planning?

FURTHER READING

1. C. A. Bartlett, "Building and Managing the Transnational: The New Organizational Challenge," in *Competition in Global Industries*, ed. M. E. Porter. Boston: Harvard Business School Press, 1986, pp. 367–404.

2. Y. Doz, *Strategic Management in Multinational Companies*. London: Oxford Press, Pergamon, 1986. J. R. Galbraith and R. K. Kazanjian, *Strategy Implementation: Structure, Systems and Process*. St. Paul, Minn.: West Publishing Co., 1986.

3. S. R. Gates and W. G. Egelhoff, "Centralization in Headquarters-Subsidiary Relationships," *Journal of International Business Studies*, Summer 1986, pp. 71–92.

4. F. Ghadar and N. J. Adler, "Management Culture and the Accelerated Product Life Cycle," *Human Resource Planning*, Vol. 12, No. 1 (1989) pp. 37–42.

5. H. V. Perlmutter and D. A. Hedman, "Cooperate to Compete Globally," *Harvard Business Review*, March–April 1986, pp. 136–152.

6. C. K. Prahalad and R. A. Bettis, "The Dominant Logic: A New Linkage Between Diversity and Performance," *Strategic Management Journal*, Vol. 7 (1986) pp. 485–501.

7. M. Schrage, "A Japanese Giant Rethinks Globalization: An Interview with Yoshihisa Tabushi," *Harvard Business Review*, July–August 1989, pp. 70–76.

8. T. T. Tyebjee, "A Typology of Joint Ventures: Japanese Strategies in the United States," *California Management Review*, Fall 1988, pp. 75–91.

9. E. L. Miller, S. Beechler, B. Bhatt, and R. Nath, "The Relationship Between the Global Strategic Planning Process and the Human Resource Management Function," *Human Resource Planning*, Vol. 9, No. 1 (1986) pp. 9–25.

NOTES

1. L. Baird and I. Meshoulam, "Managing Two Fits of Strategic Human Resource Management," *Academy of Management Review*, Vol. 13, No. 1 (1988) pp. 116–128.

2. A. V. Phatak, *International Dimensions of Management*, 2nd ed. (Boston, Mass.: PWS-KENT Publishing Co., 1989).

3. Baird and Meshoulam, "Managing Two Fits."

4. L. S. Welch and R. Luostarinen, "Internationalization: Evolution of a Concept," *Journal of General Management*, Vol. 14, No. 2 (1988) pp. 34–55.

5. J. Johanson and J.-E. Vahlne, "The Mechanism of Internationalisation," *International Marketing Review*, Vol. 7, No. 4 (1990) pp. 11–24.

6. Welch and Luostarinen, "Internationalization."

7. Phatak, *International Dimensions*.

8. "Canadian Licensing Venture Helps Firm Improve Penetration," *Overseas Trading*, Vol. 27, No. 16 (1975) p. 398.

9. Phatak, *International Dimensions*.

10. J. Stopford and L. Wells, *Managing the Multinational* (London: Longmans, 1972).

11. Stopford and Wells, *Managing the Multinational*.

12. L. Leksell, *Headquarter-Subsidiary Relationships in Multinational Corporations*, Stockholm, 1981.

13. G. Hedlund, "Organization In-between: The Evolution of the Mother-Daughter Structure of Managing Foreign Subsidiaries in Swedish MNCs," *Journal of International Business Studies*, Fall 1984, pp. 109–123.

14. S. Ronen, *Comparative and Multinational Management* (New York: John Wiley, 1986).

15. See V. Pucik, "Strategic Human Resource Management in a Multinational Firm," in *Strategic Management of Multinational Corporations: The Essentials*, ed. H. V. Wortzel and L. H. Wortzel (New York: John Wiley, 1985) p. 425.

16. S. F. Slater, N. K. Napier, and M. S. Taylor, "Human Resource Competence as a Source of Competitive Advantage in Multinational Companies:

Issues Affecting the Transfer of Distinctive Competence" (Working Paper, Boise State University, 1989).

17. A. R. Negandhi, *International Management* (Newton, Mass.: Allyn and Bacon, 1987).

18. Stopford and Wells, *Managing the Multinational*.

19. See Pucik, "Strategic Human Resource Management," p. 425.

20. Ibid.

21. C. A. Bartlett and S. Ghoshal, "Organizing for Worldwide Effectiveness: The Transnational Solution," *California Management Review*, Fall 1988, pp. 54–74.

22. J. R. Galbraith and R. K. Kazanjian, "Organizing to Implement Strategies of Diversity and Globalization: The Role of Matrix Designs," *Human Resource Management*, Vol. 25, No. 1 (1986) p. 50; see also T. T. Naylor, "The International Strategy Mix," *Columbia Journal of World Business*, Vol. 20, No. 2 (1985); and R. A. Pitts and J. D. Daniels, "Aftermath of the Matrix Mania," *Columbia Journal of World Business*, Vol. 19, No. 2 (1984) for a discussion of the matrix form.

23. W. Taylor, "The Logic of Global Business: An Interview with ABB's Percy Barnevik," *Harvard Business Review*, March–April 1991, pp. 95–96.

24. C. A. Bartlett and S. Ghoshal, "Matrix Management: Not a Structure, a Frame of Mind," *Harvard Business Review*, July–August 1990, pp. 138–145.

25. Ronen, *Comparative and Multinational Management*, p. 330.

26. P. J. Dowling, "International HRM," in *Human Resource Management: Evolving Roles and Responsibilities*, Vol. 1, ed. L. Dyer. ASPA/BNA Handbook of Human Resource Management series. Washington, D.C.: BNA, 1988.

27. Galbraith and Kazanjian, "Organizing to Implement Strategies," p. 50.

28. Bartlett and Ghoshal, "Organizing for Worldwide Effectiveness," p. 66.

29. G. Hedlund, "The Hypermodern MNC—A Heterarchy?" *Human Resource Management*, Vol. 25, No. 1 (1986) pp. 9–35.

30. J. I. Martinez and J. C. Jarillo, "The Evolution of Research on Coordination Mechanisms in Multinational Corporations," *Journal of International Business Studies*, Fall 1989, pp. 489–514.

31. V. Anderson, M. Forsgren, C. Pahlberg, and P. Thilenius, "Global Firms in Internationalized Networks," in *Proceedings of the Sixteenth Annual Conference of the European International Business Association*, ed. J. Duran, Madrid (December, 1990) p. 2.

32. M. Forsgren, "Managing the International Multi-centre Firm: Case Studies from Sweden," *European Management Journal*, Vol. 8, No. 2 (1990) pp. 261–267.

33. S. Ghoshal and C. A. Bartlett, "The Multinational Corporation as an Interorganizational Network," *Academy of Management Review*, Vol. 8, No. 2 (1990) pp. 603–625.

34. D. E. Welch and L. S. Welch, "Using Personnel to Develop Networks: An Approach to Subsidiary Management," *International Business Review*, Vol. 2, No. 2 (1993).

35. R. N. Osborn and C. C. Baughn, "Forms of Interorganizational Governance for Multinational Alliances," *Academy of Management Journal*, Vol. 33, No. 3 (1990) pp. 503–519; J. C. Jarillo and H. H. Stevenson, "Co-operative Strategies—The Payoffs and the Pitfalls," *Long-Range Planning*, Vol. 24, No. 1 (1991) pp. 64–70.

36. D. Scott-Kemmis, T. Darling, R. Johnston, F. Collyer, and C. Cliff, *Strategic Alliances in the Internationalisation of Australian Industry* (Canberra, Australia: Australian Government Publishing Service, 1990).

37. R. Luostarinen and L. S. Welch, *International Business Operations* (Helsinki: Export Consulting KY, 1990).

38. Business International, *Making Alliances Work: Lessons from Companies' Successes and Mistakes* (London: Business International, Ltd., 1990) p. 27.

39. Ibid.

40. Scott-Kemmis et al., *Strategic Alliances*.

41. D. Lei and J. W. Slocum, Jr., "Global Strategic Alliances: Payoffs and Pitfalls," *Organizational Dynamics*, Winter 1991, p. 57.

42. P. Lorange, "Human Resource Management in Multinational Cooperative Ventures," *Human Resource Management*, Vol. 25, No. 1 (1986) p. 133.

43. W. F. Cascio and M. G. Serapio, "Human Resources Systems in an International Alliance: The Undoing of a Done Deal?" *Organizational Dynamics*, Winter 1991, pp. 63–74. R. S. Schuler and E. Van Slujis, "Davidson-Marley BV: Establishing and Operating an International Joint Venture," *European Management Journal*, Vol. 10, December, 1992, pp. 428–436.

44. C. A. Bartlett, "How Multinational Organizations Evolve," *Journal of Business Strategy*, Vol. 3, No. 1 (1982). See also T. Hout, M. E. Porter, and E. Rudden, "How Global Companies Win Out," *Harvard Business Review*, Vol. 60, No. 5 (1982).

45. P. J. Dowling, "Hot Issues Overseas," *Personnel Administrator*, Vol. 34, No. 1 (1989) pp. 66–72.

46. D. A. Ondrack, "International Human-Resources Management in European and North-American Firms," *International Studies of Management and Organization*, Vol. 15, No. 1 (1985) pp. 6–32; and Phatak, *International Dimensions*.

47. P. Evans, "The Context of Strategic Human Resource Management Policy in Complex Firms," *Management Forum*, Vol. 6 (1986) pp. 105–117.

48. Ibid.

49. Phatak, *International Dimensions*.

50. Evans, "The Context of Strategic HRM."

51. A. J. Morrison, D. A. Ricks, and K. Roth, "Globalization Versus Regionalization: Which Way for the Multinational?" *Organizational Dynamics*, Winter 1991, p. 24.

52. N. Boyacigiller, "The Role of Expatriates in the Management of Interdependence, Complexity and Risk in Multinational Corporations," *Journal of International Business Studies*, Vol. 21, No. 3 (1990) pp. 357–381; D. E. Welch, "Determinants of International Human Resource Management Approaches and Activities: A Suggested Framework," *Journal of Management Studies*, forthcoming.

53. For example, L. Dyer, "Bringing Human Resources into the Strategy Formulation Process," in *Perspectives on Personnel/Human Resource Management* (3rd ed.), ed. H. G. Heneman and D. P. Schwab (Homewood, Ill.: Irwin, 1986).

54. Lorange, "HRM in Multinational Cooperative Ventures," p. 133.

55. Y. Doz and C. K. Prahalad, "Controlled Variety: A Challenge for Human Resource Management in the MNC," *Human Resource Management*, Vol. 25, No. 1 (1986) pp. 55–71.

56. R. S. Schuler and P. J. Dowling, "Survey of SHRM/I Members" (Unpublished manuscript, Stern School of Business, New York University, 1988).

57. B. Bhatt et al., "The Relationship Between the Global Strategic Planning Process and the Human Resource Management Function," in *Readings in Human Resource Management* (3rd ed.), ed. R. S. Schuler, S. A. Youngblood, and V. L. Huber (St. Paul, Minn.: West Publishing Co., 1988) pp. 427–435; see also G. Oddou and M. Mendenhall, "Succession-Planning for Global Managers: How Well Are We Preparing Our Future Decision-Makers?" *Business Horizons*, Vol. 34, No. 1 (1991) pp. 26–34.

58. Doz and Prahalad, "Controlled Variety."

59. P. J. Dowling, "International and Domestic Personnel/Human Resource Management: Similarities and Differences" (Working Paper No. 24, The Graduate School of Management, University of Melbourne, November 1986).

60. C. Reynolds, "Are You Ready to Make IHR a Global Function?" *HR News*, February 1992.

61. E. Brandt, "Global HR," *Personnel Journal*, March 1991, p. 38.

62. Ibid.

63. Reynolds, "Are You Ready?"

Chapter THREE

Recruitment and Selection of International Employees

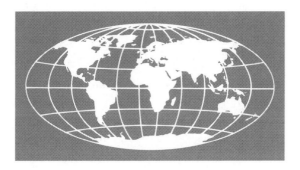

KEY ISSUES IN INTERNATIONAL RECRUITMENT AND SELECTION

The focus of this chapter is on the staffing function and its activities of recruitment and selection in an international context. We define recruitment as searching for and obtaining potential job candidates in sufficient numbers and quality so that the organization can select the most appropriate people to fill its job needs. Selection is the process of gathering information for the purposes of evaluating and deciding who should be employed in particular jobs.[1] The effective utilization of human resources is a goal of most organizations, domestic or international, but there are a number of staffing issues that multinationals must face—executive nationality staffing policies, predictors of expatriate success, expatriate failure, repatriation, equal employment opportunity (EEO), and recruitment and selection of HCNs and TCNs, for example—that are not present in a domestic environment. The aim of this chapter is to critically review the literature on these key issues to identify current and future trends in the recruitment, selection, and transfer of international employees.

EXECUTIVE NATIONALITY STAFFING POLICIES

As we discussed in Chapter 2, a multinational company can choose from four staffing options: (1) ethnocentric, (2) polycentric, (3) geocentric, and (4) regiocentric.[2] We shall consider them in detail here because each option has important implications for the recruitment and selection practices of MNEs.

The Ethnocentric Approach

An ethnocentric approach to staffing results in all key positions in a multinational company being filled by parent-country nationals (PCNs). This practice is common in the early stage of internationalization, when a company is establishing a new business, process, or product in another country and prior experience is essential. Other reasons for pursuing an ethnocentric staffing policy are a perceived lack of qualified host-country nationals (HCNs) and the need to maintain good communication links with corporate headquarters. For these reasons, an ethnocentric approach could be perfectly valid for a very experienced MNE that is normally geocentric. For example, when a multinational acquires a firm in another country, it may wish to initially replace local managers with PCNs for competency reasons or to ensure that the new subsidiary complies with overall corporate objectives and policies.

An ethnocentric policy, however, has a number of disadvantages. Zeira[3] has identified several major problems. First, an ethnocentric staffing policy limits the promotion opportunities of HCNs, which may lead to reduced productivity and increased turnover among that group. Second, the adaptation of expatriate managers to host countries often takes a long time, during which PCNs often make mistakes and make poor decisions. Third, when PCN and HCN compensation packages are compared, the often-considerable income gap in favor of PCNs is viewed by HCNs as unjustified. Finally, for many expatriates a key overseas position means new status, authority, and an increase in standard of living. Zeira states that these changes "tend to dull expatriates' sensitivity to the needs and expectations of their host country subordinates—and [are] not conducive to objective self-evaluation." Expatriates are also very expensive to maintain in overseas locations. The U. S.-based Employee Relocation Council reports that the average annual cost to send an employee overseas is $200,000 to $250,000.[4]

The Polycentric Approach

A polycentric staffing policy is one in which HCNs are recruited to manage subsidiaries in their own country and PCNs occupy positions at corporate headquarters. There are four main advantages of a polycentric policy. First, employing HCNs eliminates language barriers, avoids the adjustment problems of expatriate managers and their families, and removes the need for expensive training programs. Second, employment of HCNs allows a multinational company to take a lower profile in sensitive political situations. Related to this point, Robinson[5] has noted that a dubious reason for employing local managers is to insulate parent-company personnel from direct involvement in making extralegal payments to local government officials. It is difficult to evaluate the extent to which this factor may influence staffing decisions, but, clearly, in some countries it may well be the case. A third advantage of a polycentric policy is that the employment of HCNs is less expensive, even if a premium is paid to attract high-quality applicants. Fourth, a polycentric policy gives continuity to the management of foreign subsidiaries.

Some of these advantages address some of the shortcomings of an ethnocentric policy. A polycentric policy, however, has its own disadvantages. Perhaps the major difficulty is that of bridging the gap between the local national subsidiary managers and the parent-country managers at corporate headquarters. Language barriers, conflicting national loyalties, and a range of cultural differences (for example, personal value differences and differences in attitudes to business) may isolate the corporate headquarters staff from the various foreign subsidiaries. The result may be that a multinational firm could become a "federation" of independent national units with nominal links to corporate headquarters, a situation that would make a major strategic shift such as a move to production sharing very difficult to achieve.

A second major problem associated with a polycentric staffing policy concerns the career paths of HCN and PCN managers. Host-country managers have limited opportunities to gain experience outside their own country and cannot progress beyond the senior positions in their own subsidiary. Parent-country managers also have limited opportunities to gain overseas experience. As headquarters positions are held only by PCNs, the senior corporate management group responsible for resource allocation decisions between subsidiaries and overall strategic planning may have little overseas work experience from which to draw. In an increasingly competitive international environment, such lack of experience is a liability. It may also reinforce a cynical view among many PCNs that overseas experience is of little value in terms of career advancement.[6] Of course, in some cases the host government may dictate that key managerial positions be filled by its nationals. Alternatively, the MNE may wish to be perceived as a local company as part of a strategy of local responsiveness. (Some U.S. multinationals have taken this path as a way of "Europeanizing" in preparation for the Single European Market.)

The Geocentric Approach

This option utilizes the best people for the key jobs throughout the organization, regardless of nationality. There are two main advantages to this approach: it enables a multinational firm to develop an international executive team; and it overcomes the "federation" drawback of the polycentric approach. Phatak[7] believes the feasibility of implementing a geocentric policy is based on five related assumptions:

> (a)   highly competent employees are available not only at headquarters, but also in the subsidiaries; (b) international experience is a condition for success in top positions; (c) managers with high potential and ambition for promotion are constantly ready to be transferred from one country to another; (d) competent and mobile managers have an open disposition and high adaptability to different conditions in their various assignments; (e) those not blessed initially with an open disposition and high adaptability can acquire these qualities as their experience abroad accumulates.

As with the other staffing approaches, there are disadvantages associated with a geocentric policy. First, host governments want a high number of their citizens employed and will utilize immigration controls in order to force HCN employment if enough people and adequate skills are available. In addition to this constraint on the implementation of a geocentric policy, most Western countries require companies to provide extensive documentation if they wish to hire a foreign national instead of a local national. Providing this documentation can be time-consuming, expensive, and at times futile. Of course, the same drawback applies to an ethnocentric policy. A related issue, which will be discussed later, is the difficulty of obtaining a work permit for the accompanying spouse.

Another disadvantage is that a geocentric policy can be expensive to implement because of increased training and relocation costs. A related factor is the need to have a compensation structure with standardized international base pay, which may be higher than national levels in many countries. Finally, large numbers of PCNs, TCNs, and HCNs need to be sent abroad in order to build and maintain the international team required to support a geocentric staffing policy.[8] To successfully implement a geocentric staffing policy, therefore, requires longer lead time and more centralized control of the staffing process. This necessarily reduces the independence of subsidiary management in these issues, and this loss of autonomy may be resisted by the subsidiary.

The Regiocentric Approach

A fourth approach to international staffing is a regional policy with regard to executive nationality. The best example of this approach is a regiocentric policy, which Heenan and Perlmutter[9] define as functional rationalization on a more-than-one country basis. The specific mix will vary with the nature of a firm's business and product strategy, but one approach is for a MNE to divide its operations into geographical regions and transfer staff within these regions. For example, the MNE could create three regions: Europe, the Americas, and Asia-Pacific. European staff would be transferred throughout the European region (say a Briton to Germany, a French national to Belgium, and a German to Spain). Staff transfers to the Asian-Pacific region from Europe would be rare, as would transfers from the regions to headquarters.

One motive for using a regiocentric approach is that it allows interaction between executives transferred to regional headquarters from subsidiaries in the region and PCNs posted to the regional headquarters.[10] This approach also reflects some sensitivity to local conditions, since local subsidiaries are staffed almost totally by HCNs. Another advantage is that a regiocentric approach can be a way for a MNE to gradually move from a purely ethnocentric or polycentric approach to a geocentric approach.[11] To a certain extent, that appears to be the path taken by some multinationals, such as the Ford Motor Company. However, there are some disadvantages in a regiocentric policy. It can produce federalism at a regional rather than a country basis and constrain the organization from taking a global stance. Another difficulty is that while this approach does improve career prospects at the national level, it only moves the barrier to the regional level. Staff may advance to regional headquarters but seldom to positions at the parent headquarters.

The Ad Hoc Approach

Rather than systematically selecting one of the four approaches discussed above, a MNE may just proceed on an ad hoc basis. The danger with this approach, according to Robinson,[12] is that "the firm will opt for a policy of using parent-country nationals in foreign management positions by default, that is, simply as an automatic extension of domestic policy, rather than deliberately seeking optimum utilization of management skills."

This option is really a policy by default; there is no conscious decision or evaluation of appropriate policy. The "policy" is a result of corporate inertia, inexperience, or both. The major disadvantage here (apart from the obvious one of inefficient use of resources) is that the multinational is poorly placed to either anticipate threats or profit from opportunities. Responses are reactive rather than proactive, and a consistent organizational human resources strategy that fits the overall business strategy of the organization is difficult to achieve with an ad hoc approach.

Determinants of Policy Choice

In summary, a multinational can pursue one of several approaches to international staffing. The choice can be determined by internal or external factors. As was discussed in Chapter 2, changes in an organization's structure evolve to correspond with changes in its strategy, and HRM decisions are made in response to these strategy-structure changes. The choice of an appropriate policy on executive nationality tends to reflect organizational needs. For example, if the organization places a high priority on organizational control, then an ethnocentric policy will be adopted.[13] Transnationals endeavor to internationalize management as well as products and tend to select a regiocentric or geocentric policy.[14]

However, there are difficulties in maintaining a uniform approach to international staffing; each has its advantages and disadvantages. Therefore, strategies in different countries may require different staffing approaches (see Exhibit 3-1). For example, a U.S. multinational may take a geocentric approach toward its operations in Europe and Asia-Pacific, but an ethnocentric approach toward its operations in Africa.

EXPATRIATE FAILURE

A prominent issue in the international recruitment and selection literature is that of expatriate "failure," which may be defined as the premature return of an expatriate manager (that is, a return to the home country

E X H I B I T   3 - 1   Selecting Managers: Pros and Cons of PCNs, TCNs, and HCNs.

Parent-Country Nationals

Advantages
- Organizational control and coordination is maintained and facilitated.
- Promising managers are given international experience.
- PCNs are the best people for the job.
- There is assurance that subsidiary will comply with company objectives, policies, etc.

Disadvantages
- The promotional opportunities of HCNs are limited.
- Adaptation to host country may take a long time.
- PCNs may impose an inappropriate HQ style.
- Compensation for PCNs and HCNs may differ.

Third-Country Nationals

Advantages
- Salary and benefit requirements may be lower than for PCNs.
- TCNs may be better informed than PCNs about host-country environment.

Disadvantages
- Transfers must consider possible national animosities (e.g., India and Pakistan).
- The host government may resent hiring of TCNs.
- TCNs may not want to return to their own countries after assignment.

Host-Country Nationals

Advantages
- Language and other barriers are eliminated.
- Hiring costs are reduced, and no work permit is required.
- Continuity of management improves, since HCNs stay longer in positions.
- Government policy may dictate hiring of HCNs.
- Morale among HCNs may improve as they see the career potentials.

Disadvantages
- Control and coordination of HQ may be impeded.
- HCNs have limited career opportunity outside the subsidiary.
- Hiring HCNs limits opportunities for PCNs to gain overseas experience.
- Hiring HCNs could encourage a federation of national rather than global units.

before the period of assignment is completed). Thus, an expatriate failure represents a selection error, compounded in some cases by poor expatriate management policies.

There is some discussion in the literature about the usefulness of defining expatriate failure so narrowly. An expatriate may be ineffective and poorly adjusted yet, if not recalled, he or she will not be considered a failure. Because of an inability either to effectively handle the new responsibilities or to adjust to the country of assignment, performance levels may be diminished. If the manager is not coping well culturally, the performance of the business unit will be affected; the result may be, for example, low HCN morale or dissatisfied clients.[15] Thus, the return rate is not a perfect measure of success or failure and may underestimate the problem.[16] As will be discussed in Chapter 5, organizations need to look rather at performance evaluation in order to accurately define successful assignment completion; a more accurate measurement of expatriate failure will then be possible. Despite its limitations, however, the current definition of expatriate failure has served to highlight the problems encountered in staffing overseas subsidiaries with PCNs and TCNs.

The Costs of Failure

The costs of failure can be both direct and indirect. Direct costs usually include salary, training, and travel and relocation expenses, which can average U.S. $55,000 to U.S. $80,000, depending on currency exchange rates and the location of the assignment.[17] The costs rise if the "failed" manager is replaced by another PCN.

The "invisible" or indirect costs are harder to quantify in dollar terms but can prove to be more expensive for the company, depending on the expatriate position involved. Many expatriate positions, for example, involve contact with host-government officials and key clients.[18] Failure at this level may result in loss of market share, difficulties with host-government officials, and demands that PCNs be replaced with HCNs. The possible effect on local staff is also an indirect cost factor, since morale and productivity could suffer. Zeira and Banai[19] argue that multinational corporations should consider these factors as the real cost of expatriate failure, rather than the direct costs for salary and repatriation.

Failure also, of course, has an effect on the expatriate concerned, who may lose self-esteem, self-confidence, and prestige among peers.[20] Future performance may be marked by decreased motivation, lack of promotional opportunities, or even increased productivity to compensate for the failure. Finally, the expatriate's family relationships may be threatened. These are additional costs to organizations that are often overlooked. As Guptara[21] states: "A company that sends out people who may not be suitable for working cross-culturally is being grossly negligent."

Failure Rates Compared

The international literature also indicates that expatriate failure is a persistent and recurring problem, especially for American companies, where it has been reported to fluctuate between 25 and 40 percent, rising to 70 percent in developing countries.[22] One of the earliest empirical studies on expatriate failure rates was that by Tung.[23] This study surveyed a number of U.S., European, and Japanese multinationals. As Exhibit 3-2 shows, all the multinationals in the study reported significant expatriate failure rates, although those for U.S. companies were higher than the rates for European and Japanese companies.

EXHIBIT 3-2   Expatriate Failure Rates

Recall Rate %	% of Companies
U.S. multinationals	
20–40	7
10–20	69
<10	24
European multinationals	
11–15	3
6–10	38
<5	59
Japanese multinationals	
11–19	14
6–10	10
<5	76

Source: R. L. Tung, "Selection and Training Procedures of U.S., European, and Japanese Multinationals." Copyright © 1982 by The Regents of the University of California. Reprinted from the *California Management Review*, Vol. 25, No. 1, pp. 57–71. By permission of The Regents.

Brewster[24] conducted a study of twenty-five MNEs across five industries from five European countries. He reports low rates of early recall, findings that concur with the European failure rates reported by Tung.[25] Likewise, in a pilot study, Hamill[26] investigated the IHRM practices and policies of seven British multinationals. He found that the failure rate among British expatriates was significantly lower (less than 5 percent) than that reported for U.S. multinationals. The British rates are similar to Australian expatriate failure rates. In their study of international HRM policies of four MNEs operating internationally from Australia, Dowling and Welch[27] found that expatriate failure was not a major concern. A further study by Welch[28] of three Australian multinationals and one U.S. subsidiary found that, although precise records were not kept, the four companies estimated failure rates of less than 5 percent. Bjorkman and Gertsen[29] report that their study of Scandinavian firms found expatriate failure rates of less than 5 percent. Thus, it appears that expatriate failure has been of greater concern for U.S. multinationals than others. However, it should be pointed out that the non-American studies were conducted several years after Tung's study, and a simple explanation for the differences noted here may be that companies operating internationally have since become more aware of the problems associated with expatriate failure and have learned to avoid them.

Reasons for Failure

As part of her study, Tung[30] asked respondents to indicate reasons for expatriate failure in their companies. There were national differences in the responses. The American companies cited, in descending order of importance: (1) inability of spouse to adjust, (2) manager's inability to adjust, (3) other family reasons, (4) manager's personal or emotional maturity, (5) inability to cope with larger overseas responsibility. The Japanese responses were almost reversed: (1) inability to cope with larger overseas responsibility, (2) difficulties with new environment, (3) personal or emotional problems, (4) lack of technical competence, and (5) inability of spouse to adjust. For the European companies, "inability of spouse to adjust" was the only consistent reason given by respondents.

Tung notes that the relatively lower ranking of "inability of spouse to adjust" by Japanese respondents is not surprising, given the role and status to which Japanese society relegates the spouse. However, other social factors may contribute to this finding. Because of the competitive nature of the Japanese education system, the spouse commonly opts to remain in Japan with the children, particularly where male offspring are concerned. Thus, in many cases, the spouse is not a factor in expatriate failure. Tung[31] also points out that the length of the overseas assignment is also a factor: three to four years is the average assignment for Japanese firms, compared with two to three years for American firms. This longer assignment allows the expatriate more time to adjust to the foreign situation. As well, Japanese firms do not expect the expatriate to perform up to full capacity until the third year; the first year of the foreign assignment is seen mainly as a period of adjustment to the foreign environment. Allen[32] examined the differences between Japanese postings to the United States and vice versa. He found that some Japanese firms post to the United States only those senior managers who have a significant history with the company and can make contact with top executives in Japan. He also found that Japanese firms will sometimes send a younger potential successor with the senior manager, who acts as the junior manager's mentor while in the United States.

Respondents in Hamill's[33] study suggested that the reasons for the lower British expatriate failure rate were that British managers were more internationally mobile than U.S. managers and that British companies had developed more effective expatriate policies. (For example, many overseas assignments were an integral part of individuals' career development.)

Australian studies have found that early recalls were attributed as much to lack of technical skills as to the failure of the spouse to adjust. One U.S. personnel director who was interviewed by Dowling and Welch[34] pointed out that attributing expatriate recall to "failure of spouse to adjust" was at times a simplistic explanation. He postulated that, apart from the probability of the expatriate blaming his wife (all the expatriates in this study were male) for his own failure to adjust, some astute spouses may see the expatriate's poor performance and trigger the early recall to limit damage to the expatriate's career. Welch[35] notes that the respondents in her study perceived an expatriate posting as a desirable appointment—an opportunity to travel and live overseas—and that those selected tended to generate a feeling of envy and a recognition of status from fellow workers, relatives, and neighbors. This attitude is partly due to a feeling among Australians of being isolated from the rest of the world and partly to a willingness to travel, similar to the view reported by Hamill. This positive outlook on the foreign assignment may have assisted the Australians in the study to adjust to the demands of the foreign location.

E X H I B I T   3 - 2   IHR in the News

City of Love Drives Foreigners to Despair

Psychiatrist says Paris is a mental health hazard

by Stuart Wavell, Paris

Paris, the eternal City of Love and a million street cafes, where the divine ambrosia of Gauloises and fresh croissants mingles with expensive scents and a hint of drains, may be dangerous to your mental health.

The beguiling face that the city presents to millions of entranced tourists looks very different to many foreign residents, who experience feelings of persecution and despair. Parisian behaviour can make the Japanese contemplate suicide and drive the British into profound depression.

The disorder has been named "the Paris syndrome" by Dr. Hiroaki Ota, a psychiatrist who has treated or hospitalised 139 disturbed Japanese in the past few years. Two have tried to kill themselves.

Desperate British residents are regular callers at SOS Help, an English-language helpline allied to the Samaritans. "We have a significant proportion of callers with considerable psychiatric problems" a spokesman said last week. "There is a particular paranoia that sets in here."

Germans, Scandinavians and Americans also suffer from distress, which is blamed on Parisians' arrogance, hostility and fearsome bureaucracy. Apart from Italians, only the gregarious Irish, with 15 pubs in the city, seem immune to the malady.

Jonathan, a 39-year-old British computer engineer, explained last week how an accumulation of small incidents can lead to the conviction that an "implacable and malign system" is ranged against the innocent foreigner.

"The other week my car was towed away because my French neighbour complained about it to the police, although it was parked perfectly legally," he said. "My upstairs neighbour stamps on the floor at six in the morning to punish me for other tenants' noise. Once she leapt out and attacked me on the stairs. And someone keeps ripping my name tag off the entryphone.

(continued)

"I fell in love with Paris, and I can't believe it's turning into a nightmare. Parisians are so bloody rude. I speak good French, but if you stumble over a word in a shop, they'll cut you dead and turn to the next customer."

Difficulty in learning French is at the root of the trauma experienced by the Japanese, Dr. Ota believes. As a result: "You don't have time to explain yourself, and no one listens to you." He also cites the culture shock of encountering hostile shop assistants, the city's prolific dog messes and the perils of pedestrian crossings.

"It's like a disease, and it only happens in Paris," said his French wife Fabienne. "In London or Dusseldorf, people will really make an effort to help you.

"This syndrome can affect a family profoundly. The husband returns from a long day at the office, frustrated that he has been unable to communicate. His wife has spent all day at home, and she is frustrated too."

A large contingent among the 30,000-strong British community flock together in the city's outer suburbs in a misguided attempt to replicate Purley or Guildford, according to the Rev. Martin Draper, Chaplain of St. George's Anglican Church in Paris. "The Anglican churches in the suburbs are like little British parishes, with their Cubs and Brownies," he said.

"It's perfectly possible to live in that English world for three or four years, so that your only contact with France is intimidating— when you need those dreadful foreigners for the plumbing or some bureaucracy."

Isolation is a principal complaint fielded by Message, a mother's support group in the fashionable suburb of St. Germain en Laye. "We get some pretty desperate calls," said Julie Duthie, the organiser. "It's very difficult to meet French women. A lot of them go out to work or are too preoccupied with their extended families."

French men fuel their sense of insecurity. "I am scared of them," said Duthie. "I don't like socialising with them. They come across as so superior and intimidating that they make you feel stupid. One woman I know is living a double life because her husband won't let her talk about British friends."

(continued)

EXHIBIT 3-3 *(continued)*

SOS Help often has to soothe the clash between English and French temperaments by referring callers to doctors. "English reserve is just a question of manners, but the French have this coldness which assumes they are intellectually superior to everyone else," a spokesman said. "They assume you have the intelligence of a seven-year-old if you speak with an accent."

Kay, a 52-year-old British widow, speaks perfect French and has lived near the centre of Paris for 11 years, but plans to return to Britain.

"I have finally had to admit to myself that I don't like the French and that Parisians bring a particular refinement to French cruelty," she said. "I worked in two French offices where they made it clear that because I was British I was inferior and couldn't enjoy the same rights. It was so unpleasant that I had to leave.

"I'm going to try to rediscover my British identity in Britain, but after spending so long in France I may find myself in limbo, not at home in either society."

Source: The Sunday Times (London), 3 November 1991, p. 19. © Times Newspapers Ltd. 1991. Reprinted with permission.

In a later article,[36] Tung identifies what she terms the common denominators of successful performance among European and Japanese multinationals. These are: long-term orientation regarding overall planning and performance assessment; the use of more rigorous training programs to prepare candidates for overseas assignments (particularly by Japanese multinationals); provision of a comprehensive expatriate support system; overall qualification of candidates for overseas assignments; and restricted job mobility (due mainly to company loyalty). Tung adds three additional factors that she feels may account for European and Japanese companies' success with expatriation relative to the U.S. experience: international orientation, longer history of overseas operations, and language capability. She concludes that U.S. multinationals could learn about expatriate management from the experience of their Japanese and European counterparts.

Other researchers have since addressed the reasons for expatriate failure. For example, Gregersen and Black[37] studied 220 American expatriates in four Pacific Rim countries. They found a positive correlation between "intent to stay in the overseas assignment" and "commitment to the local company," "adjustment to interaction with HCNs," and "adjustment to general living conditions." Adjustment to the work role itself, however, was negatively associated with intent to stay. The findings suggest that failure is seldom a consequence of a lack of technical skills, which is not surprising, given the emphasis on relevant technical skills during the expatriate selection process. In their discussion of the significance of the work role and intent to stay, Gregersen and Black link challenges at work with cultural adjustment. They argue that once the expatriate has mastered, or nearly completed, the assigned work, other factors may surface and assume relative importance. For instance, because work is no longer so time-consuming, the expatriate may pay more attention to cultural interactions. These can become distorted when combined with lack of challenge at work and thus sow seeds for failure.

It should be pointed out that, for assignments involving U.S. and other Western expatriate families, the spouse carries a heavy burden. Upon arrival in the country of assignment, the responsibility for settling the family into its new home falls on the spouse, who may have left behind a career, along with friends and social support networks (particularly relatives). Servants may be involved, for which the spouse is seldom prepared. It is often not possible for the spouse to work in the country of assignment. The well-being and education of the children also concern the spouse. Though the majority of spouses are female, trailing male spouses face similar problems of adjustment.[38] All these factors can contribute to a failure of the spouse to adjust, which may affect the performance of the expatriate manager. "The negative impact of the accompanying spouse's career continuity, self-esteem and identity can be personally and professionally devastating. Not only can the marriage partnership's balance and health be jeopardized by the psychological assault to the trailing spouse, but so can the performance level of the employee who has been transferred."[39] In fact, when one adds cultural adjustment problems to such a situation, it is perhaps not so surprising to find that some couples seek to return home prematurely.

PREDICTORS OF EXPATRIATE SUCCESS

Given the costs of expatriate failure, selecting the right people for overseas assignments is important. According to the relevant literature, certain traits and characteristics have been identified as predictors of expatriate success; although these traits may not guarantee an expatriate's success, without them, the possibility of failure is enhanced. These traits or characteristics are technical ability, managerial skills, cultural empathy, adaptability, diplomacy, language ability, positive attitude, emotional stability and maturity, and adaptability of family.[40] According to Murray and Murray,[41] while managerial or technical competence is regarded as the primary competence for expatriate success, effectiveness and coping skills are also required. Effectiveness skills are defined as the ability to successfully translate the managerial or technical skills into the foreign environment, whereas coping skills enable the person to become reasonably comfortable, or at least survive, in a foreign environment.

The Use of Selection Tests

Although there is a consensus among scholars and practitioners that personal characteristics (or traits) are important, there is considerable debate about how such personal characteristics can be reliably and accurately measured. Personality and psychological tests have been used in the selection process, but the effectiveness of such tests as predictors of cultural adjustment is questioned. For example, Torbiorn[42] comments that though desirable personality traits are specified and recommended, the tests or criteria to assess these traits are seldom convincingly validated. Willis[43] states that if tests are used they should be selected with care and regard for reliability and validity: "While some tests may be useful in suggesting potential problems, a review of a number of studies indicates little correlation between test scores and performance." As well, most of the relevant tests have been devised in the United States and, therefore, may be "culture bound." Use of such tests on non-American nationals adds another question mark to their reliability and validity as predictors of expatriate success. Another constraint is that in some countries (Australia being one) there is controversy about the use of psychological tests.[44]

The difficulty of predicting success, then, seems to be related to the lack of valid and reliable screening devices to identify, with certainty, managers who will succeed in a foreign assignment.[45] The crucial variables affecting the adjustment of the individual and family are not only difficult to identify or measure, but the complex relationship between personality factors and ability to adjust to another culture is not well understood.[46] Discussing this problem, Gertsen[47] points out that the use of personality traits to predict intercultural competence is further complicated by the fact that personality traits are not defined and evaluated in the same way in different cultures. She states, "The most serious problem, however, is that attitudes do not always result in the implicitly expected behavior. If a person has very positive attitudes towards a culture but is unable to express this in his behavior, it has no effect." She concludes that attitudes are relevant only to the extent that they determine a person's actual communicative behavior in another culture and that other personality traits are relevant in the same way.

One drawback of models based on traits or characteristics is the subjective nature of the scoring of the abilities, especially those classified as personal and environmental characteristics. Nevertheless, models derived from this approach have value in that they provide some guidelines that can be applied during the selection process, rather than mere reliance on the potential manager's domestic record as a predictor.[48]

Research on Selection Criteria

One of the few studies reported in the literature that examines expatriate selection practices is Tung's[49] empirical study of 80 U.S. multinationals. She found that selection criteria tended to differ according to job category. In Tung's study, job categories were classified as chief executive officer, functional head, troubleshooter, and operative. Tung grouped variables contributing to expatriate success into four general areas: technical competence on the job; personality traits or relational abilities; environmental variables; and family situation. The U.S. multinational respondents indicated that the most important criteria for the selection of the chief executive officer for a foreign subsidiary would be communication skills, managerial talent, maturity, emotional stability and adaptability to new environmental settings. For a functional head, the criteria were maturity, emotional stability, and technical knowledge. Knowledge of the host-country's language was considered important for functional head and operative jobs.

Tung's study also asked respondents to indicate their procedures for assessing the criteria they used to select overseas staff. Only 3 percent of companies reported formally assessing technical competence, which did not surprise Tung, since most candidates are internal recruits. For management positions, 52 percent of respondents indicated that they interviewed both candidate and spouse to assess the family situation. Forty percent interviewed both candidate and spouse for technical positions. Only 1 percent of firms indicated that they did not conduct interviews with both the candidate and spouse. These figures for interviews with both candidates may seem high, but they are less impressive when one

considers the fact that inability of the spouse to adjust is the most frequently cited reason for expatriate failure.

In a more recent empirical investigation, Brewster[50] found that only
16 percent of the European companies in his study interviewed the potential expatriate and spouse. Speculating on reasons for the differing results between his findings and those of Tung's[51] study, Brewster suggests
that methodological approaches may be part of the answer. He points out
that Tung's study relied on questionnaire responses and companies that
have particular approaches to expatriate selection are more likely to respond to a questionnaire. Brewster adds that the situation may have
changed in the intervening years between Tung's study and his own but
concludes that the most likely explanation for the differing results is that
companies that have a very detailed knowledge of the spouse have included that fact in a questionnaire response as "interview," whereas in
his study that categorization was clarified during face-to-face discussions.

Another significant finding of Tung's early work was that, although
most respondents indicated that relational abilities were an important selection criteria, only 5 percent assessed a candidate's relational ability
through a formal procedure such as judgment by seniors or psychological
tests. This omission is perhaps not as surprising as Tung's study suggests.
Hixon,[52] in his study of expatriate management, found that selection was
based on technical ability and willingness to reside overseas. Mendenhall, Dunbar, and Oddou,[53] in their review of expatriate selection practices, conclude that U.S. companies seem to focus their selection efforts
on one single criterion—that of technical competence, despite the importance of all the other criteria correlated to overseas success. McEnery and
DesHarnais[54] surveyed forty Michigan firms and found that functional or
technical skills were the most important selection criteria used.

Even though companies may agree that relational skills and/or abilities are important criteria (see Exhibit 3-4), it is difficult to accurately assess them. Given the confusion surrounding the personality and psychological tests reported above, it is not surprising to find that companies
primarily rely on technical skills and past performance. Guptara[55] argues
that companies hesitate to use psychometric tests because the crude nature of tests developed so far for this purpose yield uncertain results. In
addition, though some multinational companies use elaborate psychometric analysis designed to determine the prospect's "adaptability" to a foreign culture and society, failure rates continue to approach one-third.[56]

Unlike adjustment skills, technical and managerial competence can
be determined on the basis of past performance. Since expatriates are
usually internal recruits,[57] personnel evaluation records need only be

EXHIBIT 3-4   Key Characteristics of the International Manager

(% of respondents who ranked a characteristic as among the five most important)

Strategic awareness	71
Adaptability in new situations	67
Sensitivity to different cultures	60
Ability to work in international teams	56
Language skills	46
Understanding international marketing	46
Relationship skills	40
International negotiation skills	38
Self-reliance	27
High task-orientation	19
Open, non-judgmental personality	19
Understanding international finance	13
Awareness of own cultural background	2

Source: K. Barham and M. Devine, "The Quest for the International Manager: A Survey of Global Human Resource Strategies," the Economist Intelligence Unit, London, Special Report No. 2098 (1990), p. 21. Reprinted with permission.

examined and checked with the candidate's past and present superiors. However, past performance may have little or no bearing on one's ability to achieve a task in a foreign cultural environment.[58] In fact, traits that may make a person a good performer in the domestic environment may be liabilities overseas. In an attempt to address the problem, Zeira and Banai[59] advocate an open-system approach to identifying valid selection criteria for international executives. They recommended that

> research literature dealing with selection of international executives should be broadened to include an analysis of the expectations of the host environments in addition to those of the MNCs. This broadening of the spectrum would make it possible for MNCs to base the selection of their international executives on the expectations of the real environment in which EMs [expatriate managers] operate and with which they must cope. Selection based on both the MNCs and the host environments' expectations would further better prediction of the extent of candidates' suitability for their respective host countries.

This discussion has indicated that the cultural environment in which expatriates operate is an important factor in determining successful performance. Reliance on technical skills as a predictor of success is, therefore, limiting. According to Mendenhall and Oddou, "Technical competence has nothing to do with one's ability to adapt to a new environment, deal effectively with foreign coworkers, or perceive and if necessary imitate the foreign behavioral norms."[60] Mendenhall and Oddou[61] further claim that a multidimensional approach is important in the successful selection of expatriates and propose a four-dimensional model that attempts to link specific behavioral tendencies to probable overseas performance. Their four dimensions in the expatriate adjustment process are:

1. The self-oriented dimension, the degree to which the expatriate expresses an adaptive concern for self-preservation, self-enjoyment, and mental hygiene.

2. The others-oriented dimension, the degree to which the expatriate is concerned about host-national coworkers and desires to affiliate with them.

3. The perceptual dimension; reflects the expertise the expatriate possesses in accurately understanding why host-nationals behave the way they do.

4. The cultural-toughness dimension, a mediating variable which recognizes that acculturation is affected by the degree to which the culture of the host country is incongruent with that of the home country.

Mendenhall and Oddou recommend that the expatriate selection process focus on evaluating the candidate's strengths and weaknesses in these four dimensions. They derive two major propositions from their study. First, expatriate acculturation is a multidimensional process rather than a unidimensional phenomenon. Thus, selection procedures of multinational firms should be changed from their present one-dimensional focus on technical competence as the primary criterion to a multidimensional focus based on criteria relating to the dimensions identified in their review. Second, comprehensive acculturation training programs incorporating each of the four dimensions outlined above should be designed for expatriates. To carry out these propositions, Mendenhall and Oddou suggest a number of proposals for enhancing the expatriate selection process. Specifically, they recommend that the expatriate selection process should focus on evaluating the applicant's strengths and weaknesses in the dimensions of expatriate acculturation identified in their review:

- For the self-oriented dimension, a number of psychological tests are available to measure stress levels and Type A behavior patterns.[62] Technical expertise is already assessed in most organizations.

- For the perceptual dimension, psychological tests with established validity could assess the flexibility of an individual's perceptual and evaluative tendencies. They could be used in conjunction with in-depth evaluations from other sources such as a consultant psychologist and the applicant's superiors. Use of testing may also encourage self-reflection regarding motivation for the assignment.

- The above approach could also be used to gauge degree of others-orientation.

- The toughness of the culture of the country to which a future expatriate will be assigned can be assessed by comparing the host country's political, legal, socioeconomic, and business systems to those in the parent country. If there is considerable disparity (that is, if the host country is "culturally tough"), only applicants with high scores on the battery of evaluation devices should be considered for the assignment. For assignments to countries similar to the parent country (for example, an assignment to Australia from the United States), applicants with more marginal evaluation scores may be considered. This point is very similar to the notion of similarity/dissimilarity between cultures as a selection factor proposed by Tung in her selection model.

Another approach to address this concern is offered by Ronen,[63] whose model appears to incorporate the success factors identified by Tung and by Mendenhall and Oddou. Ronen's model has five categories of attributes for success: job factors; relational dimensions (similar to the perceptual dimension of Mendenhall and Oddou's model); motivational state; family situation; and language skills. While the model is useful in bringing previous work together into a framework, it has limitations. According to Ronen,

> The relative importance of each category is difficult to establish. Returning IAs [international assignees] and managers' evaluations, however, do offer some information in this regard, as reported earlier. Unfortunately, the lack of systematic evaluation of such data renders speculative any statement about the relative importance of these dimensions in contributing to an international assignee's level of effectiveness.

Our discussion has revealed that establishing criteria for expatriate selection remains problematic. Predictors of success have been identified, but it remains unclear as to how these should be measured. Part of the problem is the design of appropriate tests, but other factors are involved.

One factor is time. Expatriates are often selected quickly to staff unexpected overseas vacancies, precluding a lengthy screening process.[64]

The Importance of the Family

Another factor in selection is the importance of the family. The contribution that the family, particularly the spouse, makes to the success of the overseas assignment is now well documented, having been the subject of further research since landmark studies, such as that of Tung, were published. For example, Black and Stephens[65] examined the influence of the spouse on American expatriate adjustment. Surveying 220 U.S. expatriates and their spouses working in Japan, Taiwan, and Hong Kong, they found that a favorable opinion about the overseas assignment by the spouse is positively related to the spouse's adjustment and that the adjustment of the spouse is highly correlated to the adjustment of the expatriate manager. Despite this important link, however, Black and Stephens relate that only 30 percent of the firms sought the spouse's opinion concerning the international assignment, and they conclude:

> Given (a) that spouse opinion about accepting the international assignment is related to spouse adjustment, (b) that spouse adjustment is positively related to expatriate adjustment and expatriate intentions to stay or leave and (c) that premature returns are quite costly, it seems that firms could benefit from more careful attention to the opinion of the spouse concerning the assignment before the expatriate is transferred overseas.[66]

Other studies seem to confirm the U.S. results. Australian research into the psychological impact of relocation on the partners of fifty-eight expatriate and repatriate managers[67] found that the amount of control the partner felt over the decision to relocate was significantly correlated to her satisfaction with life in the predeparture and early stages of expatriation. As important, the more comprehensive the company assistance, especially during the early stages of the expatriation process, the higher the level of psychological adjustment to relocation made by the expatriate partner. Like the Black and Stephens study, the Australian study supports the need for the inclusion of the family in the selection process. Yet, when one looks at more recent studies of the expatriation practices of various MNEs, the inclusion of the spouse and family in the selection process continues to be either overlooked or treated in a peripheral way. Brewster's[68] study of twenty-five European MNEs found that only 16 percent interviewed the spouse during the selection process. Bjorkman's[69] study of expatriation practices in Scandinavian firms found that less than one-third of the firms surveyed carried out interviews with the spouse, a result similar to that reported by Gertsen,[70] who argues that the Danish firms in her study were reluctant to interview the spouse because this would be interfering in the employee's private life. Welch[71] found a similar reluctance on the part of Australian companies to include spouses in the formal selection process.

Thus, this growing body of research indicates that companies are aware of the importance of the family but are experiencing difficulties in incorporating the family into the selection process. Companies are reluctant to intrude into matters normally outside their domain and to become involved in issues of civil liberties. Can a company, for example, insist that a spouse, who is not an employee of the company, undergo a personality test? What one finds in practice is that companies alert to the key role the family plays resort to informal methods, such as taking the couple to dinner or putting the couple in contact with a repatriate couple who once lived in the location concerned.[72] Brewster comments that personal knowledge of the potential expatriate was emphasized by most of the companies in his study and that personal knowledge extended to knowledge of, and often acquaintance with, the family.[73] However, what is clear from the above discussion is that the understandable reluctance to become involved in an employee's private life constrains the company's ability to select the most appropriate couple.

Figure 3-1 graphically illustrates the selection process discussed above, and Exhibit 3-5 delineates some of the difficulties experienced by Japanese families in Britain.

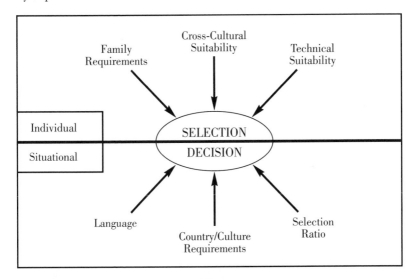

FIGURE 3-1   Factors in Expatriate Selection

EXHIBIT 3-5   IHR in the News

Island-Hoppers

Ten years ago there were 10,000 Japanese living in Britain. Today there are at least 44,000. The tide of Japanese investment is bringing a tide of Japanese expatriates—and with them everything from sushi bars to sumo wrestling.

The typical Japanese expatriate is still a company man spending three to five years abroad. Most commonly he (rarely she) will be a banker in his 20s or 30s; a small minority will be senior executives sent over to run a London headquarters or (less often) a plant in Wales or the north-east. Recently, more students are arriving too.

The biggest snag for a Japanese expatriate with a family is providing an education for his children. Stepping off the exams escalator at home risks sacrificing a job-for-life in a prestigious company. Parents with no option but to bring their children to Britain with them scramble for places in schools that teach the Japanese national curriculum.

The best known is the Japanese School in Acton, West London. It caters for 980 pupils—up from 657 in 1987—and is staffed by Japanese teachers on three-year secondments from the Ministry of Education in Tokyo. But three new schools have opened since the mid-1980s to ensure the maximum choice for Taro-chan. One, the Gyosei International School in Milton Keynes, takes 1,000 pupils and is the biggest Japanese school in Europe. Britain now has eight private Japanese schools, and six Saturday schools attached to Japanese-owned factories in Wales and the north-east.

Even with the schools problem resolved, there are other headaches. Top of the list for most is the language. English (or rather American) is Japan's second language. But eight years of parroting verbs and learning about sub-clauses is poor preparation for the patter of London cabbies and Geordie shop stewards. One woman who has lived in Britain for a decade summed up her frustration: what makes life so difficult is that the poor people do not speak English.

(continued)

Another worry is social anarchy. Many Japanese find ethnic diversity a puzzle. The levels of violence and crime in contemporary Britain are profoundly shocking to them. Most dislike the lack of deference displayed by the poor to the rich and—even worse, in their eyes—the lack of consideration shown by the rich for the poor. One acute young banker mused that he could see where Karl Marx got his idea of the class struggle from.

A mini-industry has developed to make the Japanese feel at home. Those moving to Britain can choose among eight Japanese estate agents to find them a house, and seven Japanese removal companies to shift the mod cons which keep all Japanese houses ultra-clean and super-efficient. Once here, they look for a location that reflects their position in the social pecking-order. Around London it is St. John's Wood and Hampstead for bosses; Finchley, Golders Green and Ealing for middle managers; Croydon for the lower ranks.

The unadventurous can live as though they have never left Tokyo: reading Japanese newspapers, buying their spectacles in Japanese opticians and suits in Japanese tailors, playing mahjong in Japanese clubs and singing "New York, New York" in karaoke bars. London has more than 60 Japanese restaurants and eight Japanese food shops to stave off the torments of English food. In the provinces there are regular food parcels from relatives in Japan and weekly lorry loads of supplies from London shops.

As they become more established, the Japanese are also growing more adventurous. There is plenty that they like about Britain: huge houses and (relatively) easy commuting, cheap and readily accessible golf courses. And the women enjoy their freedom and status. Japanese firms have recently started to worry that company wives do not want to go home. Perhaps Britain will change Japan as much as Japan is changing Britain.

Source: The Economist, 14 September 1991, p. 40. © The Economist, London, September 1991. Reprinted with permission.

OTHER FACTORS AFFECTING EXPATRIATE SELECTION

Once an organization has gone through the selection process, it may find that the preferred candidate is not available or rejects the offered assignment. Other interrelated factors can intervene at the acceptance stage, such as the following. (See Exhibit 3-6 for a ranked list of factors.)

Work Permit Refused

As discussed in Chapter 1, international companies are usually required to demonstrate that a HCN is not available before the host government will issue the necessary work permit and entry visa for the desired PCN or TCN. In some cases, the MNE may wish to use an expatriate and has selected a candidate for the international assignment, only to find the transfer blocked by the host government. Some countries, such as the United States, are changing their legislation to facilitate employment-related immigration,[74] which will make international transfers somewhat easier. It is therefore important that HR staff keep abreast with changing legislation in the countries in which the MNE is involved.

An important, related point is that generally a work permit is granted to the expatriate only. The accompanying spouse or partner is not per-

EXHIBIT 3-6   Factors Stopping Companies Giving International Experience to Managers

(% respondents who ranked a factor as among the five most important constraints in their organisation)

Disruption of children's education	77
Spouse/partner reluctant to give up own career	67
Fear of losing influence/visibility at corporate centre	54
Organisation finds difficulty in re-absorbing returning managers	52
Lack of co-ordinated approach across the company	48
Managers find reintegration difficult on return	31
Immigration/employment laws & host country restrictions	29
Financial constraints	29
Lack of perceived need	19
Elderly relatives	17
Host country subsidiaries unwilling to accept managers	8
Subsidiaries in non-parent countries unwilling to release managers	8

Source: K. Barham and M. Devine, "The Quest for the International Manager: A Survey of Global Human Resource Strategies," the Economist Intelligence Unit, London, Special Report No. 2098 (1990), p. 28. Reprinted with permission.

mitted to work in the host country. Increasingly, MNEs are finding that the inability of the spouse to work in the host country may cause the selected candidate to reject the offer of an international assignment. If the international assignment is accepted, the lack of a work permit for the accompanying spouse or partner may cause difficulties in adjustment and even contribute to failure.

Dual-Career Couples

A worldwide trend is the increase in the number of dual-career couples. This trend is predicted to continue and is posing a dilemma for both companies and employees alike, affecting staff availability for transfer. In the past, working spouses were less common, spouses were generally female, and they were prepared to follow their partner's career transfers, both domestic and international. This past situation is reflected in the use of terms such as "the trailing spouse" to refer to the housebound female who accompanied her husband. But this situation has changed. As Reynolds and Bennett[75] point out, fewer employees are willing to relocate, either domestically or internationally, without the support of their spouses. Citing figures from the U.S. Department of Labor (which predicts that 81 percent of all marriages will be dual-career partnerships by 1995) and results from their study of 160 American, Australian, Canadian, and European multinational corporations, Reynolds and Bennett argue that the career-couple challenge is an issue that multinational employers cannot ignore. A U.K.-based study's[76] results support this contention. As shown in Exhibit 3-6, 67 percent of respondents in this study listed "spouse/partner reluctant to give up own career" as a major constraint to international assignment. The increase in the number of female managers is a related issue here.

Confronted with this situation, some companies are endeavoring to come up with solutions to the dual-career challenge. According to Reynolds and Bennett,[77] "Most companies still use informal or *ad hoc* approaches to addressing the problems of their expatriate career couples. In isolation or with industry colleagues, companies are beginning to generate innovative programs and interventions to assist this special breed of couples." Strategies include intercompany networking, job-hunting/fact-finding trips, intracompany employment, and commuter marriage support. Despite such innovative approaches, Reynolds and Bennett found that the attitude that "this is a problem the couples responsible should resolve" still prevails in many companies. Such an attitude contributes to the problem of staff immobility rather than solving it.

The impact of career orientation upon adjustment and intention to stay in a foreign location is an emerging area of research. A recent study of the impact of a spouse's career orientation on managers during transfers from the United States to Japan[78] found that, although most spouses who worked before the international assignment did not find employment afterward, a significantly higher proportion of career-oriented spouses found employment. In their discussion of this finding, Stephens and Black comment that career-oriented spouses may have had a higher employment rate in the foreign country because they were more qualified or because they had more to lose and therefore tried harder to find employment or, perhaps, because their spouses' companies provided job-finding assistance. They concluded, though, with the caution that this finding should not necessarily lead companies to believe that job-finding assistance for spouses is not important, and that "if organizations wish to take advantage of the career development aspects of international transfers and the benefits to the firm inherent in effective relocation programmes, they must consider the impact of international transfers on both partners in dual-career couples."

Family Considerations

Apart from the accompanying partner's career, there are other family considerations. Disruption to children's education is an important consideration, and the selected candidate may reject the offered assignment on the grounds that a move at this particular stage in his or her child's life is inappropriate. The care of aging or invalid parents is another consideration. (Both factors are noted in Exhibit 3-6.)

EQUAL EMPLOYMENT OPPORTUNITY ISSUES

In the recruitment and selection process, MNEs must address the issue of equal employment opportunity (EEO) for employees in all employment locations. The legal definition and coverage of relevant laws are immediate problems. The United States has a comprehensive statute (Title VII of the Civil Rights Act of 1964) to cover many EEO situations. However, it should be noted here that a recent decision of the U.S. Supreme Court[79] held that this act does not apply outside the territorial borders of the United States. The case involved an American citizen who claimed that he had been illegally discriminated against while working overseas for a U.S. corporation. A naturalized citizen born in Lebanon, the plaintiff began working for Aramco Corporation in Texas in 1979 and was transferred by the company to work in Saudi Arabia in 1980, where he worked until 1984, when he was discharged. The Court rejected the person's claim that he had been harassed and ultimately discharged by Aramco Corporation on account of his race, religion, and national origin. The decision has important implications for the status and protection of Americans working abroad for U.S. firms.

Many countries (for example, Britain and Australia) have separate legislation to cover racial and sex discrimination (generally reflecting the much later development in other countries of the debate about the position of women in society). Some countries have little or no EEO legislation, particularly in parts of the Middle East, Africa, Asia, and Latin America, where women tend to have a lower social status and are not universally employed.[80] Equal employment opportunity laws are expressions of social values with regard to employment and reflect the values of a society or country. The selection procedures of MNEs often must be defended against illegality and must take into consideration the increasingly conflicting national laws on employment. For example, mandatory retirement/hiring ages are illegal in the United States and some other countries but legal in still other countries. Determining which law applies where, and which has precedence, is a problem without a specific solution.

To date, very few women have been sent on expatriate assignments by Western MNEs. Adler[81] conducted a survey of international HR practices in over 600 U.S. and Canadian companies and found that of the 13,338 expatriates identified, only 3 percent (402) were female. Female expatriates tended to be employed by companies with over 1,000 employees in the banking, electronics, petroleum, and publishing industries. One explanation that could be offered with regard to these data is that the data simply reflect the preferences of males and females, and the majority of females do not wish to be sent on an expatriate assignment. Such an explanation assumes that both males and females are offered the opportunity of expatriate assignments, which Adler reports is not the case. Another explanation (also offered for minority groups) is that the data reflect the limited number of females with sufficient experience to be sent abroad.

Another explanation is that many MNEs are concerned with the various social norms with regard to women that prevail in many countries. For example, some Middle Eastern countries would not issue a work visa to a female expatriate even if the MNE selected her. Adler argues that such examples are the exception rather than the rule, and in many countries social norms regarding the role of women do not apply to female expatriates because they are seen by locals as foreigners. Expatriate women may be exempt in many situations, but the disadvantages of being a minority cannot be entirely dismissed. For example, some of the traditional methods of entertainment in Asian business culture involve the sexual exploitation of women and clearly exclude female colleagues.[82]

Equal opportunity for female HCNs is a complex issue for MNEs. Many MNEs already experience difficulties in the recruitment and selection of HCNs, particularly in less-developed countries where relatively low educational and economic levels limit the sources of potential talent.[83] The relative status of women in some countries may further restrict employment practices, particularly EEO objectives. In Western countries, the tendency is toward opening all occupations to both sexes, mainly through the introduction of sex discrimination legislation.[84] In general, however, the less developed the country, the less equal are the sexes with regard to job opportunities and education. There are many countries in which the customs, attitudes, or religion are hostile to the presence of women in the professions or business and in society in general. Ball and McCulloch[85] provide details of sexist legislation in several countries, including Pakistan, Saudi Arabia, and India. Even in countries where legislation states that there should be equality of the sexes, the reality may not comply with this. As Jelinek and Adler[86] have stated, the cultures of countries, particularly many Asian countries, "perpetuate the scarcity of indigenous female managers."

Several researchers have focused on the opportunities for foreign MNEs operating in Japan to employ female HCNs.[87] Many MNEs have difficulty attracting well-qualified Japanese men due to cultural reasons and traditional employment arrangements provided by Japanese corporations, so MNEs should consider employing Japanese women for managerial positions. According to Kaminski and Paiz, over one-third of Japanese women hold university or college degrees, but they are not actively recruited by Japanese companies because of cultural preferences for hiring males. Compared to the United States, Japanese women have a relatively low workforce participation rate, and they are mainly employed in traditional occupations (as secretaries, hostesses, or teachers, for example). Although they tend to have good educational qualifications, professional women in Japanese companies play a temporary or support role and do not advance as men do. In the Japanese economy, a full employment policy and lifetime employment are available only to men.[88] The corporate expectation is that women will leave the workforce by the age of 25 to raise a family and may return ten or twenty years later in a part-time position. Japanese national statistics, however, indicate that this employment pattern for females is changing as more women obtain qualifications and remain in the workforce for longer periods.

The limited opportunities and wage disparity for women employed in Japanese companies should assist foreign MNEs in recruiting female employees. Another important factor influencing the need for MNEs to consider hiring females is that the (predominantly male) elite in Japan and many other countries would prefer employment in the civil service or a leading company rather than work for a foreign MNE. Although the idea of women holding managerial level positions is relatively new in Japan, Kaminski and Paiz predict an evolutionary increase in the participation rate of women in the Japanese workforce, particularly as professionals in foreign MNEs. Such a pattern is likely to develop in many other countries as well. As Adler[89] concludes, "There is no doubt that the most successful North American companies will draw on both men and women to manage their international operations. The only question is how quickly and how effectively companies will manage the introduction of women into the worldwide managerial work force."

REPATRIATION

Perhaps the most important, yet seemingly least understood, factor affecting staff availability for international assignments is the way in which the organization handles staff repatriation, the process of returning to the home country. It should be noted that not all international assignments end with the transfer home. On completion of the assignment, the expatriate may be transferred to another overseas post, especially if the firm is endeavoring to build the international team of managers required for a geocentric staffing policy. Generally, though, the MNE brings the expatriate back to the home country. The process of repatriation can be divided into four related phases, as illustrated in Figure 3-2.

> ***1.*** *Preparation* involves developing plans for the future and gathering information about the new position. The firm may provide a checklist of items to be considered before the return home (such as closure of bank accounts and settling bills) or a thorough preparation of employee and family for the transfer home. However, there is little evidence in the literature that preparation for repatriation is seen by the MNE to be as important as predeparture training.[90]

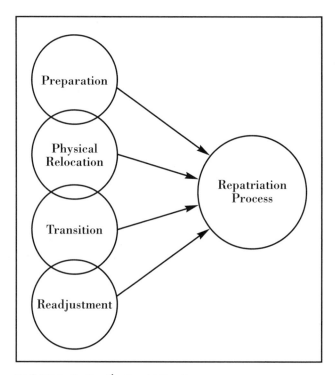

FIGURE 3-2 The Repatriation Process
Source: D. Welch, T. Adams, B. Betchley, and M. Howard, "The View from the Other Side: The Handling of Repatriation and Other Expatriation Activities by the Royal Australian Airforce," in *Proceedings of the AIB Southeast Asia Conference*, ed. O. Yau and B. Stening, Brisbane (June, 1992).

2. *Physical relocation* refers to removing personal effects, breaking ties with colleagues and friends, and traveling to the next posting, usually the home country. Most international companies use removal firms or relocation consultants to handle the physical relocation, both for the movement out as well as return home of the employee and family, and this will be formalized in company policies.

3. *Transition* means settling into temporary accommodation, making arrangements for housing and schooling, and carrying out other administrative tasks (such as renewing driver's license, applying for medical insurance, opening bank accounts). Some companies hire relocation consultants to assist in this phase also.

4. *Readjustment* involves coping with reverse culture shock and career demands.[91]

Readjustment Problems

Of the four phases, the one which seems to be the least understood and most poorly handled by organizations is the readjustment phase, which can be a traumatic experience.[92] During the transition from the country of assignment back into the home country, expatriates and their families face previously familiar surroundings after living abroad for a significant period.[93] Expatriates expect life in a new country to be different, but they are not prepared for home to have changed; they experience culture shock in reverse. Several things contribute to reverse culture shock, and these can be divided into job-related and social factors.

Job-Related Factors

"Out of Sight, Out of Mind"   The expatriate fears that an extended overseas stay may cause a loss of visibility and isolation from the parent company, which will adversely affect his or her career path.[94] The expatriate can become anxious that the company has not planned adequately, and that he or she will be placed in a mediocre or makeshift job. Upon return, the manager may find that these fears have materialized: Peers have been promoted ahead of the repatriated manager, and the repatriate is placed in a position that is, in effect, a demotion. Worse, the repatriate may find that, since there is no suitable position available, she or he is retrenched. This anxiety about career progression upon repatriation can affect productivity during the last couple of months of the international assignment as well as inhibit work adjustment upon repatriation.[95] In an effort to alleviate such anxiety, some international companies either sign a contract or otherwise formally agree that the expatriate will return to a position at the same grade level at the home base, although the actual reentry position will depend on openings available at the time of repatriation.[96] Special assignments may be used until a suitable position becomes available, and some repatriates may be offered another overseas assignment. There is no guarantee of promotion upon return, however, unless a higher position exists and the expatriate's performance overseas warrants such a promotion.

International Experience Devalued   Some managers report that on returning home they feel that the skills they acquired overseas are not valued[97] as the reentry position is unrelated to the work they were doing overseas, or because they are not consulted about activities and strategies involving the foreign subsidiary to which they had been attached. In other words, repatriates tend to become an underutilized resource. There are few programs that exploit the international experience and cosmopolitan view that the expatriate has gained while overseas, and the return position is frequently a lateral move rather than a promotion.[98] As Harvey[99] points out, expatriate managers should be accorded a higher value by the organization, considering their experience in managing the foreign operations. The fact that they were selected for the overseas assignment in the first place indicates, in most cases, that they were highly thought of. The degrading of the repatriate's recent experience can be coupled with a negative career progression; that is, a less challenging job with less responsibility and status than the previous international assignment. Such treatment, according to Tung's research,[100] is evident in many U.S. multinationals. The devaluing of the international experience may be explained by the fact that U.S. companies tend to focus more readily on the domestic market, while companies operating from countries with smaller domestic markets must rely more heavily on international markets for revenue.[101]

Loss of Status and Pay   Usually, the overseas assignment is a form of promotion: It carries greater autonomy, a broader area of responsibility (because of the smaller size of the overseas subsidiary), and, at the top management level, a prominent role in the local community. The result is higher status. Some expatriates use the term *kingpin* to describe this increased status. Upon return, the repatriate is expected to resume his or her position within the home company, with the loss of status and autonomy. In effect, the repatriate is treated as just another company executive. This shift may cause readjustment problems. For example, a repatriate can find that, whereas overseas he was the key decision maker, now he has to seek permission. As one repatriate described his feeling, "Over there, you are the big fish in the small pond. Back home, you return to being the small fish in a big pond."[102] Compounding the problem is the loss of expatriate premiums. As Conway[103] states, "More commonly, employees are brought home to resume life on a scale that may be significantly less comfortable than what they had grown used to abroad. Pay is usually lower in absolute terms." Also, the returning manager may no longer be able to afford to buy a home similar to the one sold a few years before.[104] A recent U.S. study suggests that the current practice of providing expatriates with better housing than they had at home may contribute to repatriation problems. That is, a drop in the standard of housing conditions has a negative impact on the adjustment of the repatriate.[105]

Changes in the Workplace   Since life is not static, the expatriate will also encounter changes in the formal and informal operations and in the information channels in the home organization. Technological advances in the company may render the repatriate's functional skills and knowledge obsolete. Unless there was sufficient contact with the expatriate during the overseas assignment, the expatriate is unprepared for these changes. Coupled with the other job-related problems, these changes make work adjustment a difficult process.

Social Factors

The international experience can distance the expatriate socially and psychologically—a situation that also involves the expatriate's family. People may feel alienated in their own country, particularly if they have been out of contact with family, friends, and local events. Expatriates and their families may have enjoyed interaction with the social and economic elite during their international assignment, and the return home may bring with it some measure of social disappointment, along with the loss of the compensation premium. In addition, repatriates may have developed a broader cultural perspective; they can now compare home-country conditions with other ways of life and environments. Many repatriates report that people show little interest in hearing about their expatriate experiences, which can make conversation uncomfortable.[106]

It must be stressed here that the family is also experiencing its own readjustment problems. Many spouses encounter difficulties in reentering the workforce. Reestablishing social networks can also be difficult, especially if the family has been repatriated to a different state or town in the home country. Those returning to their previous domestic locations find that friends have moved away or reentered the workforce and are no longer available for social activities. Teenage children, in particular, may find it difficult to rejoin peer groups. Studies of Japanese repatriates are finding that reentry is particularly acute for children, who face difficulties reintegrating into both their peer groups and the

Japanese educational system.[107] As was true of cultural adjustment abroad, reentry problems encountered by the employee at work and by the spouse and family "spill over" and can exacerbate the entire reentry situation.[108]

Company Responses

Mendenhall, Dunbar, and Oddou[109] report that human resource professionals may be unaware of the challenges facing repatriated managers. Harvey[110] concurs, noting that "even though many executives have experienced difficulties upon repatriation, multinational companies have seemingly not addressed the issues related to repatriation with the same level of interest as preparing executives for expatriation."

One reason for this oversight is that the problem is not as dramatical or readily identifiable as expensive. Repatriate turnover is not as visible as expatriate failure, nor are precise figures available, although figures of 20 and 25 percent have been estimated for the U.S. situation.[111] Black and Gregersen calculate that a U.S. MNE spends around $1 million on each expatriate over the duration of a foreign assignment. They argue convincingly that if approximately one in four repatriates exits the firm within a year of repatriation, "this represents a substantial financial and human capital loss to the firm, especially if the skills, knowledge, and experience that the individual gains are important to the firm and scarce in the internal or external labor markets."[112] It appears that until top management is confronted with the cost of repatriate turnover (as has occurred with expatriate failure rates), repatriation will continue to be given low priority.

Despite their importance, formal repatriation programs are reportedly scarce among companies.[113] Harvey[114] surveyed Society for Human Resource Management International (SHRM/I) members to ascertain U.S. companies' current approaches to repatriation. He found that 31 percent indicated some formal repatriation programs, but of these only 22 percent instituted the repatriation training before departure and only 35 percent included the spouse. Those who did not have a repatriation training program were asked to give reasons for not having such a program. The most frequently mentioned reasons were lack of expertise in establishing a program (47 percent); cost of program to train repatriates (36 percent); and no perceived need for repatriation training by top management (35 percent). Harvey concludes that "the lack of acceptance of repatriation programs among the survey respondents tends to illustrate the absence of organized efforts by large sophisticated multinationals to assist expatriated personnel. . . . The almost total lack of attention to family members would appear to be one of the most egregious errors being made."

Several authors offer suggestions for an effective repatriation training program. For example, Conway[115] suggests that the organization view the overseas assignment as a total system, with repatriation integrated into orientation and selection. He also feels that the trend toward using external consultants for orientation and relocation may preclude the organization from obtaining relevant feedback, particularly from repatriates. Phatak[116] suggests the use of written agreements covering the return position and the length of the assignment and the use of a mentor or contact person at headquarters as ways of improving the reentry phase.

More important, as we mentioned in the opening to this section, repatriation has an impact on staff availability for international assignments. Reentry positions signal the importance given to the overseas assignment by the organization.[117] If the repatriate is promoted or given a position that capitalizes on the overseas experience, other members of the organization interpret the overseas assignment as a positive career move. If the company does not reward expatriate performance, tolerates a high turnover among repatriates, or is seen to terminate a repatriate's employment upon reentry, then the workforce may interpret the acceptance of an expatriate assignment as a high-risk decision in terms of future career progression within the organization. The company's ability to attract high-caliber staff for expatriate posting is thereby lessened, and this can have a negative effect on the company's overseas activities in the long run. In short, repatriation is an important factor in effective expatriate management and should be viewed as an integral part of the overseas assignment.[118]

RECRUITMENT AND SELECTION OF HCNs AND TCNs

As Heenan and Perlmutter,[119] Berenbeim,[120] and other writers have observed, over time a MNE will tend to move from a dominantly ethnocentric staffing policy to a polycentric and/or regiocentric policy. One effect of both polycentric and regiocentric policies is to markedly reduce the number of PCNs sent on overseas assignments. There are a number of reasons why a MNE would want to reduce the population of PCN employees on overseas assignments. One obvious factor is the cost of maintaining expatriates and their families abroad. By replacing PCNs with

HCNs or TCNs, MNEs can achieve substantial savings. A second reason why MNEs are often quite willing to replace PCNs is that managerial and technical competence has increased in many countries, and there are now large numbers of qualified and experienced local employees to take the place of expatriate employees. Thus, many MNEs are finding that one of the important reasons for initially using PCNs (lack of suitably qualified local employees) no longer applies. As Kobrin[121] has succinctly noted, "all things being equal, a local national who speaks the language, understands the culture and the political system, and is often a member of the local elite should be more effective than an expatriate alien."

As discussed earlier, a third factor that has often heavily influenced MNE staffing policy has been the pressure from many governments to limit the number of PCNs and increase the number of HCNs. This pressure may be explicit (immigration visa quotas for PCNs) or implicit (informal comments by government officials during negotiations to obtain various licenses or approvals for projects). Thus, many newly developing countries in Asia and Africa require MNEs to commit themselves to extensive training of HCNs before PCN employees are given work visas. This use of immigration regulations is not limited to newly developing countries. Most industrialized countries (including the United States) have immigration rules that require companies to demonstrate why they need to hire a foreign national rather than a local national. Successful MNEs incorporate such requirements into their planning process when they are considering new investments or developments. For example, in the mid-1980s Australia offered a once-only opportunity for foreign banks to enter the local market, and Citibank was one of the successful applicants for a banking license. Banks, along with oil and construction companies, remain heavy users of PCN employees because all three industries require very specific (sometimes firm-specific) skills frequently not found in foreign locations. Over a year before the licenses were to be awarded, Citibank sent one of its senior HR managers on a year-long assignment to Sydney to assess the staffing implications of an application to the Australian government for a banking license. Once an assessment was made as to how many PCN visas would be required, a detailed summary was prepared for the immigration department showing the history of Citibank's investment in training Australian nationals (Citibank already held a limited banking license that allowed it to operate a merchant banking operation and finance company), with career examples of Australian nationals who were now employed by Citibank in Australia, other foreign locations, and in the United States. This proved to be a successful strategy: Citibank received one of the sixteen licenses on offer and all of the visas it requested and is now one of the leading foreign banks in Australia.

Selecting HCNs

The same general criteria for selecting PCNs apply to selecting HCNs, although more training is usually needed, as HCNs often lack detailed knowledge of the organization and its products or services. Desatnick and Bennett[122] emphasize the importance of careful preparation, plus the investment of time and effort, in the recruitment and selection of HCNs. This process involves a realistic assessment of the skills available in the local labor market and the ability to tailor the recruitment and selection process to fit local conditions. For example, college recruiting is an integral part of U.S. recruitment practice, but this is much less the case in other Western countries, where business tends to have fewer direct links with educational institutions. Unless the company has the experience, it may also be advisable to employ a local recruiting source. Selection procedures and interviews need to follow local customs. In some countries, questions regarding a person's family, hobbies, parents, or religious convictions are unacceptable, since these are considered private areas.[123]

Selecting TCNs

As discussed earlier, multinational companies have found advantages in recruiting TCNs because they tend to cost less and they often come from a country similar to the MNE's home country. MNEs also find it advantageous to hire TCNs who have already been working for the organization and thus are familiar with its management policies and practices. In addition, TCNs are unlikely to experience conflict between loyalty to the organization and loyalty to the host country. (Ball and McCulloch[124] provide examples of HCNs giving preference to local suppliers when imported goods were less expensive and of superior quality.) Not surprisingly, one difficulty of hiring TCNs is that host countries that place importance on employment of their own citizens may regard the employment of large numbers of TCNs to be as unacceptable as a large number of PCNs. Third-country nationals tend to be most numerous where a MNE has established a regional headquarters (for example, a Pacific Basin regional headquarters in Melbourne or Singapore), as employees from countries in the region are assigned to the regional headquarters to gain wider experience or to fill specific positions.

In a controversial article, Kobrin[125] argues that many U.S. companies have overdone the replacement of U.S. expatriates with HCNs. In addition to the reasons discussed above (lowering costs, responding to local pressures, and so on) Kobrin believes that U.S. MNEs may have substituted HCNs and TCNs for expatriates in response to "the difficulties that Americans have had in adjusting to other cultural environments rather than for the usual reasons of effectiveness and efficiency. . . . Put directly, Americans may not have been able to handle international assignments and many U.S. firms may have 'solved' the problem by virtually getting out of the expatriate business." He argues that, in doing so, U.S. MNEs could become composed primarily of employees who identify with the local subsidiary rather than the worldwide organization. Such conditions raise major strategic management and control issues such as how to encourage managers to identify with firm-wide rather than local objectives, how to maintain strategic control over personnel and the informal organization, and how to internationalize U.S. managers if they are not sent on expatriate assignments.

Kobrin's explanation as to why American managers are not being sent on expatriate assignments has major implications for the recruitment, selection, and training of managers in U.S. MNEs. He notes that "the problem is exacerbated by the scandalously low levels of international awareness and language competence found in graduates of American universities and business schools," which may be another difficulty U.S. MNEs must face when they recruit future managers. This latter point is reinforced by a Gallup poll conducted for the National Geographic Society that surveyed 18- to 24-year-olds from nine countries.[126] American respondents in this survey were ranked *last* in terms of general geographic knowledge (a variable that would correlate reasonably well with "international awareness").

American MNEs may have to become more selective in their recruiting by emphasizing international awareness, language skills,[127] and so on and investing more heavily in training to develop an international cadre of managers. They may also have to consider increasing the number of TCNs, whom they recruit at U.S. schools.[128] There is some evidence to indicate that some U.S. MNEs are aware of the issues discussed by Kobrin. In a recent survey of U.S. managers responsible for international HRM, respondents rated issues such as "the necessity to learn to think globally" and "the changing role of the U.S. expatriate in the world" among the most important current issues in international HRM.[129] Even with a sufficient cadre of qualified expatriates, however,

U.S. MNEs are increasing their use of TCNs and HCNs mainly for cost and political reasons. As they do, the issues of training and retraining TCNs and HCNs will grow in importance and MNEs will have to give more consideration to career opportunities and career paths for TCNs and HCNs, as described in Chapter 5.

SUMMARY

This chapter has identified a number of issues and trends in the area of international staffing. The work of Tung[130] and others suggest that expatriate failure is a general problem for many MNEs and, it would appear, a particular problem for U.S. MNEs. Future research should, first, confirm whether expatriate failure continues to be a major staffing issue and, second, examine the incidence of failure by job category (CEO, functional head, operative, or troubleshooter) to determine the extent of the problem for each category and whether reasons for failure vary by job category. In addition, the model of expatriate acculturation proposed by Mendenhall and Oddou[131] could be tested by examining case histories of successful and unsuccessful expatriates or through a more formal empirical validation strategy.

Our discussion of the predictors of expatriate success has revealed the difficulty of selecting the right candidate for the overseas assignment and the importance of including family considerations in the selection process. Societal trends such as dual-career families will continue to constrain the organization's ability to attract the best candidate for the overseas assignment. Such pressures are encouraging organizations to be more flexible in the way they handle the expatriation process. Concern is now focused on acknowledging the importance of repatriation, on utilizing the international experience to the benefit of the global organization, and on ensuring that high-potential employees are available for overseas assignments.

Another area that needs to be addressed by researchers is the influence (or lack of influence) of human resource planning on international staffing. Torbiorn[132] has noted the impact of lack of planning in this area: "The mass of possible selection criteria proposed in the literature is rarely likely to be matched by a wide range of available candidates and the man chosen is often simply the man who happens to be there." Such situations are inevitable at times, but this cannot be a permanent strategy. Mendenhall and Oddou[133] have also noted that too often expatriates are hurriedly selected because of the need to resolve a staffing crisis in an overseas subsidiary. To address this situation, they argue, top management would need to provide institutional and political support in three areas: First, the personnel department must have accurate forecasts of staffing needs in foreign subsidiaries; second, the length of time budgeted for the selection and training process must be increased; and third, expatriate selection and training should begin early in a manager's career so that the organization can develop a pool of internationally oriented managers.

QUESTIONS

1. Outline the main characteristics of the ethnocentric, polycentric, regiocentric, and geocentric approaches to international staffing.

2. What are the main advantages and disadvantages of a polycentric approach to international staffing?

3. Why is an ad hoc approach to international staffing invariably a dysfunctional strategy for MNEs?

4. What are the most important criteria MNEs should use when selecting PCNs? What factors may influence these criteria?

5. Many MNEs perceive serious limitations with regard to assigning female managers to overseas locations. What are these perceived limitations, and do you think these perceptions will change over time?

FURTHER READING

1. P. L. Blocklyn, "Developing the International Executive," *Personnel*, March 1989, pp. 44–48.

2. R. Brislin et al., *Intercultural Interactions, A Practical Guide*, Beverly Hills, Calif.: Sage, 1986.

3. P. J. Dowling and T. W. Nagel, "Nationality and Work Attitudes: A Study of Australian and American Business Majors," *Journal of Management*, Vol. 12 (1985) pp. 99–106.

4. W. A. Evans, D. Sculli, and W. S. L. Yau, "Cross-cultural Factors in the Identification of Managerial Potential," *Journal of Management*, Vol. 13, No. 1 (1987) pp. 52–59.

5. P. R. Harris and R. T. Morgan, *Managing Cultural Differences*, 2nd ed. Houston, Tex.: Gulf, 1979.

6. R. M. Hodgetts and F. Luthans, "Japanese HR Management Practices," *Personnel*, April 1988, pp. 42–45.

7. D. B. Ondrack and H. F. Schwind, "A Comparative Study of Personnel Problems in International Companies and Joint Ventures in Japan," *Journal of International Business Studies*, Spring–Summer 1977, pp. 45–55.

8. J. S. Black, "Work Role Transitions: A Study of American Expatriate Managers in Japan," *Journal of International Business Studies*, Summer (1988) pp. 277–294.

9. J. S. Black, M. Mendenhall, and G. Oddou, "Toward a Comprehensive Model of International Adjustment: An Integration of Multiple Theoretical Perspectives," *Academy of Management Review*, Vol. 16, No. 2 (1991) pp. 291–317.

NOTES

1. R. S. Schuler and V. L. Huber, *Personnel and Human Resource Management*, 5th ed. (St. Paul, Minn.: West Publishing Co., 1993).

2. See R. D. Robinson, *International Business Management: A Guide to Decision Making*, 2nd ed. (Hinsdale, Ill.: Dryden, 1978); D. A. Heenan and H. V. Perlmutter, *Multinational Organization Development* (Reading, Mass.: Addison-Wesley, 1979); and S. H. Robock and K. Simmonds, *International Business and Multinational Enterprises*, 4th ed. (Homewood, Ill.: Irwin, 1989).

3. Y. Zeira, "Management Development in Ethnocentric Multinational Corporations," *California Management Review*, Vol. 18, No. 4 (1976) pp. 34–42.

4. M. Fergus, "Employees on the Move," *HR Magazine*, May 1990, p. 45.

5. Robinson, *International Business Management*.

6. See L. Smith, "The Hazards of Coming Home," *Dun's Review*, October 1975, pp. 71–75.

7. A. V. Phatak, *International Dimensions of Management*, 2nd ed. (Boston: PWS-KENT Publishing Company, 1989).

8. M. Borg, *International Transfers of Managers in Multinational Corporations* (Sweden: University of Uppsala, 1987).

9. Heenan and Perlmutter, *Multinational Organization Development*.

10. Y. L. Doz and C. K. Prahalad, "Controlled Variety: A Challenge for Human Resource Management in the MNC," *Human Resource Management*, Vol. 25, No. 1 (1986) pp. 55–71.

11. A. J. Morrison, D. A. Ricks, and K. Roth, "Globalization Versus Regionalization: Which Way for the Multinational?" *Organizational Dynamics*, Winter 1991, pp. 17–29.

12. Robinson, *International Business Management*, p. 297.

13. Borg, *International Transfers of Managers.*

14. C. Bartlett and S. Ghoshal, "Organizing for Worldwide Effectiveness: The Transnational Solution," *California Management Review*, Fall 1988, pp. 54–74.

15. M. E. Mendenhall and G. Oddou, "The Overseas Assignment: A Practical Look," *Business Horizons*, September–October 1988, pp. 78–84.

16. C. Brewster, *The Management of Expatriates*, Human Resource Research Centre Monograph Series, No. 2, Cranfield School of Management, Bedford, U.K. (1988); M. Gertsen, "Expatriate Selection and Training," in *Proceedings of the Fifteenth Annual Conference of the European International Business Association*, ed. R. Luostarinen, Helsinki (December, 1989) pp. 1251–1280.

17. M. Mendenhall and G. Oddou, "The Dimensions of Expatriate Acculturation: A Review," *Academy of Management Review*, Vol. 10 (1985) pp. 39–47.

18. M. G. Harvey, "The Multinational Corporation's Expatriate Problem: An Application of Murphy's Law," *Business Horizons*, Vol. 26, No. 1 (1983) pp. 71–78.

19. Y. Zeira and M. Banai, "Present and Desired Methods of Selecting Expatriate Managers for International Assignments," *Personnel Review*, Vol. 13, No. 3 (1984) pp. 29–35.

20. Mendenhall and Oddou, "The Dimensions of Expatriate Acculturation"; and R. L. Desatnick and M. L. Bennett, *Human Resource Management in the Multinational Company* (New York: Nichols. 1978).

21. P. Guptara, "Searching the Organization for the Cross-Cultural Operators," *International Management*, August 1986, p. 40.

22. Mendenhall and Oddou, "The Dimensions of Expatriate Acculturation."

23. R. L. Tung, "Selection and Training of Personnel for Overseas Assignments," *Columbia Journal of World Business*, Vol. 16, No. 1 (1981) pp. 68–78.

24. Brewster, *The Management of Expatriates.*

25. Tung, "Selection and Training of Personnel."

26. J. Hamill, "International Human Resource Management in British Multinationals," in *Proceedings of the Thirteenth Annual Meeting of the European International Business Association*, ed. D. Van Den Bulke, Antwerp (December, 1987) pp. 267–277.

27. P. J. Dowling and D. Welch, "International Human Resource Management: An Australian Perspective," *Asia-Pacific Journal of Management.* Vol. 6, No. 1 (1988) pp. 39–65.

28. D. E. Welch, "The Personnel Variable in International Business Operations: A Study of Expatriate Management in Australian Companies," Ph.D. diss., Monash University, Melbourne, 1990.

29. I. Bjorkman and M. Gertsen, "Corporate Expatriation: An Empirical Study of Scandinavian Firms," in *Proceedings of the Third Symposium on Cross-Cultural Consumer and Business Studies*, Honolulu (December, 1990).

30. R. L. Tung, "Selection and Training Procedures of U.S., European and Japanese Multinationals," *California Management Review*, Vol. 25, No. 1 (1982) pp. 57–71.

31. R. L. Tung, "Human Resource Planning in Japanese Multinationals: A Model for U.S. Firms?" *Journal of International Business Studies*, Fall 1984, pp. 139–149.

32. L. A. Allen, "Working Better with Japanese Managers," *Management Review*, Vol. 77, No. 11 (1988) pp. 55–56.

33. Hamill, "International Human Resource Management in British Multinationals."

34. Dowling and Welch, "International Human Resource Management: An Australian Perspective."

35. Welch, "The Personnel Variable in International Business Operations."

36. R. L. Tung, "Expatriate Assignments: Enhancing Success and Minimizing Failure," *Academy of Management Executive*, Vol. 1, No. 2 (1987) pp. 117–126.

37. H. B. Gregersen and J. S. Black, "A Multifaceted Approach to Expatriate Retention in International Assignments," *Group & Organization Studies*, Vol. 15, No. 4 (1990) pp. 461–485.

38. M. Harvey, "The Executive Family: An Overlooked Variable in International Assignments," *Columbia Journal of World Business*, Spring 1985, pp. 84–93; A. Thompson, "Australian Expatriate Wives and Business Success in South East Asia, *Euro-Asian Business Review*, Vol. 5, No. 2 (1986) pp. 14–18; J. E. Harris, "Moving Managers Internationally: The Care and Feeding of Expatriates," *Human Resource Planning*, Vol. 12, No. 1 (1989) pp. 49–53.

39. C. Reynolds and R. Bennett, "The Career Couple Challenge," *Personnel Journal*, March 1991, p. 48.

40. Harvey, "The Executive Family: An Overlooked Variable"; Phatak, *International Dimensions of Management*.

41. F. T. Murray and A. H. Murray, "Global Managers for Global Businesses," *Sloan Management Review*, Vol. 27, No. 2 (1986) pp. 75–80.

42. I. Torbiorn, *Living Abroad: Personal Adjustment and Personnel Policy in the Overseas Setting* (New York: John Wiley, 1982).

43. H. L. Willis, "Selection for Employment in Developing Countries," *Personnel Administrator*, Vol. 29, No. 7 (1984) p. 55.

44. P. J. Dowling, "Psychological Testing in Australia: An Overview and an Assessment," in *Australian Personnel Management: A Reader*, ed. G. Palmer, Sydney: Macmillan, 1988.

45. Phatak, *International Dimensions of Management*.

46. A. L. Hixon, "Why Corporations Make Haphazard Overseas Staffing Decisions," *Personnel Administrator*, Vol. 31, No. 3 (1986) pp. 91–94.

47. Gertsen, "Expatriate Selection and Training," p. 1257.

48. G. M. Baliga, and J. C. Baker, "Multinational Corporate Policies for Expatriate Managers: Selection, Training, Evaluation," *Advanced Management Journal*, Vol. 50, No. 4 (1985) pp. 31–38. See also J. S. Black, "The Relationship of Personal Characteristics with the Adjustment of Japanese Expatriate Managers," *Management International Review*, Vol. 30, No. 2 (1990) pp. 119–134, for a review and discussion of cross-cultural adjustment.

49. Tung, "Selection and Training of Personnel for Overseas Assignments."

50. Brewster, *The Management of Expatriates*.

51. Tung, "Selection and Training of Personnel for Overseas Assignments."

52. Hixon, "Why Corporations Make Haphazard Overseas Staffing Decisions."

53. M. E. Mendenhall, E. Dunbar, and G. Oddou, "Expatriate Selection, Training and Career-Pathing: A Review and a Critique," *Human Resource Planning*, Vol. 26, No. 3 (1987) pp. 331–345.

54. J. McEnery and G. DesHarnais, "Culture Shock," *Training and Development Journal*, Vol. 44, No. 4 (1990) pp. 43–47.

55. Guptara, "Searching the Organization for the Cross-Cultural Operators."

56. M. A. Conway, "Reducing Expatriate Failure Rates," *Personnel Administrator*, Vol. 29, No. 7 (1984) pp. 31–38.

57. For example, according to the *Price Waterhouse Cranfield Project on International Human Resource Management 1991 Report*, most organizations surveyed filled management vacancies predominantly from among current employees.

58. Hixon, "Why Corporations Make Haphazard Overseas Staffing Decisions."

59. Y. Zeira, and M. Banai, "Selection of Expatriate Managers in MNCs: The Host-Environment Point of View," *International Studies of Management and Organization*, Vol. 15, No. 1 (1985) pp. 36–37.

60. Mendenhall and Oddou, "The Overseas Assignment: A Practical Look."

61. Mendenhall and Oddou, "The Dimensions of Expatriate Acculturation: A Review."

62. For a review of the Type A literature, see V. A. Price, *Type A Behavior Pattern: A Model for Research and Practice* (New York: Academic Press, 1982).

63. S. Ronen, "Training the International Assignee," in *Training and Career Development*, ed. I. Goldstein (San Francisco: Jossey-Bass, 1989) p. 430.

64. Mendenhall, Dunbar, and Oddou, "Expatriate Selection, Training and Career-Pathing: A Review and a Critique."

65. J. S. Black and G. K. Stephens, "The Influence of the Spouse on American Expatriate Adjustment and Intent to Stay in Pacific Rim Overseas Assignments," *Journal of Management*, Vol. 15, No. 4 (1989) pp. 529–544.

66. Black and Stephens, "The Influence of the Spouse," p. 541.

67. H. De Cieri, P. J. Dowling, and K. F. Taylor, "The Psychological Impact of Expatriate Relocation on Partners," *The International Journal of Human Resource Management*, Vol. 2, No. 3 (1991) pp. 377–414.

68. Brewster, *The Management of Expatriates*.

69. I. Bjorkman, "Expatriation and Repatriation in Finnish Companies: A Comparison with Swedish and Norwegian Practice," Working Paper, Swedish School of Economics and Business Administration (1990).

70. Gertsen, "Expatriate Selection and Training."

71. Welch, "The Personnel Variable."

72. Welch, "The Personnel Variable."

73. Brewster, *The Management of Expatriates*.

74. C. Shusterman, "A Welcome Change to Immigration Law," *Personnel Journal*, September 1991, pp. 44–48.

75. Reynolds and Bennett, "The Career Couple Challenge."

76. K. Barham, and M. Devine, *The Quest for the International Manager: A Survey of Global Human Resource Strategies*, Ashridge Management Resource Group/The Economist Intelligence Unit, Special Report No. 2098 (1990).

77. Reynolds and Bennett, "The Career Couple Challenge," p. 48.

78. G. K. Stephens and S. Black, "The Impact of Spouse's Career-Orientation on Managers during International Transfers," *Journal of Management Studies*, Vol. 28, No. 4 (1991) p. 425.

79. E.E.O.C. v. Arabian American Oil Co., 111 S. Ct. 1227 (1991). For an excellent commentary on this case, see G. L. Clark, "The Geography of Civil Rights," *Environment and Planning D: Society and Space*, 1992, *10*, pp. 119–121.

80. See Desatnick and Bennett, *Human Resource Management*.

81. N. J. Adler, "Women in International Management: Where Are They?" *California Management Review*, Vol. 26, No. 4 (1984) pp. 78–89.

82. Similar results were found by R. Stone ("Expatriate Selection and Failure," *Proceedings of the Second International Conference on Personnel and Human Resource Management*, Hong Kong, December 1989) in his study of Australian and Asian managers' attitudes toward female expatriate managers working in Asia.

83. Desatnick and Bennett, *Human Resource Management*.

84. See C. E. Landau, "Recent Legislation and Case Law in the EEC on Sex Equality in Employment," *International Labour Review*, Vol. 123, No. 1 (1984) pp. 53–70.

85. D. A. Ball and W. H. McCulloch, *International Business: Introduction and Essentials* (Plano, Tex.: Business Publications, 1988).

86. M. Jelinek and N. J. Adler, "Women: World-Class Managers for Global Competition," *Academy of Management Executive*, Vol. 2, No. 1 (1988) pp. 11–19.

87. M. Kaminski and J. Paiz, "Japanese Women in Management: Where Are They?" *Human Resource Management*, Vol. 23, No. 3 (1984) pp. 277–292; and P. Lansing and K. Ready, "Hiring Women Managers in Japan: An Alternative for Foreign Employers," *California Management Review*, Vol. 26, No. 4 (1988) pp. 469–481.

88. M. A. Devanna, "Women in Management: Progress and Promise," *Human Resource Management*, Vol. 26, No. 4 (1987) pp. 469–481.

89. N. J. Adler, "Pacific Basin Manager: A Gaijin, Not a Woman," *Human Resource Management*, Vol. 26, No. 2 (1987) pp. 169–191.

90. M. G. Harvey, "Repatriation of Corporate Executives: An Empirical Study," *Journal of International Business Studies*, Spring 1989, pp. 131–144.

91. D. Welch, T. Adams, B. Betchley, and M. Howard, "The View from the Other Side: The Handling of Repatriation and Other Expatriation Activities by the Royal Australian Airforce," in *Proceedings of the AIB Southeast Asia Conference*, ed. O. Yau and B. Stening, Brisbane (June, 1992).

92. Conway, "Reducing Expatriate Failure Rates"; R. Moran, "Coping with Re-entry Shock," *International Management*, December 1989, p. 67; Harvey, "Repatriation of Corporate Executives."

93. S. Ronen, *Comparative and Multinational Management* (New York: John Wiley, 1986); N. Adler, *International Dimensions of Organizational Behavior*, 2nd ed. (Boston: PWS-KENT International, 1991).

94. Moran, "Coping with Re-entry Shock"; Phatak, *International Dimensions of Management*.

95. Welch, "The Personnel Variable"; S. Black and H. B. Gregersen, "When Yankee Comes Home: Factors Related to Expatriate and Spouse Repatriation Adjustment," *Journal of International Business Studies*, Vol. 22, No. 4 (1991) pp. 671–694. See also N. K. Napier and R. B. Peterson, "Expatri-ate Re-entry: What Do Expatriates Have to Say?" *Human Resource Planning*, Vol. 14, No. 1 (1991) pp. 19–28.

96. Brewster, *The Management of Expatriates*.

97. J. E. Beck, "Expatriate Management Development: Realizing the Learning Potential of the Overseas Assignment," in *Best Papers Proceedings, Academy of Management 48th Annual Meeting*, ed. F. Hoy, Anaheim, California (August, 1988) pp. 112–116; R. L. Tung, "Career Issues in International Assignments," *Academy of Management Executive*, Vol. 2, No. 3 (1988) pp. 241–244.

98. Moran, "Coping with Re-entry Shock"; R. L. Tung and E. L. Miller, "Managing in the Twenty-first Century: The Need for Global Orientation," *Management International Review*, Vol. 30, No. 1 (1990) pp. 5–18; N. Adler, *International Dimensions of Organizational Behavior*.

99. Harvey, "Repatriation of Corporate Executives."

100. Tung, "Career Issues in International Assignments."

101. Bjorkman and Gertsen, "Corporate Expatriation." This may be the case for MNCs, but a Finnish study of 180 repatriates from international assignments involving government-sponsored foreign aid projects found that for 63 percent of respondents the period overseas had a neutral affect on their careers (T. Peltonen, "A Study of the Foreign Development Assignments Immediate Impact on Professional Careers," Master's thesis, Helsinki School of Economics and Business Administration, Helsinki, Finland, February, 1992).

102. Welch, "The Personnel Variable."

103. Conway, "Reducing Expatriate Failure Rates," p. 38.

104. Phatak, *The International Dimensions of Management*.

105. Black and Gregersen, "When Yankee Comes Home."

106. M. G. Harvey, "The Other Side of Foreign Assignments: Dealing with the Repatriation Dilemma," *Columbia Journal of World Business*, Vol. 17, No. 1 (1982) pp. 52–59; R. Savich, and W. Rodgers, "Assignment Overseas: Easing the Transition Before and After," *Personnel*, August 1988, pp. 44–48.

107. W. Enloe and P. Lewin, "Issues of Integration Abroad and Readjustment to Japan of Japanese Returnees," *International Journal of Intercultural Relations*, Vol. 11 (1987) pp. 223–248.

108. Black and Gregersen, "When Yankee Comes Home."

109. Mendenhall, Dunbar, and Oddou, "Expatriate Selection, Training and Career-Pathing."

110. Harvey, "Repatriation of Corporate Executives," p. 337.

111. Adler, *The International Dimensions of Organizational Behavior.*

112. Black and Gregersen, "When Yankee Comes Home," p. 672.

113. See Adler, *International Dimensions of Organizational Behavior*; Black and Stephens, "The Influence of the Spouse."

114. Harvey, "Repatriation of Corporate Executives," p. 140.

115. Conway, "Reducing Expatriate Failure Rates."

116. Phatak, *The International Dimensions of Management.*

117. Adler, *International Dimensions of Organizational Behavior*; Harvey, "Repatriation of Corporate Executives."

118. D. Welch, "Determinants of International Human Resource Management Approaches and Activities: A Suggested Framework," *Journal of Management Studies* (forthcoming).

119. Heenan and Perlmutter, *Multinational Organization Development.*

120. R. E. Berenbeim, *Managing the International Company: Building a Global Perspective* (New York: The Conference Board, 1983).

121. S. J. Kobrin, "Expatriate Reduction and Strategic Control in American Multinational Corporations," *Human Resource Management*, Vol. 27, No. 1 (1988) pp. 63–75.

122. Desatnick and Bennett, *Human Resource Management.*

123. P. E. Illman, *Developing Overseas Managers and Managers Overseas*, (New York: Amacom, 1980); Phatak, *International Dimensions of Management*; C. Fetterlof, "Hiring Local Managers and Employees Overseas," *The International Executive*, May–June 1990, pp. 22–26.

124. Ball and McCulloch, *International Business.*

125. Kobrin, "Expatriate Reduction."

126. *Geography: An International Gallup Survey*, a survey conducted for The National Geographic Society (Princeton, N.J.: The Gallup Organization, 1988).

127. A strong case can be made for the proposition that English is now the language of world business, but it is also the case that English speakers who refuse to use any other language are frequently perceived to be ethnocentric in their attitudes and behavior. A number of writers have made the point that bilingualism is *qualitatively* different from monolingualism because it gives a "stereo quality" to perception and interpretation. See G. Hedlund, "The Hypermodern, MNC—A Heterarchy?" in *Human Re-*

source Management, Vol. 25, No. 1 (1988) p. 31, for a discussion of this issue and further references.

128. See B. Luck-Nunke, "Recruiting European Nationals to Return to Their Home Countries," *Personnel Administrator*, July 1984, pp. 41–45.

129. P. J. Dowling, "Hot Issues Overseas," *Personnel Administrator*, Vol. 34, No. 1 (1989) pp. 66–72.

130. Tung, "Selection and Training of Personnel for Overseas Assignments" and "Selection and Training Procedures"; Brewster, *The Management of Expatriates*; Bjorkman and Gertsen, "Corporate Expatriation"; Dowling and Welch, "International Human Resource Management."

131. Mendenhall and Oddou, "The Dimensions of Expatriate Acculturation."

132. Torbiorn, *Living Abroad*, p. 51.

133. Mendenhall and Oddou, "The Dimensions of Expatriate Acculturation."

Chapter **F O U R**

Performance Appraisal

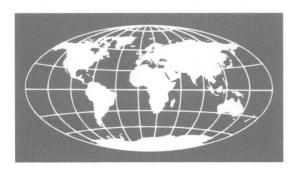

Once MNEs staff their international operations, they need to appraise the performance of both employees and the operation as a whole. This chapter focuses on performance appraisal in an international context. Although it is similar in some respects to performance appraisal in domestic operations, there are some significant differences. This chapter will highlight these differences.

There are aspects of international business that require a substantial modification of the traditional appraisal criteria that have been developed for a domestic business environment. As we discussed in Chapter 3, HR management needs to recognize that technical competence is a necessary but not sufficient condition for successful performance in international management positions. Cross-cultural interpersonal skills, sensitivity to foreign norms and values, understanding of differences in labor practices or customer relations, and ease of adaptation to unfamiliar environments are just a few of the managerial characteristics most multinational firms seek and evaluate. In addition to appraising these basic operational and managerial level skills, HR departments must develop an appropriate appraisal system for evaluating managers on attributes associated with successful performance at a strategic level.[1] Such a system should also apply to expatriate employees other than managers. Designing a performance-appraisal system to meet these demands is not easy. The various factors that need to be considered are discussed in the pages to follow.

TYPES OF EXPATRIATE TASK ROLES

In addition to operational managers, Hays[2] describes three other types of expatriate task roles:

- The *structure reproducer* carries the assignment of building or reproducing in a foreign subsidiary a structure similar to that which he or she knows from another part of the company. He or she could be building a marketing framework, implementing an accounting and financial reporting system, or establishing a production plant, for example.

- The *troubleshooter* is the individual who is sent to a foreign subsidiary to analyze and solve a particular operational problem.

- The *operational element* is the individual whose assignment is to perform as an acting element in an already existing operational structure.

Because these three roles are regarded as technical and staff specialist positions and may be of shorter duration than expatriate management assignments, their performance appraisal may be composed of evaluations from the subsidiary staff *and* from the home office. For these positions, strategic criteria may be much less relevant than operational and specialist managerial criteria. Cross-cultural skills, however, are as important for success in these positions as they are for the expatriate management positions.

DIFFERENT CRITERIA

Because of these different roles, we need to distinguish between operational, managerial, and strategic criteria when considering performance appraisal in MNEs. Operational and managerial criteria are relevant to the performance of technical and staff experts plus more junior expatriate management positions. Strategic criteria should be used when evaluating the performance of the senior managers and chief executive of the subsidiary or foreign affiliate. Commenting on the issues involved when evaluating the performance of this latter group, Pucik has noted:[3]

> The successful execution of competitive global strategy requires managers and executives with excellent environment-scanning abilities, familiar with conditions of business and market opportunities not in one, but in a number of countries and regions, and sensitive to special constraints facing multinational corporations, such as the relationship with the host governments. For example, interaction with top government officials and legislators is a function reserved in the home office to the chief executive and his staff. In foreign subsidiaries, the same task may fall on the shoulders of managers a number of layers below the corporate ladder. The proposition that an appraisal on the strategic level ought to be focused on the congruence of current managerial performance with long-term corporate objectives is today widely accepted at least as a theory, while its practical application is often bogged down by the constraint of organizational realities. In what form should long-term goals be expressed to be measurable against performance? What aspects of performance should be considered?

The difficulty in answering these questions makes the appraisal of managerial performance on an international level extremely complex. Because of this difficulty and the fact that they are really more descriptive of the performance of the subsidiary unit, strategic criteria are used here to describe the appraisal process of the unit rather than the individual manager. Since there is clearly a significant relationship between the activities of the senior managers and the performance of the subsidiary, a discussion of the issues related to evaluating the performance of the foreign subsidiary is quite relevant here. In this regard, the appraisal of the chief executive (or another senior manager) is similar to that of a general manager in charge of a strategic business unit. Thus, in addition to data on the results of the foreign subsidiary, the appropriate regional general manager (of the Asia-Pacific region, for example) can also evaluate the subsidiary's chief executive using an appraisal form that is similar to that used to evaluate domestic-based senior managers. This method allows the MNE to collect appraisal data that is more comparable across subsidiaries so that promotion and transfer decisions may be made more objectively. However, this personal appraisal data must also be considered in the context of the constraints facing strategic-level appraisal of foreign subsidiaries.

CONSTRAINTS ON STRATEGY-LEVEL APPRAISAL IN MNEs

In developing a suitable mix of objectives to be used as the framework of management appraisal on a strategic level, it is necessary to consider the implications of five major constraints that affect global strategy-level appraisal in MNEs.

Whole versus Part

To pursue a competitive global strategy, a MNE must necessarily focus on global performance rather than subsidiary or regional market performance. In the long run, the sum of short-term optimal sub-portfolio investments may not lead to optimal long-term performance for the MNE as a whole. The limitation of short-term local profit-maximization strategies can be seen when competitive pressure requires a multinational firm to operate and compete actively in markets where, if isolated from other markets, it would not compete. A typical case, described by Pucik,[4] is one in which a MNE enters a market where an international competitor is a dominant market leader. The objective of entering the market is to challenge the competitor's cash flow with aggressive pricing policies. The balance sheet of this particular subsidy might be continually in the red, but this strategy, by tying up the competitor's resources, may allow substantially higher returns in another market. The difficulties in quantifying such a global strategy in terms of the usual return-on-investment objectives are obvious.

Noncomparable Data

Frequently, the data obtained from subsidiaries may be neither interpretable nor reliable. For example:[5]

- Sales in Brazil may be skyrocketing, but there are reports that the Brazilian government may impose tough new exchange controls within a year, thus making it impossible for the MNE to repatriate profits. Does this mean that the MNE is performing effectively? Is the subsidiary performing effectively?

- Sales in Peru may be skyrocketing, but no one told the headquarters managers that under Peruvian accounting rules, sales on consignment are counted as firm sales. How should the headquarters accounting system handle these sales relative to sales from other subsidiaries, which do not consider sales on consignment as firm sales?

Physical measures of performance may be easier to interpret than in the examples, but difficulties may still arise. For example, notions of what constitutes adequate quality control checks can vary widely from one country to another, import tariffs can distort pricing schedules, a dock strike in one country can unexpectedly delay supply of necessary components to a manufacturing plant in another country, and local labor laws may require full employment at plants that are producing at below capacity. These factors can make objective appraisal of subsidiary performance problematic.

Volatility of the International Environment

The turbulence of the international environment requires that long-term goals be flexible in order to respond to potential market contingencies. An inflexible approach may mean that subsidiaries could be pursuing strategies that no longer fit the new environment. The interrelationship between the monitoring of relevant changes and the appraisal process is one important area in which corporate planning and human resource activities closely overlap. Consider, for example, the impact on international business of major international events such as the Tiananmen Square incident in Beijing in 1989, the Persian Gulf War in 1991, and the collapse of communist rule beginning in 1989 throughout Eastern Europe and the former Soviet Union.

The implications of some international developments may remain unclear for a considerable period of time. For example, in 1997 the British colony of Hong Kong will revert to the control of the People's Republic of China (PRC). Although the PRC, looking ahead to this transition of power, has passed laws that will allow Hong Kong to continue its capitalist economy for at least fifty years, there is considerable debate as to whether the Chinese government will deliver on this commitment. One result of this debate has been a dramatic migration from Hong Kong (mainly to Canada and Australia), which has created serious skill shortages in the Hong Kong labor market. Thus, foreign businesses in Hong Kong have experienced a significant increase in labor costs and face the uncertainty of business growth beyond 1997. Because subsidiaries operate under such volatility and fluctuation, they must tailor long-term goals to the specific situation in a given market. It is important to reconcile the tension between the need for universal appraisal standards with specific objectives in the subsidiaries.[6]

Separation by Time and Distance

Judgments concerning the congruence between long-term MNE strategy and activities in subsidiaries are further complicated by the physical distances involved, time-zone differences, the infrequency of contact between the corporate head-office staff and subsidiary management, and the cost of the reporting system. Developments in sophisticated worldwide communications systems such as Fax machines and video telephone conferences do not fully substitute for "face-to-face" contacts between subsidiary managers and MNE corporate staff. For some areas, such as the People's Republic of China and most of Eastern Europe and Russia, the telecommunications system is so overloaded that reliable telephone and Fax services cannot be assumed. It is often necessary to meet personally with a manager to fully understand the problems that managers must deal with. For this reason, many MNE corporate HR managers spend a considerable amount of time traveling in order to meet expatriate and local managers in foreign locations.

Variable Levels of Market Maturity

Without the supporting infrastructure of the parent company, the market development in foreign subsidiaries is generally slower and more difficult to achieve than at home, where established brands can support new products and new business areas can be cross-subsidized by other divisions. As a result, more time is needed to achieve results than is customary in a domestic market, and this fact ought to be recognized in the appraisal process. Further, variations in customs and work practices between the parent country and the foreign subsidiary must be considered. For example,

> One does not fire a Mexican manager because worker productivity is half the American average. In Mexico, that would mean that this manager is working at a level three or four times as high as the average Mexican industrial plant. Here we need relevant comparative data, not absolute numbers; our harassed Mexican manager has to live with Mexican constraints, not European or American ones, and these can be very different. The way we measure worker productivity is exactly the same, but the numbers come out differently because of that environmental difference.[7]

In summary, there are a number of significant constraints that must be considered when evaluating the performance of a foreign subsidiary. Because this evaluation is primarily based on strategic factors, it affects the evaluation and success of the subsidiary chief executive most directly. But there are also other factors affecting the performance of the chief executive and the other expatriate managers.

FACTORS ASSOCIATED WITH EXPATRIATE PERFORMANCE AND APPRAISAL

The assessment of expatriate performance is enhanced by a consideration of the variables that influence success or failure in a foreign assignment, and these factors should be considered, but are not always, before the assignment is made. These variables are the environment, the task, and the personality of the individual. The factors associated with the national environment to which an expatriate is assigned can be critical to the success of the individual. Variables associated with the particular job to be performed abroad are considered to be task variables. The individual factors are those associated with the characteristics and the situation of the person being considered for the international assignment.[8] In analyzing the performance of an expatriate, these variables should be considered as potential reasons for any performance deficiencies. After describing each variable, we can look at some ways in which performance can be appraised.

Environment

The environment has an impact on any job, but it becomes of primary importance in the role of the expatriate. As environments differ greatly, their potential for fostering successful performance also varies. Some environments can yield a relatively easy adaptation by an expatriate, while others impose tremendous difficulties. (This is similar to the notion of "cultural toughness" discussed in Chapter 3.) Many factors that can be expected or taken for granted in one's home country (for example, potable tap water) may not exist in the host country. It is likely that expatriate managers and their families will have some difficulty adjusting to a new environment, which will impact on the manager's work performance. This difficulty should be taken into account when assessing work performance. Similarly, the type of business and stage of the international business will influence the success of the expatriate.

Task

In attempting to predict how well an individual will perform in the expatriate assignment, consideration must be given to the general type of job assignment overseas. That is, the specific task variables should be assessed. Task variables are generally considered to be more under a MNE's control than environmental factors. Because of this relative control, the task variables can be better assessed and more easily changed. This, of course, may vary according to the position of the expatriate being appraised.

As various categories of job assignments are examined, it becomes clear that the ability of the individual to perform a particular job is critical to the success of the assignment. It is generally thought that most MNEs are able to obtain a reasonably accurate assessment of an individual's basic capability for the job, in terms of the task involved, from performance evaluations prior to the expatriate assignment. Many individuals and firms rank job ability as the primary ingredient relating to their expected probability of success in the international assignment (the "domestic equals overseas performance equation" mentioned in Chapter 3).

Certain types of tasks, however, require significantly more interaction with local culture than others. Thus the task variables and environmental factors can be interrelated. The process of establishing a new marketing system or operating as chief executive officer, for example, may depend heavily on an individual's ability to interact effectively with the local culture and environment. On the other hand, a technical troubleshooter probably requires considerably less ability to efficiently operate within a foreign environment. Clearly, in job assignments and tasks that require an ability to relate effectively and closely with the local culture, the social and cultural skills of the individual become more critical to the success of the assignment.

Another factor relating to task variables that warrants consideration is the similarity of the job the individual is assigned abroad to the job he or she held domestically. Some types of tasks require an individual to operate within a given structure, while other tasks demand the creation of the structure. Individuals vary greatly in their ability to conceive and implement a system and their tolerance for lack of structure and ambiguity. Some MNEs have experienced failure abroad because they assumed that an individual could be effective in setting up a structure, such as a marketing system, based on evidence of good performance within the existing marketing structure in the domestic corporation.[9]

Personality Factors

Personality factors appear to play a role in explaining an international manager's ability to adapt to a foreign environment. Thus much of the expatriate effectiveness literature is concerned with assessing personality variables. As the environment and the job may be largely predetermined in any particular instance, the choice of the individual is one of the few decisions under the control of the MNE. Personality variables appear to play an important role in helping to increase the probability of successful performance of international managers.[10]

For example, an individual's position along the dogmatism/authoritarianism scale, which can be determined with some accuracy, has a significant influence on his or her performance as an international manager. Dogmatism is a relatively closed conception of beliefs and disbeliefs about reality, and authoritarianism is a preoccupation with power and status considerations and a general hostility toward out-groups. Authoritarian personality traits and dogmatism tend to represent one end of the scale; the other end is represented by the corresponding opposites of openness, social sensitivity, and empathy.[11] These variables are relevant to the performance of international managers because open-minded individuals seem to adapt more easily to new environments. Those who score high on authoritarianism/dogmatism often have difficulty accepting and adjusting to a new culture and therefore may be somewhat less effective in accomplishing tasks with the local culture.[12]

In summary, the environment, the job or tasks, and the individual are important factors that interact to narrow the types of expatriate assignment choices with the highest probability of successful performance. These factors have significant implications for assessing the performance of international employees. The circumstances of a particular assignment will dictate which factors are of primary importance.

CRITERIA USED FOR PERFORMANCE APPRAISAL OF INTERNATIONAL EMPLOYEES

Now that we have an understanding of the variables likely to influence expatriate performance, we can discuss the criteria by which performance is to be appraised and evaluated. These criteria are generally a function of the nature of the specific type of expatriate assignment (for example, Hays's structure reproducer, troubleshooter, and so on),[13] the stages of international business development, and the international HRM philosophy or approach of the MNE.

As discussed in Chapter 2, the approach of the MNE to human resource management influences which criteria are used and who sets the standards. With an ethnocentric approach, standards are set and administered by expatriates. With a polycentric approach, standards are largely determined and administered by local staff in the host country. As the stage of international business development changes, appraisal criteria also change. For example, a change in focus from technology transfer and narrow objectives to a more global approach with longer-term objectives requires a considerable change in emphasis with regard to performance appraisal.

The type and relevance of performance criteria vary according to the form of control exercised by the parent over the subsidiary. Whether this control is loose or tight, subsidiary performance has implications for the overall financial performance of the MNE. Hence, it is important to understand the key issues associated with subsidiary unit appraisal. For example, MNEs commonly use arbitrary transfer pricing and other financial tools for transactions between subsidiaries to minimize foreign-exchange risk exposure and tax expenditures. Thus, the financial results recorded for any particular subsidiary do not always reflect accurately its contribution to the achievements of the corporation as a whole. Therefore, such results cannot and should not be used as a primary input in managerial appraisal.[14]

Another consideration is that all financial figures are generally subject to the problem of currency conversion, including sales and cash positions. In a MNE, it may not be known how much is sold in any given time period. Further complications arise because some currencies are not convertible to foreign currencies. For example, a profit of 300 million Indian rupees from that branch operation may be meaningless if you cannot bring the money out of India.[15]

To a certain extent, then, the success of subsidiaries is in many ways a product of the accounting and financial operations of the MNE. An extremely important aspect of both of these disciplines is to give management feedback on results in an accurate, concise way, so that managers know how they are performing and are able to plan properly for the future. In both disciplines, the international dimension is a rapidly growing area, simply because MNE managers would like to know what is going on. The nature of the international monetary system and local accounting differences, however, preclude an accurate measurement of results. How, then, can the MNE measure results? Many MNEs appear to measure cash flow very precisely. If various subsidiaries, after suitable development periods, are generating healthy cash surpluses, then the MNE is probably performing satisfactorily, regardless of the indications of more traditional accounting ratios. Most MNEs would have little cause for concern if cash deficits were being incurred (as when a major expansion is under way) as long as sufficient credit was available and there were prospects for surpluses in the future. In short, MNE managers work, by necessity, with somewhat cruder evaluative techniques than their domestic counterparts.

The use of transfer pricing and other financial tools is necessary because of the complexity of the international environment. Multinationals cannot allow subsidiaries to become autonomous in financial management terms. As Drucker[16] has commented:

> And when it comes to finance, the "autonomous" subsidiary becomes a menace. The splintering of financial-management decisions is responsible in large measure for the poor performance of the U.S.-based multinationals during these past years of an over-valued dollar, when most of them lost both market standing and profitability—unnecessarily. We do know how to minimize the impacts of exchange-rate fluctuations on both sales and profits. Now that fluctuating exchange rates, subject to sudden wide swings and geared primarily to capital movements and to governmental decisions, have come to be the norm, localized financial management then requires taking financial operations away from all operating units, including the parent, and running them as systems operations—the way old hands at the game, such as Exxon and IBM, have for many years.

Pucik[17] has suggested that in order to properly evaluate a subsidiary's performance and, therefore, the performance of the senior managers, a set of parallel accounts adjusted for the influence of financial manipulation may need to be maintained, or new measures of control developed, that are less susceptible to the influence of factors such as exchange-rate fluctuations, cash-flow and liquidity, and transfer pricing. Another alternative would be not to use measures such as the subsidiary's profit or return on equity to evaluate a manager but to use achievement of long-range goals such as market share growth, safety and health improvements, and environmental impact. Concern for the impact of business on the environment is becoming so important that some MNEs are now linking staff salaries to performance. (See Exhibit 4-1.)

Much of this discussion focuses on using financial data to evaluate how well an expatriate manager operates a foreign subsidiary. This results-oriented approach does not consider the way results are obtained and the behaviors used to obtain these results.[18] Concern with such issues led to the enactment of the U.S. Foreign Corrupt Practices Act (FCPA), which may prompt an increased use of behavioral as well as

EXHIBIT 4-1   IHR in the News

Management Pay

ICI to Link Staff Salaries to Environmental Performance

by Diane Summers, Labour Staff

ICI, the chemicals conglomerate, is to be one of the first UK companies to link the pay of its managers to performance in meeting environmental targets. The targets will form part of a drive by the company to improve its environmental record.

For ICI's most senior managers, who are already paid wholly on the basis of performance, environmental issues will be moved to the top of their list of priorities. The company's eventual aim is for all white-collar workers' pay to reflect environmental performance. Negotiations with unions on the reform of pay structures are currently taking place.

The move forms part of a plan by ICI to double environmental spending to £1bn worldwide and reduce output of harmful wastes by at least 50 per cent over the next five years. Sir Denys Henderson, ICI's chairman, said recently that the aim was to make the company's environmental performance "measurably better."

A number of other companies, particularly in the chemical and natural resource sectors, are also thought to be considering the introduction of environmental performance-related pay. The idea has already gained acceptance in the U.S.: Exxon, the U.S. oil company of which Esso is a subsidiary, set its managers extensive environmental targets after the public furore surrounding the 11m-gallon oil spill by the Exxon Valdez off Alaska last year.

Ms. Vicky Wright, head of compensation practice at Hay management consultants, said that, while ICI appeared to be leading the field, a number of other organisations that Hay was working with were also looking at ways of linking company objectives more closely to performance management.

"Organisations are getting away from simple profit targets and are looking at issues like the environment and developing customer relations," said Ms. Wright.

continued

EXHIBIT 4-1   *(continued)*

Relating pay to environmental performance at ICI marks a "distinct change of emphasis," according to Mr. John Coleman, group environmental affairs manager. Historically, safety, health and environmental targets have been grouped together, with safety "tending to predominate," he said.

Now ICI has decided to separate environmental from health and safety objectives and give them equal priority, said Mr. Coleman. Broad corporate objectives on the environment are to be translated into targets for the company's individual businesses.

From there, the performance-related pay targets will "cascade downwards, in theory quite a long way," according to Mr. Coleman. The company is currently reviewing ways of strengthening and extending its overall performance-related pay structure, he added.

Source: Financial Times (London), December 5, 1990, p. 12. Reprinted with permission.

---

results data to appraise the performance of expatriate managers in foreign subsidiaries. Enacted in 1977, the FCPA addresses the problem of questionable foreign payments by MNEs and their managers. This act was amended by Congress in 1988 to include substantial increases in the authorized criminal fines for organizations and new civil sanctions for individuals violating the FCPA.[19]

Appraisal of other expatriate employees is likely to be conducted by the subsidiary's chief executive officer, the immediate supervisor of the individual, and the individual's home country manager. The performance appraisal form of the home country is likely to be used, reflecting some results and behavioral criteria. If the assignment is being used to groom the expatriate for further international assignments, those in the foreign location evaluating the individual may add comments about the person's ability to deal with cultural issues, both on and off the job.

While some companies are developing information systems to assist in performance appraisal, the widespread use of computer-generated data is hampered by the legal constraints imposed by some host governments or by concerns about personal privacy. This is, however, a dynamic issue.

APPRAISAL OF HCN AND TCN EMPLOYEES

The discussion so far has omitted the issue of appraising the performance of HCN and TCN employees. This reflects the scarcity of research on the topic and the general lack of an acceptable way to address the situation.[20] In practice, U.S. MNEs have often used the same appraisal form for HCNs and TCNs (and expatriates if they are not heading the subsidiary) as for their domestic employees. Sometimes the forms are translated from English; sometimes they are not. Both approaches have drawbacks. The use of English-worded forms may not be readily understood by HCN and TCN managers and their employees (nor do they easily apply to all jobs in all situations). Even when the forms are translated and then returned to the home office, they still may not be readily understood by the domestic staff.

The practice of performance appraisal itself confronts the issue of cultural applicability.[21] Performance appraisal in different nations can be interpreted as a signal of distrust or even an insult. In Japan, for instance, it is important to avoid direct confrontation to "save face," and this custom affects the way in which performance appraisal is conducted. A Japanese manager cannot directly point out a work-related problem or error committed by a subordinate. "Instead, he is likely to start discussing with the subordinate about the strong points of that person's work, continuing with a discussion about the work on a relatively general level. Then he might continue to explain the consequences of the type of mistake committed by the subordinate, still without directly pointing out the actual mistake or the individual employee. From all this, the subordinate is supposed to understand his mistake and propose how to improve his work."[22] Evaluation of employee performance, therefore, requires cultural sensitivity, and many MNEs have been hesitant about doing performance appraisals of their HCN and TCN employees. One way to overcome this dilemma is to use host-country nationals to assist in devising a suitable system for appraising the local staff in the subsidiary and to advise on the conduct of the appraisal. This approach evinces local responsiveness but does not apply to the expatriate and TCN employees who may also be working in that subsidiary. The MNE may therefore desire a more global approach.

Pepsi-Cola International (PCI),[23] with operations in over 150 countries, has devised a common performance appraisal system that focuses on motivating managers to achieve and maintain high standards of performance. Administrative consistency is achieved through the use of a performance appraisal system of five feedback mechanisms: Instant Feedback, coaching, accountability-based performance appraisals, development feedback, and a human resource plan.

The common system provides guidelines for performance appraisal yet allows for modification to suit cultural differences. For example, the first step—Instant Feedback—is based on the principle that any idea about any aspect of the business or about an individual's performance is raised appropriately and discussed in a sensitive manner. The Instant Feedback message can be delivered in any culture; the important thing is not *how* it is done but *that* it is done.

In practice at PCI, the successful delivery of Instant Feedback requires some adjustment to local cultures. Americans use it because it fits a fast-paced way of doing business. In most Asian cultures, feedback may be tough and direct but is never given in public; nor, in some Asian cultures, does head-nodding during Instant Feedback signify agreement, only that the message has been heard. Some Latins will argue very strongly if they do not agree with the feedback, and some employees, Indian nationals, for example, will insist on a great deal of specificity. The purpose of Instant Feedback is always to improve business performance, not to criticize cultural styles. Using this system, PCI tries to balance the cultural and administrative imperatives of successfully managing the performance of a diverse workforce.[24]

SUMMARY

In this chapter we have discussed the MNE's need to determine if performance problems are due to management failure or to environmental constraints. To make this judgment, MNEs need to acquire accurate information. We discussed several types of information that can be gathered and the difficulties in gathering that information. A firm's communications requirements expand when it develops international markets because of the need for more information to properly evaluate subsidiary performance.[25]

In addition to the challenges in appraising the performance of each subsidiary manager, we discussed the challenges of comparing subsidiary managers in different countries. For example, it is difficult to compare the performance of a French subsidiary manager with that of a Singapore subsidiary manager because each manager works under quite different environmental conditions. It is equally as challenging to evaluate the performance of the employees (the majority of whom are HCNs) who work in the subsidiary. This task, however, is almost always left to the subsidiary manager in conjunction with HCN managers and local environmental conditions.

We concluded that MNEs make broad assessments of how well their chosen strategies are working. They may anticipate certain monetary and real growth in markets in given countries, and in a general way their managers can evaluate overall financial results subject to all the difficulties noted in this chapter. The micro details about evaluating the performance of TCNs and HCNs, quality control, production norms, pay rates, supplier relations and much more can be analyzed with some of the same tools and techniques used by the parent company, allowing for some appreciation for local conditions and cultures. The need for appreciating and then adapting to the needs of the local conditions, however, cannot be overstated. But as the example of Pepsi Cola International indicates, MNEs can provide some guiding principles that can be used internationally, with some local adaptations.

QUESTIONS

1. Discuss the major factors associated with appraisal of expatriate managerial performance.

2. What are some of the factors that influence appraisal of expatriate performance in subsidiary units?

3. Why is it important to distinguish between short-term and long-term objectives when assessing expatriate managerial performance?

4. In what ways would the role of a manager working in a less-developed country (LDC) differ from that of a manager in a developed Western economy?

5. It is often claimed that U.S. managers are less skilled in cross-cultural interaction than are their European counterparts.[26] In your view, is this a fair comment?

FURTHER READING

1. C. P. Dredge, "Corporate Culture: The Challenge to Expatriate Managers and Multinational Corporations," in *Strategic Management of Multinational Corporations: The Essentials*, ed. H. V. Wortzel and L. H. Wortzel (New York: John Wiley, 1985).

2. J. M. Geringer, P. W. Beamish, and R. C. daCosta, "Diversification Strategy and Internationalization: Implications for MNE Performance," *Strategic Management Journal*, Vol. 10 (1989) pp. 109–119.

3. S. E. Jackson, ed., *Human Resource Management Approaches for Effectively Managing Diversity* (New York: Guilford Publications, 1992).

4. L. Leksell and U. Lindgren, "The Board of Directors in Foreign Subsidiaries," in *International Business Knowledge: Managing International Functions in the 1990s*, ed. W. A. Dymsza and R. G. Vambery (New York: Praeger, 1987).

5. P. Lorange, "Human Resource Management in Multinational Cooperative Ventures," *Human Resource Management*, Vol. 25, No. 1 (1986) pp. 133–148.

6. I. Torbiorn, "The Structure of Managerial Roles in Cross-Cultural Settings," *International Studies of Management and Organization*, Vol. 15, No. 1 (1985) pp. 52–74.

NOTES

1. This section is based in part on V. Pucik, "Strategic Human Resource Management in a Multinational Firm," in *Strategic Management of Multinational Corporations: The Essentials*, ed. H. V. Wortzel and L. H. Wortzel (New York: John Wiley, 1985), and is used with permission.

2. Richard Hays, "Expatriate Selection: Insuring Success and Avoiding Failure," *Journal of International Business Studies*, Vol. 5, No. 1 (1974) pp. 25–37.

3. Pucik, "Strategic Human Resource Management," p. 429.

4. Pucik, "Strategic Human Resource Management."

5. J. Garland, R. N. Farmer, and M. Taylor, *International Dimensions of Business Policy and Strategy*, 2nd ed. (Boston: PWS-KENT, 1990).

6. Pucik, "Strategic Human Resource Management."

7. Garland, Farmer, and Taylor, *International Dimensions of Business Policy and Strategy*, p. 193.

8. This section is adapted from S. F. Slater and N. K. Napier, "Human Resource Competence as a Source of Competitive Advantage in Multinational Companies: Issues Affecting the Transfer of Distinctive Competence" (Working Paper, Boise State University, 1989). Used with permission. One of the dangers of performance appraisal is that, because the focus is so much on a particular individual, the teamwork aspect gets lost. In an international location, it is perhaps desirable to focus more on how the PCN has settled in and is operating as part of a team rather than as an individual at the possible detriment of the team.

9. M. Conway, "Reducing Expatriate Failure Rates," *Personnel Administrator*, July 1984, pp. 31–37.

10. See I. Torbiorn, *Living Abroad: Personal Adjustment and Personnel Policy in the Overseas Setting* (New York: John Wiley, 1982).

11. See E. Dapsin, "Managing Expatriate Employees," *Management Review*, July 1985, pp. 47–49; W. Davidson, "Administrative Orientation and International Performance," *Journal of International Business Studies*, Fall 1984, pp. 11–23; and M. Mendenhall and G. Oddou, "The Overseas Assignment: A Practical Look," *Business Horizons*, September–October 1988, pp. 78–84.

12. See M. Harvey, "The Executive Family: An Overlooked Variable in International Assignments," *Columbia Journal of World Business*, Spring 1985, pp. 84–92; M. Harvey, "The Other Side of Foreign Assignments: Dealing with the Repatriation Dilemma," *Columbia Journal of World Business*, Vol. 17, No. 1 (1982) pp. 53–59; and Hays, "Expatriate Selection."

13. Hays, "Expatriate Selection."

14. Pucik, "Strategic Human Resource Management."

15. Garland, Farmer, and Taylor, *International Dimensions of Business Policy and Strategy*.

16. P. Drucker, "The Changing Multinational," *Wall Street Journal*, January 1, 1986, p. 12.

17. Pucik, "Strategic Human Resource Management."

18. R. W. Beatty, "Competitive Human Resource Advantages Through the Strategic Management of Performance," *Human Resource Planning*, Vol. 12, No. 3 (1989) pp. 179–194.

19. K. F. Brickley, *Corporate Criminal Liability: A Treatise on the Criminal Liability of Corporations, Their Officers and Agents*, Cumulative supplement (Deerfield, Ill.: Clark Boardman Callaghan, 1992).

20. Personal conversations with Mark Mendenhall and Patrick Morgan, August 17, 1989.

21. N. J. Adler, *International Dimensions of Organizational Behavior*, 2nd ed. (Boston: PWS-KENT Publishing Company, 1991); S. Schneider, "National vs. Corporate Culture: Implications for Human Resource Management," *Human Resource Management*, Vol. 27 (1988) pp. 231–246; and G. P. Latham and N. K. Napier, "Chinese Human Resource Management Practices in Hong Kong and Singapore: An Exploratory Study," in *Research in Personnel and Human Resource Management*, Vol. 6, ed. G. Ferris, K. Rowland, and A. Nedd (Greenwich, Conn.: JAI, 1989).

22. J. V. Koivisto, "Duality and Japanese Management: A Cosmological View of Japanese Business Management." Paper presented at the European Institute of Advanced Studies in Management Workshop, *Managing in Different Cultures*, Cergy, Group Essec, France, November 23–24, 1992.

23. J. Fulkerson and R. S. Schuler, "Managing Worldwide Diversity at Pepsi-Cola International," *Human Resource Management Approaches for Effectively Managing Workforce Diversity*, ed. S. E. Jackson (New York: Guilford Publication, 1992).

24. For a complete description of PCI's system, see R. S. Schuler, J. R. Fulkerson, and P. J. Dowling, "Strategic Performance Measurement and Management in Multinational Corporations," *Human Resource Management*, Vol. 30, No. 3 (1991) pp. 365–392.

25. Garland, Farmer, and Taylor, *International Dimensions of Business Policy and Strategy.*

26. For example, see Chapter 1 of V. Terpstra and K. David, *The Cultural Environment of International Business*, 2nd ed. (Cincinnati, Ohio: South-Western, 1985).

Chapter F I V E

Training and Development

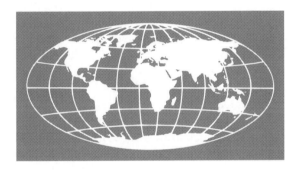

As we discussed earlier, the complex and ever-changing global environment requires flexibility; however, the organization's ability to devise strategic responses may be constrained by a lack of suitably trained, internationally oriented personnel. An emphasis on the training and development of expatriates is important, but in order to compete successfully in a global market, an increasing number of multinationals recognize that it is vital to train all categories of employees—including host-country and third-country nationals—so that high-caliber staff are available when and where required. In this chapter we first give an overview of the strategic operations of the organization as it internationalizes, to provide a contextual setting for the remainder of the chapter, which addresses the many issues involved in international training and development: the types of training programs, the frequency of their use, and cultural and language training.

THE SHIFT TO A GLOBAL MARKETPLACE

In the past, many MNEs tended to focus virtually all of their managerial development efforts on their expatriate managers.[1] This approach to training and development matched a number of other assumptions about doing business internationally. For example, a MNE assumed it could continue to grow and prosper simply by providing the same kinds of goods and services it had in the past. Managers believed that replicating the staffing of the existing MNE in foreign locations—including maintaining the same perspectives, know-how, and skills at various levels— would keep the firm on track. Management development efforts were considered successful if they produced similarly qualified replacements for individual executives whenever they might be needed. The best and most efficient way to manage the MNE was believed to be a top-down, vertical chain of command. All major decisions were made at corporate headquarters by the CEO and senior managers (or, in the case of European countries, by the managing board). Line managers at lower organization levels were expected to manage the day-to-day operation of their assigned units in accordance with uniform company policies and directives, including detailed operating plans and budgets. They were not expected to concern themselves with any broader, longer-range issues.

Of course, not all companies were quite this rigid, but, in retrospect, many will admit they were. Today the situation is quite different for most MNEs. The business environment has become turbulent, fiercely competitive, and increasingly global in scope. Multinationals headquartered all over the world are increasingly recognizing the need for change and the need to manage their affairs in a much more flexible and dynamic way. Many MNEs are now focusing on what, when, and how to change rather than how to maintain the status quo. In order to maintain growth and profitability, MNEs have had to address the following issues:

- The need to determine in which businesses the MNE should operate and which competitive strategies must be followed to compete successfully in these businesses.
- The need to formulate detailed competitive strategies and develop viable implementation plans for these businesses.
- The need to be aware of and responsive to changing markets and changing technologies all over the world.
- The need to become more flexible and resilient in dealing with unexpected political, economic, and competitive challenges and opportunities.

Accomplishing these tasks requires a very different overall management system.[2] Characteristics of such a management system include the following:

- Major strategic decision-making responsibilities are distributed to teams of line executives in charge of business units throughout the organization (including those overseas). Each organization level deals with a different set of strategic issues and so adds value in a different way. An interaction dialogue between the various parts and levels of the organization enables managers to reach agreement on appropriate strategies and to allocate available resources.

- Information gathering and information sharing become integral parts of each line manager's job, whether at home or abroad.

- There is recognition of local needs and the need to provide training, development, and promotion opportunities for HCNs and TCNs as well as PCNs.

- Close teamwork is needed in planning and smoothly implementing strategically necessary change without undermining the viability of ongoing operations.

The demands of managing business internationally call for different perspectives and skills and a much greater tolerance for ambiguity and uncertainty. These requirements must be taken into account when planning management training and development programs for MNEs, regardless of whether these programs take place in the home country or abroad.

LINKING STRATEGY AND STRUCTURE WITH INTERNATIONAL TRAINING AND DEVELOPMENT

The type of international operation is a key consideration in planning and establishing international training and development needs in a MNE. Each of the following four types of operations calls for different international training and development needs.

Limited Relationships

The first type of operation is the MNE with international sales through export offices, sales representatives, joint ventures, or distributor relationships. Businesses in this category generally limit their management development efforts to their own managers, but some also offer to help their partners' managers. Furthermore, if they see these export arrangements as temporary—as stepping stones to country businesses or mother-daughter organizations—they may also provide some business management training and development to the sales representatives, key liaison executives, or even heads of various partner organizations. Assuming these executives have all lived in the particular country, they are high-potential candidates for future management positions in the MNE. They already know the territory and the business, and they need opportunities to develop their strategic leadership skills and their general operating management skills.

Subsidiaries

The second type of operation is the firm with national subsidiaries. Because of the current emphasis on the management of businesses, subsidiaries are now likely to be represented on several lines of business strategy teams. Sometimes it is necessary to have an expatriate head up a country subsidiary at first, but there is general agreement that over time the entire management team should be from the host country. Training and development opportunities need to be provided to local managers to enable them to learn how the subsidiary operates and to develop the skills required to fulfill their managerial roles.

If the MNE decides to establish regional businesses, the managers from the various subsidiaries need to meet with each other to discuss recent developments and mutual problems, to share ideas and information and possible solution suggestions, and to begin to understand the reasons for their differing points of view. Some MNEs provide for temporary transfers between subsidiaries as a way of addressing these problems.

Regional Businesses

The third type of operation is the firm with regional businesses. If the senior managers have lived in different countries within the region, there should be an awareness of the cultural and geographic differences that must be balanced in arriving at overall strategies and business plans for the region. There are a number of training and development issues involved in operating regional businesses. First, future expatriate regional managers require several developmental assignments overseas before they are able to take up senior positions at regional headquarters. Second, host- and third-country nationals also require developmental assignments and training in strategic leadership skills and financial analysis.

In the future, it is likely that executives who have headed major regional businesses will be prime candidates to become CEOs of those same businesses on a global scale. To prepare them for future assignments and to ensure that current global business strategies appropriately balance the interests of all regions, leading-edge companies are including their regional business leaders as members of the top management teams running each of their global businesses.

Global Businesses

The final type of operation is the MNE that is a world-class company with several global businesses. Such firms report that management development programs need to emphasize worldwide information sharing on economic, social, political, technological, and market trends and to focus on building teamwork across related business lines as well as across functional and country-regional lines.

It is important to note that in practice this rather simple progression for categorizing international business development options and international management development options is more complex than it seems. The provision of relevant international training and development for managers will always be a challenging task. As Pucik[3] has noted, "Probably the most formidable task recently facing many multinational firms is the development of a cadre of managers and executives who have an understanding of the global market environment deep enough to enable them to survive and come out ahead." Part of the challenge lies in the fact that many MNEs have in the past paid too little attention to the issue of international training and development. Many MNEs traditionally relied on developing a cadre of career international management employees who moved from one international assignment to the next. (This system is often referred to as the "colonial model" because many European MNEs followed this pattern in the first half of this century.) Many MNEs are now recognizing that they need to provide international experience to many levels of managers (regardless of nationality) and not just to a small cadre of PCNs. Thus, many MNEs are now developing larger pools of employees with international experience through increasing use of short-term development assignments ranging from a few months to several years. However, some very successful global corporations have carried on the practice of developing a small cadre of international employees rather than internationalizing everyone. This practice not only saves on training costs but also saves on the costs of premature repatriation of those otherwise qualified individuals who were reluctantly internationalized.

Those multinational corporations that provide training and development opportunities for their TCN and HCN employees as well find such training is necessary to develop a true cadre of international managers and to be able to localize products and services as needed. It is also necessary in order to motivate TCN and HCN employees. Thus, multinationals must address the growing need for international training and development and deal with controversial questions concerning how many employees will be trained, what the overall purpose of the training is, and who should receive training (PCNs, HCNs, and/or TCNs). In reality, most MNEs continue to direct most of their training and development resources to PCNs. We will, therefore, look first at expatriate training before considering TCN and HCN training and development.

TRAINING AND DEVELOPMENT
FOR EXPATRIATE MANAGERS

Most training for expatriate assignments center around predeparture programs and seem primarily concerned with developing cultural awareness. As Earley[4] points out, "A major objective of intercultural training is to help people cope with unexpected events in a new culture." This cultural preparation is necessary because functional ability alone does not determine success. Cultural training also enables individuals to adjust more rapidly to the new culture and be more effective in their new roles.[5]

An organization's rationale for investing resources in training for international assignments rests primarily on the cost of expatriate failure. As Robock and Simmons[6] note, "However imperfect training may be as a substitute for actual foreign living experience, it is valuable if it can reduce the often painful and agonizing experience of transferring into another culture and avoid the great damage that culture shock and cultural misunderstanding can do to a firm's operating relationship." Copeland[7] agrees that "the cost of training is inconsequential compared to the risk of sending inexperienced or untrained people."

Scope and Use of Expatriate Training

As part of her study of expatriate management, Tung[8] reviewed training programs designed to improve the relational skills considered crucial to effective expatriate performance. She divided the training programs into five categories: (1) area studies programs that include environmental briefing and cultural orientation; (2) culture assimilators; (3) language training; (4) sensitivity training; and (5) field experiences. Tung concluded that each of the five types of training focuses on a different kind of learning process. The program selected depends on the type of job, the country of assignment, and the time available for training. To determine the types of training programs used by U.S., European, and Japanese multinationals, Tung,[9] in a later study, asked respondents to indicate which of these six training programs were used. The results showed that the U.S. multinationals tended to use training programs for expatriates less frequently than the European and Japanese firms (32 percent compared with 69 percent and 57 percent, respectively). According to Ronen,[10] this finding is consistent with earlier research. Given this finding, the higher expatriate failure rate experienced by U.S. companies at the time of the study is less surprising.

Tung also asked those respondents who reported no formal training programs to give reasons for omitting these programs. Again, differences were found between the three regions. The U.S. companies cited a trend toward employment of local nationals (45 percent); the temporary nature of such assignments (28 percent); the doubtful effectiveness of such training programs (20 percent); and lack of time (4 percent). The reasons given by European multinationals were the temporary nature of such assignments (30 percent); lack of time (30 percent); a trend toward employment of local nationals (20 percent); and the doubtful effectiveness of such programs. Responses from the Japanese companies were lack of time (63 percent); and doubtful effectiveness of such programs (37 percent).

Most of the U.S. and European companies that had training programs recognized the need for more rigorous training for their CEOs and functional heads than for their troubleshooters and operatives. The Japanese, on the other hand, appeared to provide slightly more rigorous training for their operatives. According to Tung, a possible explanation for this difference could be that Japanese CEOs have more extensive records of overseas work experience and have less need for the more rigorous programs than the relatively less-experienced operatives.

Recent studies confirm Tung's findings. The emphasis placed by European and Scandinavian multinationals on predeparture training, particularly language training, continues to be stronger than that of U.S. MNEs.[11] A 1984 study of one thousand U.S. MNEs found that only 25 percent offered extensive predeparture orientation training programs.[12] Another study, conducted in 1989, surveyed U.S. firms regarding relocation programs and found that only 13 percent of respondents indicated that they would offer expatriates an orientation program.[13] In their review of U.S. practices, McEnery and DesHarnais[14] estimate that between 50 and 60 percent of U.S. companies operating abroad do not provide any preparation. Those that do provide only brief environmental summaries and some cultural and language preparation, and only around half of these programs would last longer than a week. McEnery and DesHarnais draw attention to the lack of preparation given to the spouse and family before departure overseas. On this point, however, U.S. firms are not alone. European, Scandinavian, and Australian firms also place less priority on providing predeparture training for the spouse and family.[15]

Among the various reasons cited by business organizations for the low use of cross-cultural training is that top management just does not believe the training is necessary or effective.[16] This view of cross-cultural training needs to change; training and development of expatriates should begin where selection ends. An effective approach to expatriate development includes the following basic aspects:

- development of expatriates before, during, and after foreign assignment
- orientation and training of expatriate families before, during and after foreign assignments
- development of the headquarters staff responsible for the planning, organization, and control of overseas operations.

In designing international training and development for their expatriates, MNEs need to recognize the importance of multiple home-country and host-country role relationships, shown in Figure 5-1. In addition, international training and development programs need to recognize the importance of bringing about attitudinal and behavioral changes in the expatriates and their families.

A contributing factor here is that organizations use the overseas assignment for various purposes. Transfers can be made for three main reasons:[17]

a. For staffing—Viewed as temporary assignments, the flow of personnel is from the headquarters to the foreign subsidiary and back again.

b. For management development—Headquarters staff are transferred to subsidiaries to learn how to manage in a foreign environment. The transfer could also be made for training in a special technical skill that might exist in a particular subsidiary.

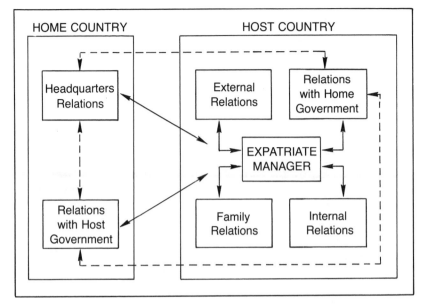

F I G U R E 5 - 1   Major Relations between the Expatriate Manager and Other Parties Interested in International Business

Source: A. Rahim, "A Model for Developing Key Expatriate Executives," *Personnel Journal,* April 1983, p. 313. Reprinted with permission.

Host-country nationals can also be transferred to headquarters to learn how the organization works.

c. For organization development—The use of transfers for coordination and control. Managers (usually PCNs) are transferred to a variety of international locations to foster their own development but, at the same time, to build a team of international managers from which the organization can draw managerial and technical skills. This use of staff transfers allows the total organization to develop a global focus as well as assist in the coordination and control of the global network through the corporate culture transferred via such staff.

Effective Cross-Cultural Training

Once an employee has been selected for an expatriate position, cross-cultural training becomes the next critical step in attempting to ensure the expatriate's effectiveness and success abroad. (This training is in addition, of course, to the task-specific knowledge necessary for the position.) Depending on the assigned country, the employee and his or her family may be confronted with a culture markedly different from their own. These contrasts can extend beyond the language barrier and encompass aspects of social life, political climate, and religious differences.[18]

Studies indicate that there are three areas that contribute to a smooth transition to a foreign post: cultural training, language instruction, and assistance with practical, day-to-day matters.[19] The first two phases necessarily begin prior to the international assignment. Because these phases take time, the notification of posting should be done well in advance of the departure. Business conditions, however, cannot always be planned so precisely. Recognizing this, human resource specialists must nevertheless encourage the line managers (who typically make the selection and assignment decisions) to anticipate their global needs. The last category, practical assistance, begins once the employee arrives in the host country.

Cultural Training

To be effective, the expatriate employee must adapt to and not feel isolated from the host country. A cultural training program can be extremely beneficial. The potential benefits of cultural or cross-cultural training are widely acknowledged, yet this type of training is not offered by most U.S. MNEs.[20]

Cultural training seeks to foster an appreciation of the host country's culture so that expatriates can behave accordingly. Sieveking, Anchor, and Marston[21] cite the culture of the Middle East to emphasize this point. In that region, emphasis is placed on personal relationships, trust, and respect in business dealings. Coupled with this is an overriding emphasis on religion that permeates almost every aspect of life. Without an understanding (or at least an acceptance) of the host-country culture in such a situation, the expatriate is likely to face considerable difficulty during the international assignment. As discussed in Chapter 4, flexibility appears to be an important characteristic for the expatriate.

Baliga and Baker[22] suggest that the expatriate receive training concentrated in the assigned region's culture, history, politics, economy, religion, and social and business practices. They advocate a training program focused on a particular location as opposed to one in which employees are made aware of broad differences in cultures and encouraged merely to be open to them. Only with precise knowledge of the varied components of their host culture can the expatriate and family grasp how and why people behave and react as they do. According to Harris,[23] it is also important to include the family in cultural training programs. "In the past, the family has not received an appropriate amount of attention," he has noted. "The biggest problem for Americans overseas is not technical know-how, rather it is some kind of spousal and/or child problem."

Because of the skills and complexities involved, many MNEs employ specialists such as Moran, Stahl & Boyer in the United States or the Center for International Briefing (known as Farnham Castle) in Britain to conduct cultural training programs.[24] These training programs enable the employee, spouse, and children to become more flexible and adaptive by exposing participants to new information and experiences. In addition to these specialists, there are "how-to" books such as Copeland and Griggs's *Going International*.[25] Recent research suggests that the most effective cultural training programs use a variety of source material. For example, an interesting paper by Earley[26] suggests that MNEs should use both documentary and interpersonal methods to prepare managers for intercultural assignments.

Some European MNEs, such as Philips, have incorporated cultural training into their career planning process. For example, employees may be posted to an overseas subsidiary for three or four years to fulfill both operational and management development objectives. Some U.S. MNEs such as Hercules Incorporated, Ford, Dow Chemical, Monsanto, Westinghouse, and General Electric have successfully applied a similar approach to training and development. Such an approach is less common with U.S. MNEs, however, and this may be one reason for the reported high failure rate for U.S. expatriates.

One developmental technique useful for orienting international employees is to send them on a preliminary trip to the host country.[27] A well-planned trip overseas for the candidate and spouse provides a preview that allows them to assess their suitability for and interest in the assignment. Such a trip also serves to introduce expatriate candidates to business outside their own country and helps encourage more informed predeparture preparation. The Ford Motor Company, for example, provides a one-week visit to the foreign location for both employee and spouse, during which time the employee visits the Ford subsidiary to meet future colleagues and discuss job requirements. The couple looks at prospective houses and schools and gets a feel for the new location and its cultural environment. The Australian latex manufacturer Ansell International offers a similar reconnoiter visit when posting staff to its production plants in Southeast Asia. The company finds that this method allows couples to experience firsthand some of the cultural differences so they can make a more informed decision about the overseas assignment.

Effective and comprehensive cultural training programs can ease transition and help to develop productive expatriates. They can also prevent mistakes such as that of the highly paid expatriate who brought two miniature bottles of brandy with him into Qatar (a Muslim country in the Middle East), was discovered by customs, and was promptly deported, causing his firm to be "disinvited" and ordered never to return.

Language Training

Language training is a seemingly obvious orientation needed for a successful and productive experience abroad and should form part of any long-term management development program for future global executives.[28] As noted in Chapter 3, there is general recognition that English is the language of world business, and it is quite possible to conduct routine operations around the world using English only, but an exclusive reliance on English diminishes the incentive to develop the linguistic capacity of the MNE and the ability to process foreign-language data in a timely manner.

It is also important to note that multilingual employees of MNEs from non-English-speaking countries are able to monitor the activities of their English-speaking competitors by reading English-language publications. (The voluminous business press in an open society such as the United States frequently gives detailed accounts of the strategic plans of large companies.) For example, many engineers and managers in Japanese computer companies have a sufficient command of English to enable them to understand English-language trade journals and conference presentations, often sources of valuable business intelligence. In contrast, their English-speaking counterparts employ only a handful of engineers capable of following Japanese-language materials and of making the proper inference between publicly available information and its underlying strategic significance—a task that an outside translation service is not equipped to handle.

It appears that the importance of language training is not appreciated by many MNEs—in particular U.S. MNEs. A 1989 survey by Columbia University of 1,500 senior executives in twenty countries shows some interesting differences between U.S. and foreign executives.[29] Participants were asked to rate the importance of a number of attributes "for the CEO of tomorrow." For the attribute "trained in a foreign language" 19 percent of the U.S. respondents gave a rating of very important compared to 64 percent of foreign (non-U.S.) respondents. A similar difference was obtained (U.S., 35 percent; foreign, 70 percent) in ratings for the attribute "experienced outside home country." Commenting on this survey, Lester Korn (chairman of Korn/Ferry International, a leading executive search firm) stated:[30]

> A "Copernican revolution" must take place in the attitude of American CEOs as the international economy no longer revolves around the U.S., and the world market is shared by many strong players. . . . While U.S. executives have identified this change, they still place far less importance on having an international outlook than do the foreign executives surveyed.

Clearly, the ability to speak a foreign language can improve the expatriate's effectiveness and negotiating ability. As Baliga and Baker[31] point out, it can improve managers' access to information regarding the host country's economy, government, and market. In addition, expatriates can more easily fit into their adapted country socially whether or not English is spoken by foreign nationals. As we noted in Chapter 3, Mendenhall and Oddou[32] make the important point that willingness to communicate does not refer to level of fluency in a foreign language but rather the expatriate's confidence and willingness to use the host culture's language.

However, as we point out at the beginning of this chapter, the shift to the global marketplace is forcing companies to come to terms with the demands of international business. One outcome has been a change in emphasis on employee language skills. Major U.S. companies are requesting that U.S. business schools include foreign languages in their curricula and are giving hiring preference to graduates with foreign language skills. A similar trend is evident in the United Kingdom, and in Australia.

Practical Training

Practical assistance makes an important contribution toward the adaptation of the expatriate and his or her family to their new environment. Being left to fend for themselves would most likely result in a negative response toward the host country's culture. Lanier[33] states that the MNE needs to assist the expatriate family in establishing a new support network. The sooner a pattern of day-to-day life involving friends, banks, shopping, laundry, transportation, and so on is established, the better the prospects are that the expatriates will adapt successfully. A useful method of adaptation involves interaction between the expatriate's family and other established expatriate families. These encounters allow the exchange of information, facilitating adaptation, and serve to build a stable network of relationships for the expatriate's family. If fluency in the host-country language is important for successful adaptation, further language training for the expatriate and family should occur after arrival. Orientation programs and local language programs are normally organized by the personnel staff in the host country. Adaptation and assimilation, however, go in both directions:

> In order to help close the cultural gap, it is not always enough to just take the expat and family and explain what the local culture/language is all about. It is equally important to take the local employees and explain to them who are these "gringos" and why are they so strange. This helps with mutual assimilation.[34]

Exhibit 5-1 shows both the diversity and the frequency of approaches taken by MNEs.

EXHIBIT 5-1 Preparing Managers for International Postings

(% respondents ranking an activity as among the five most important methods in their organizations)

Arranging for managers to visit host country	79
Language training for managers	73
Briefing by host-country managers	67
In-house general management course	44
Cross-cultural training for managers	42
Cross-cultural training for family	38
General management course at business school	29
Language training for family	23
Training in negotiating within business norms of host country	17

Source: K. Barham and M. Devine, "The Quest for the International Manager: A Survey of Global Human Resource Strategies," the Economist Intelligence Unit, London, Special Report No. 2098 (1990), p. 33. Reprinted with permission.

Contingency Approaches to Expatriate Training

Because not all expatriate assignments are the same, expatriate training is likely to vary. To understand possible variations in expatriate training, Tung[35] proposed a contingency framework for deciding the nature and level of rigor of training. She argued that the two determining factors were the degree of interaction required in the host culture and the similarity between the individual's native culture and the new culture. The related training elements involved the content of the training and the rigor of the training. Essentially, Tung argued that if the expected interaction between the individual and members of the host culture was low and the degree of dissimilarity between the individual's native culture and the host culture was low, then the content of the training should focus on task- and job-related issues rather than culture-related issues, and the level of rigor necessary for effective training should be relatively low. If there was a high level of expected interaction with host nationals and a large dissimilarity between the cultures, then the content of the training should focus on the new culture and on cross-cultural skill development as well as on the new task, and the level of rigor for such training should be moderate to high.

This model does specify some criteria (degree of expected interaction and cultural similarity) for making training method decisions, but the conclusions the model allows the user to make are fairly general. The model helps the user determine when to emphasize task issues and when to emphasize culture learning along with skill development and task issues, but it does not help the user determine which specific training methods to use or what might constitute more or less rigorous training.

A more recent model presented by Mendenhall and Oddou and Mendenhall, Dunbar, and Oddou in some ways moves beyond Tung's model and provides more specific guidelines.[36] Like Tung, Mendenhall, Dunbar, and Oddou acknowledge the importance of degree of expected interaction and similarity between the native and host cultures in determining the cross-cultural training method. In addition, they propose that the following are three key elements related to training: (1) training methods; (2) low, medium, and high levels of training rigor; (3) duration of the training relative to degree of interaction and culture novelty. The key elements of this model are shown in Figure 5-2.

Using the Mendenhall, Dunbar, and Oddou model, if the expected level of interaction is low and the degree of similarity between the individual's native culture and the host culture is high, the length of the

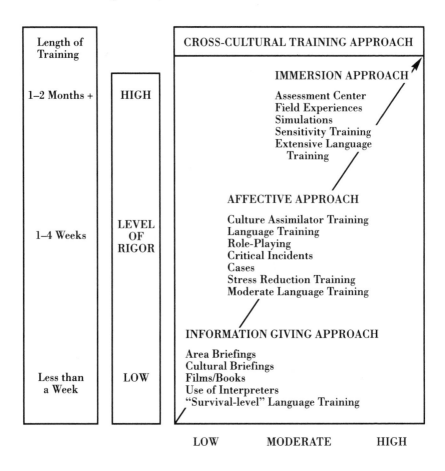

Length of Training		CROSS-CULTURAL TRAINING APPROACH
		IMMERSION APPROACH
1–2 Months +	HIGH	Assessment Center Field Experiences Simulations Sensitivity Training Extensive Language Training
		AFFECTIVE APPROACH
1–4 Weeks	LEVEL OF RIGOR	Culture Assimilator Training Language Training Role-Playing Critical Incidents Cases Stress Reduction Training Moderate Language Training
		INFORMATION GIVING APPROACH
Less than a Week	LOW	Area Briefings Cultural Briefings Films/Books Use of Interpreters "Survival-level" Language Training

| | LOW | MODERATE | HIGH |

DEGREE OF INTEGRATION

Length of stay	1 Month or less	2–12 Months	1–3 Years

FIGURE 5-2   The Mendenhall, Dunbar, and Oddou Cross-Cultural Training Model

Source: M. E. Mendenhall, E. Dunbar, and G. R. Oddou, "Expatriate Selection, Training and Career-Pathing: A Review and Critique." *Human Resource Management,* Fall 1987, p. 340. Reprinted by permission of John Wiley & Sons, Inc.

training should probably be less than a week and methods such as area or cultural briefings via lectures, movies, or books would provide the appropriate level of training rigor. On the other hand, if the individual is going overseas for a period of two to twelve months and is expected to have some interaction with members of the host culture, the level of training rigor should be higher and its length longer (one to four weeks). In addition to the information-giving approaches, training methods such as culture assimilators and role-plays may be appropriate.[37]

If the individual is going to a fairly novel and different host culture and the expected degree of interaction is high, the level of cross-cultural training rigor should be high and training should last as long as two months. In addition to the less rigorous methods already discussed, sensitivity training, field experiences, and intercultural experiential workshops may be appropriate training methods in this situation.

The model presented by Mendenhall, Dunbar, and Oddou seems to be a significant improvement over the more general model offered by Tung. It provides a grouping of specific methods by level of rigor and also discusses the duration of training relative to the criteria of interaction and culture similarity. Despite these important improvements, the model tells us little about the training and learning processes and, therefore, why the particular determinations are made. Also, the content of the training seems to be primarily "cultural" in nature, with little integration of the individual's new tasks and the new host culture. Finally, although both models make intuitive sense, the theoretical grounding is never made explicit, and, therefore, in the absence of empirical data to support the models, it is difficult to evaluate their soundness for use and success in the real world.

More recently, Black and Mendenhall have developed a much more extensive theoretically based model using Bandura's Social Learning Theory.[38] Although it is too early for empirical research on their propositions, they appear to offer a useful way to determine the appropriate content and method of expatriate training programs and to evaluate their success.

It is possible that the selection of training methods is influenced by factors such as degree of ethnocentrism. A study by Hall and Gudykunst has shown that the lower the level of perceived ethnocentrism in an MNE, the more training it provides in cultural awareness and personal flexibility, together with more language training and other training that orients the employee toward business practices in the relevant country.[39]

INTERNATIONAL TRAINING AND DEVELOPMENT FOR HCNs AND TCNs

The bulk of this chapter has so far focused on the expatriate, or PCN. It is important that MNEs also consider the training and development needs of their HCN and TCN employees. Such training may involve development of managerial skills or introduction to the MNE's corporate culture. Technical training for lower-level local employees is generally provided by the country subsidiary rather than corporate headquarters. However, some MNEs are now beginning to use satellite technology to deliver custom-designed training courses from home-country locations.[40]

Various Approaches

One of the main aims of managerial training for HCNs and TCNs is to teach managers how to lead, motivate, and develop employees in their own countries. As many MNEs are discovering, a quality enhancement approach requires not just making sure that employees have the skills, but also making sure that managers have good people-management skills. This generally means that HCN and TCN managers need to participate more in the company. In many cases, this means changing their entire way of operating. As one U.S. respondent to the Schuler and Dowling survey of SHRM/I members noted:[41]

> Implementing a quality improvement process, requiring a new role of managers, is tough enough in the U.S., but management labor "class" distinctions which are very prevalent in the U.K., France, and Germany, and seem almost sanctioned, *de facto*, in labor law make this task very difficult.

Thus, one of the traps that should be avoided is to try to export home-country training and development programs to other countries for local employees without any recognition that the training must be culturally adapted to meet local conditions. This said, many Japanese MNEs such as Nissan and Honda have been able to train substantial numbers of HCNs with success. This is particularly true regarding technical training for operating employees.

Another approach used by multinationals to develop their HCN and TCN employees, especially supervisors and managers, is to bring them to corporate headquarters. Fiat, the Italian automobile manufacturer, uses staff transfers as part of its training program, with HCN recruits spending time at corporate headquarters. The Swedish telecommunications company L. M. Ericsson has two levels of formal management development programs. One caters to the top 300 managers in the group, the other to the 1,500 middle managers. While the focus of course content differs for these two programs, there is a common aim—to develop informal networks among Ericsson managers throughout the entire global company. As part of its approach, the company has established the

Ericsson Management Institute. Similarly, the Pepsi-Cola International Management Institute is an umbrella system for the delivery of training programs such as sales force management or production techniques for the manufacturing of Pepsi brands. Part of this approach is the "Designate Program," which brings non-U.S. citizens to the United States for a minimum of eighteen months of training in the domestic U.S. Pepsi system. Other MNEs have similar central management training centers (for example, McDonald's Hamburger University, General Electric's Management Development Institute, Unilever's International Management Training Center, and NEC's Institute of Management). However, as Barham and Devine[42] explain, "companies do not necessarily need to establish elaborate physical facilities for management education. The Pepsi-Cola International Management Institute and the Ericsson Management Institute, for example, are concepts rather than physical locations." It is important also to note that while this approach is aimed primarily at developing managerial skills, participants are also exposed to the corporate culture, which assists them in developing a corporate perspective rather than simply reflecting their own local interests. By the same token, interaction with foreign staff also broadens the outlook of corporate staff.

This type of training and development can be a very effective and necessary part of successfully operating a truly global firm. Training HCNs and TCNs can also be done for the purpose of developing the global management teams described at the beginning of this chapter. Through rotational experiences and international meetings, bonds of friendship can develop between individuals from all parts of the globe. These bonds can be used in the future to build truly global teams.[43]

Novel Approaches

Exhibit 5-2, recounts an unusual approach to training: The "importing" by Matsushita of one hundred overseas managers a year to work alongside their Japanese counterparts. The article points out the constraints of implementing the approach as well as the importance of internationally oriented staff in maintaining global expansion.

A more radical approach, perhaps, is the Global Leadership Program at the University of Michigan. For a period of five weeks, teams of American, Japanese, and European executives learn global business skills through action learning. To build cross-cultural teams, the program utilizes seminars and lectures, adventure-based exercises, and field trips to

EXHIBIT 5-2   IHR in the News

The Glamour of Gaijins*

Osaka

Foreign managers have long been flown to Japan to learn the ropes—how to organise factories, exchange business cards, get drunk with their colleagues. Now Matsushita is taking a bolder step. It plans to import 100 foreign managers a year from overseas subsidiaries into its Japanese offices and factories. Naturally, they will learn a lot while they are there. But the real aim is to shock Matsushita's rather provincial Japanese managers into learning how to deal with foreign colleagues and issues.

Advocates of this therapy at Matsushita's Osaka headquarters wanted to be even more ambitious, bringing in 1,000 foreign employees a year. The firm is acutely aware that it is years behind Sony in developing an international corps of managers, whether Japanese or foreign. Though Matsushita has owned factories in the United States ever since it bought Motorola's consumer-products division in 1974, most of its products were exported directly from Japan until the mid-1980s. But now the company is building more foreign factories and, in MCA, owns a big Hollywood studio. Its bosses fear that its stay-at-home managers could hold it back.

Gaijins are foreigners.

(continued)

investigate business opportunities in countries such as Brazil, China, and India. The overall objective of the Global Leadership Program is to produce individuals with a global perspective.[44]

Foreign Managers

Establishing truly global operations means having a cadre of international managers (PCNs, HCNs, and TCNs) who are available to go anywhere in the world. To develop this cadre of managers, MNEs need to provide training for HCNs and TCNs in the parent country. This issue is of particular concern to U.S. MNEs, which are increasingly having to

Yet some shocks are too great: the 1,000-a-year plan was scaled down because it would have put a huge strain on overseas units. After all, there will be no extra Japanese managers going abroad to balance the numbers. The idea is that the foreigners work alongside Japanese equivalents, but not just as assistants: they will have their own responsibilities. So they will add to the headcount in Japan and have to be replaced back home.

The "100" project was launched in April. The first three foreigners arrived in August. Others will come from all around the world, which is why those who need it will be given language training—not in Japanese, but in English. Neither they nor their Japanese colleagues will use interpreters: they are supposed to communicate in English.

Even 100 a year will strain the foreign operations. Many of those sent to Japan are supposed to be senior managers and will stay for one or two years. Richard Kraft, head of Matsushita's American operations, points out that although his firm employs 12,500 people in the United States, the team of senior managers is pretty small. Sending 20 people to Japan, as is planned, will be tough. So will finding jobs for them back in America two years later. But Osaka will never be the same again.

Source: The Economist, September 21, 1991, p. 78. © The Economist, London, September 1991. Reprinted with permission.

deal with the problem of helping HCNs and TCNs adjust to working in the United States. Just as Americans doing business abroad must grapple with unfamiliar social and commercial practices, so, too, must European, Asian, and Latin American managers who are coming in growing numbers to work in the United States. To lessen the culture shock, many companies are relying on consultants to provide books, movies, and special programs that educate foreign employees about corporate life in the United States. Some have taken the language instruction, tax advice, and orientation techniques used when Americans are sent abroad and modified them to accommodate foreigners transferred to the United States. Others are trying a sort of buddy system, pairing foreign newcomers with American managers.[45]

Some MNEs are offering training and development programs that teach foreign managers how to motivate Americans and how to conduct performance appraisal interviews:

> Some of the programs designed to speed acculturation are intensive and emotionally strenuous. One U.S. manufacturer has retained trainers to stage role-playing sessions for its Japanese managers, some of whom have had special difficulty with American bluntness. During one of these, in which a Japanese manager was told to criticize an American employee's performance, "it took five runs of the same situation until he was direct enough that the American could realize he was being criticized," says Gary Wedersphan, a director of the international division of Moran, Stahl & Boyer, the consulting firm that conducted the sessions.[46]

SUMMARY

This chapter has shown that development of an internationally focused training and development program cannot be accomplished effectively without close coordination of developmental activities with the corporate strategic objectives. Issues include the nature and extent of current and future product markets, whether the MNE will have sufficient trained personnel to compete effectively in these product markets, and the need to develop an international cadre of managers who can manage international businesses in a variety of operating arrangements (joint ventures, subsidiaries, regional businesses, and so on). Analysis of these issues should provide parameters for HR staff, to enable them to plan training and developmental activities that are congruent with the MNE's strategic objectives. International training and development activities that are unrelated to overall strategic objectives are likely to be ineffective. Similarly, a MNE's strategic plan that does not consider appropriate human resource training and development programs is likely to be unsustainable.

QUESTIONS

1. Compare and contrast the traditional management system of MNEs to the management approaches used today in many global companies.
2. What are some of the challenges faced in training expatriate managers?
3. Identify the key aspects of a successful expatriate training and development program.

4. Why are dual-career couples and training of foreign managers two crucial issues in international training and development?

5. What are the issues and challenges MNEs face in developing a cadre of global managers?

FURTHER READING

1. R. Andre, "The Effects of Multinational Business Training: A Replication of INSEAD Research in an Institution in the United States," *Management International Review*, March 1985, pp. 4–15.

2. J. C. Baker, "Company Policies and Executives' Wives Abroad," *Industrial Relations*, October 1976, pp. 343–348.

3. C. Edinger, "Should You Work for a Foreigner?" *Fortune*, August 1, 1988, pp. 123–134.

4. C. Gould, "A Checklist for Accepting a Job Abroad," *New York Times*, July 17, 1988, p. 9.

5. J. Kepler, et al. *Americans Abroad: A Handbook for Living and Working Overseas*, New York: Praeger, 1983.

6. J. McEnery and G. DesHarnais, "Culture Shock," *Training and Development Journal*, April 1990, pp. 43–47.

7. R. Nath, "Role of Culture in Cross-Cultural and Organizational Research," *Advances in International Comparative Management*, 1986, pp. 249–267.

8. J. Onto, "Preparing Managers for International Careers: A Strategic Perspective," *Human Resource Management Australia*, Vol. 25, No. 3 (1987) pp. 22–33.

9. R. S. Savich and W. Rodgers, "Assignments Overseas: Easing the Transition Before and After," *Personnel*, August 1988, pp. 44–48.

10. J. W. Weiss and S. Bloom, "Managing in China: Expatriate Experiences and Training Recommendations," *Business Horizons*, May–June 1990, pp. 23–29.

NOTES

1. This discussion of the historical development of international business is adapted from R. Shaeffer, "Managing International Business Growth and International Management Development," *Human Resource Planning*, March 1989, pp. 29–36.

2. J. E. Harris, "Moving Managers Internationally: The Care and Feeding of Expatriates," *Human Resource Planning*, March 1989, pp. 49–54.

3. This section is adapted from V. Pucik, "Strategic Human Resource Management in a Multinational Firm," in *Strategic Management of Multinational Corporations: The Essentials*, ed. H. V. Wortzel and L. H. Wortzel (New York: John Wiley, 1985). Used by permission.

4. P. C. Earley, "Intercultural Training for Managers: A Comparison," *Academy of Management Journal*, Vol. 30, No. 4 (1987) p. 686.

5. J. McEnery and G. DesHarnais, "Culture Shock," *Training and Development Journal*, Vol. 44, No. 4 (1990) pp. 43–47; J. S. Black and M. Mendenhall, "Cross-Cultural Training Effectiveness: A Review and a Theoretical Framework for Future Research," *Academy of Management Review*, Vol. 15, No. 1 (1990) pp. 113–136; H. DeCieri, P. J. Dowling, and K. F. Taylor, "The Psychological Impact of Expatriate Relocation on Partners," *The International Journal of Human Resource Management*, Vol. 2, No. 3 (1991) pp. 377–414.

6. S. H. Robock and K. Simmons, *International Business and Multinational Enterprises*, 4th ed. (Homewood, Ill.: Richard D. Irwin, 1989) p. 578.

7. L. Copeland, "Making Costs Count in International Travel," *Personnel Administrator*, Vol. 29, No. 7 (1984) p. 47.

8. R. Tung, "Selecting and Training of Personnel for Overseas Assignments," *Columbia Journal of World Business*, Vol. 16 (1981) pp. 68–78.

9. R. Tung, "Selection and Training Procedures of U.S., European, and Japanese Multinationals," *California Management Review*, Vol. 25, No. 1 (1982) pp. 57–71.

10. S. Ronen, *Comparative and Multinational Management* (New York: John Wiley, 1986).

11. C. Brewster, *The Management of Expatriates*, Human Resource Research Centre Monograph Series, No. 2 (Bedford, United Kingdom: Cranfield School of Management, 1988).

12. J. C. Baker, "Foreign Language and Departure Training in U.S. Multinational Firms," *Personnel Administrator*, July 1984, pp. 68–70.

13. D. Feldman, "Relocation Practices," *Personnel*, Vol. 66, No. 11 (1989) pp. 22–25.

14. J. McEnery and G. DesHarnais, "Culture Shock."

15. K. Barham and M. Devine, *The Quest for the International Manager: A Survey of Global Human Resource Strategies*, Ashridge Management Research Group, Special Report No. 2098 (London: 1990) The Economist Intelligence Unit; D. Welch, "Determinants of International Human Resource Management Approaches and Activities: A Suggested Framework," *Journal of Management Studies* (forthcoming); I. Bjorkman, "Expatriation and Repatriation in Finnish Companies: A Comparison with Swedish and Norwegian Practice" (Working Paper No. 211, Swedish School of Economics and Business Administration, Helsinki: 1990).

16. M. Mendenhall and G. Oddou, "The Dimensions of Expatriate Accultura-tion," *Academy of Management Review*, Vol. 10 (1985) pp. 39–47; H. Schwind, "The State of the Art in Cross-Cultural Management Training," in *International Human Resource Management Annual*, Vol. 1, ed. Robert Doktor (Alexandria, Virginia: ASTD, 1985); and Y. Zeira, "Overlooked Personnel Problems in Multinational Corporations," *Columbia Journal of World Business*, Vol. 10, No. 2 (1975) pp. 96–103.

17. D. A. Ondrack, "International Transfers of Managers in North American and European MNEs," *Journal of International Business Studies*, Vol. 16, No. 3 (1985) pp. 1–19.

18. This section is adapted from N. Napier, M. Taylor, and S. Slater, "Human Resource Competence as a Source of Competitive Advantages in Multina-tional Companies: Issues Affecting the Transfer of Human Resource Man-agement Competence" (Working Paper, Boise State University, 1988).

19. M. Mendenhall and G. Oddou, "Acculturation Profiles of Expatriate Man-agers: Implications for Cross-Cultural Training Programs," *Columbia Jour-nal of World Business*, Winter 1986, pp. 73–79; R. W. Brislin, *Cross Cul-tural Encounters*; and D. Landis and R. W. Brislin, *Handbook on Intercultural Training*.

20. J. S. Black and M. Mendenhall, "Cross-Cultural Training Effectiveness: A Review and a Theoretical Framework for Future Research," *Academy of Management Review*, Vol. 15, No. 1 (1990) pp. 113–136.

21. N. Sieveking, B. Anchor, and R. Marston, "Selecting and Preparing Expa-triate Employees," *Personnel Journal*, March 1981, pp. 197–202. See also N. Sieveking and R. Marston, "Critical Selection and Orientation of Expa-triates," *Personnel Administrator*, April 1978, pp. 20–23.

22. G. Baliga and J. C. Baker, "Multinational Corporate Policies for Expatriate Managers: Selection, Training, and Evaluation," *Advanced Management Journal*, Autumn 1985, pp. 31–38.

23. Harris, "Moving Managers Internationally."

24. For more detailed information on organizations that specialize in interna-tional training, see Chapter 2, "Training Institutes for International As-signments," in R. L. Tung, *The New Expatriates: Managing Human Re-sources Abroad* (Cambridge, Mass.: Ballinger, 1988).

25. L. Copeland and L. Griggs, *Going International* (New York: Random House, 1985).

26. P. Earley, "International Training for Managers: A Comparison of Docu-mentary and Interpersonal Methods," *Academy of Management Journal*, Vol. 30 (1987) pp. 685–698.

27. J. Blue and U. Haynes, "Preparation for the Overseas Assignment," *Business Horizons*, June 1977, pp. 61–67.

28. This section is adapted from V. Pucik, "Strategic Human Resource Management."

29. This survey was reported in an article by L. B. Korn, "How the Next CEO Will Be Different," *Fortune*, May 22, 1989, pp. 111–113.

30. Ibid., p. 111.

31. G. Baliga and J. C. Baker, "Multinational Corporate Policies."

32. M. Mendenhall and G. Oddou, "Dimensions of Expatriate Acculturation."

33. A. Lanier, "Selecting and Preparing Personnel for Overseas Transfers," *Personnel Journal*, March 1979, pp. 160–163.

34. Personal communication with Patrick Morgan, August 1989.

35. This section on contingency is adapted from J. S. Black and M. Mendenhall (citing Tung). "A Practical but Theory-Based Framework for Selecting Cross-Cultural Training Methods," *Human Resource Management*, Vol. 28, No. 4 (1989) pp. 511–539.

36. M. Mendenhall and G. Oddou, "Acculturation Profiles of Expatriate Managers"; M. Mendenhall, E. Dunbar, and G. Oddou, "Expatriate Selection, Training and Career-Pathing: A Review and Critique," *Human Resource Management*, Vol. 26 (1987) pp. 331–345.

37. For further information on the use of cultural assimilators, see R. W. Brislin, "A Culture General Assimilator: Preparation for Various Types of Sojourns," *International Journal of Intercultural Relations*, Vol. 10 (1986) pp. 215–234; and K. Cushner, "Assessing the Impact of a Culture General Assimilator," *International Journal of Intercultural Relations*, Vol. 13 (1989) pp. 125–146.

38. J. S. Black and M. Mendenhall, "A Practical but Theory-based Framework."

39. P. Hepner Hall and W. B. Gudykunst, "The Relationship of Perceived Ethnocentrism in Corporate Cultures to the Selection, Training, and Success of International Employees," *International Journal of Intercultural Relations*, Vol. 13 (1989) pp. 183–201.

40. J. P. Giusti, D. R. Baker, and P. J. Graybash, "Satellites Dish Out Global Training," *Personnel Journal*, June 1991, pp. 80–84.

41. R. S. Schuler and P. J. Dowling, "Survey of SHRM/I Members" (Stern School of Business, New York University, 1988).

42. Barham and Devine, "The Quest for the International Manager."

43. A number of writers have also made the point that this form of developmental transfer can also function as a coordination and control strategy.

See A. Edstrom and J. Galbraith, "Transfer of Managers as a Coordination and Control Strategy in Multinational Organizations," *Administrative Science Quarterly*, Vol. 22 (1977) pp. 248–263; and C. K. Prahalad and Y. L. Doz, "An Approach to Strategic Control in MNCs," *Sloan Management Review*, Vol. 22, No. 4 (1981) pp. 5–13.

44. J. Main, "How 21 Men Got Global in 35 Days," *Fortune*, November 6, 1989, pp. 57–60.

45. This section is based on A. Bennett, "American Culture Is Often a Puzzle for Foreign Managers in the U.S.," *Wall Street Journal*, February 12, 1988, p. 33.

46. Ibid.

Chapter S I X

Compensation

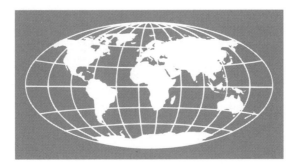

To successfully manage international compensation and benefits requires knowledge of the laws, customs, environment, and employment practices of many foreign countries; familiarity with currency fluctuations and the effect of inflation on compensation; and an understanding of why and when special allowances must be supplied and which allowances are necessary in what countries—all within the context of shifting political, economic, and social conditions.

Human resource managers spend a great deal of time developing effective compensation and benefit programs for international employees because these highly skilled, educated professionals and managers are high-cost employees. The Schuler and Dowling survey of SHRM/I members[1] found that the most common challenge mentioned about expatriate compensation was managing the expense. One respondent noted, 'We have operated for many years overseas. The weak dollar at the moment makes it very expensive to have U.S. expatriates overseas. Housing becomes exorbitant in strong-currency countries." American expatriates have become so expensive, in fact, that many American multinationals have repatriated all but their most essential overseas employees.[2] During the last decade, the average number of American expatriates per company fell from 112 to 67.[3]

Many companies estimate that an expatriate employee costs them three times as much as a domestic employee. Estimates have even ranged as high as five times as much. Nonetheless, there will always be a core group of international employees to compensate. Due to the complexity and expense of compensating expatriates, most of the discussion in this chapter addresses expatriate compensation. Issues unique to compensating TCNs and HCNs are also described because they are becoming more important to the success of many multinational corporations.

OBJECTIVES OF INTERNATIONAL COMPENSATION

When developing international compensation policies, a firm seeks to satisfy several objectives. First, the policy should be consistent and fair in its treatment of all categories of international employees. The interests of the multinational are best served if all international employees are relatively satisfied with their compensation package and perceive that they are treated equitably. Second, the policy must work to attract and retain personnel in the areas where the multinational has the greatest needs and opportunities. Third, the policy should facilitate the transfer of international employees in the most cost-effective manner for the MNE. Fourth, the policy should be consistent with the overall strategy, structure, and business needs of the multinational. Finally, compensation should serve to motivate employees. Some professional international HR managers would say that motivation is the major objective of their compensation programs.[4]

APPROACHES TO INTERNATIONAL COMPENSATION

The area of international compensation is complex and one that IHRM professionals commonly describe as "a headache." This is mainly because the international compensation package has not only to meet the multiple objectives outlined above but also to cater to the three categories of employees: expatriates, TCNs, and locals (HCNs). Whether to establish an overall policy for all employees or to distinguish between PCNs and TCNs is one of the first issues facing MNEs when designing international compensation policies. It is, therefore, not surprising to find several approaches to international compensation.

Home-based Policy

This approach links the base salary for expatriates and TCNs to the salary structure of the relevant home country.[5] For example, a U.S. executive transferred to France would have his or her compensation package built upon the U.S. base-salary level rather than that applicable to the host country, France.

One advantage of this approach is that international staff members (that is, expatriates and TCNs) are treated equitably in relation to their home countries, which assists repatriation. However, international staff are paid different amounts for performing the same function in the host location, according to their different home base-salary levels. This means, for example, that in the London branch of a U.S. bank, a U.S. expatriate and an Australian (TCN) may perform the same banking duties but the American will receive a higher salary than the Australian because of the differences in U.S. and Australian base-salary levels. In addition, as Anderson notes, "international assignees and local staff members are paid different amounts for performing the same function in the host location as a result of differences between home and host country salary structures."[6]

Despite the perceived inequity that may result, this approach can work well if international assignees are repatriated to their home countries after a two- to three-year foreign assignment and they still regard their counterparts at home as their peers. But after being away from home for, say, ten years, a British expatriate has a hard time accepting a salary that is 20 percent to 30 percent less than a German counterpart's simply because of an accident of birth. As Reynolds[7] has observed, "There is no doubt that paying each expatriate according to his or her home country can be less expensive than paying everyone on an American scale, but justifying these differences can be very difficult indeed." Nonetheless, the trend has been for U.S. companies to switch to this approach for third-country nationals. Evidently, the reduction in expenses outweighs the difficulty of justifying any pay differentials.

However, as the number of nationalities among the international workforce increases, the home-based approach becomes expensive,[8] and this may force the globalizing firm to look for an alternative method.

Host-based Policy

With this approach, the base salary for international transfer is linked to the salary structure in the host country, but the significant international supplements (such as cost-of-living adjustments, housing, schooling, and other premiums) are usually connected to home-country salary struc- tures. As Anderson[9] explains, this approach, on a case-by-case basis, "orients itself to the higher of host or home gross salary level and the lowest of host, home, or their reference point's taxes."

The host-based approach is effective in attracting expatriates or TCNs to a location that pays higher salaries than those received in the home country, but it poses problems upon repatriation when the person's salary reverts to home-country levels. Inequity between expatriates and third-country nationals can still result as the foreign service premiums and benefits tend to still be linked to home-country levels. In some cases, according to Anderson,[10] companies posting staff overseas on such a basis for periods of six years or longer will progressively phase out home-country–linked benefits after the fourth year of assignment. This has the effect of minimizing the differentials between the three na- tional groups in the particular host country. Of course, it only applies where international assignments are of an indefinite duration or where staff are assigned to high-pay countries and are unlikely to be repatri- ated to their country of origin.

Region-based Policy

A third approach some companies have found attractive is to compen- sate expatriates working in their home regions (for example, an Italian working in Germany) at somewhat lower levels than those who are work- ing in regions far from home (such as an American working in Saudi Arabia).

According to Reynolds,[11] a U.S. firm can realize significant cost sav- ings by switching from an American compensation system (where all in- ternational transferees are paid United States–based salaries) to a re- gionally based one. He illustrates this point with the example of a U.S. consumer goods company that paid all its foreign service employees as if they were Americans, even though 70 percent of its internationally mo- bile workforce were non-Americans. One option would have been to adopt the home-base approach for each foreign service employee. This would have saved the company money, but most TCNs were unlikely ever to be repatriated and many were from countries where the corpora- tion did not even have operations. It was finally decided that the sound- est solution was to take a regional approach. Those who made interconti- nental moves remained on the American scale, and regional expatriates were paid on separate scales appropriate to their regions. This approach works very well and has reduced compensation costs significantly.

DESIGNING INTERNATIONAL COMPENSATION PACKAGES

The most widely used approach for expatriates is the home-based because it emphasizes "keeping the expatriate whole" (that is, maintaining relativity to PCN colleagues and compensating for the costs of international service).[12] The basis of this policy implies that foreign assignees should not suffer a material loss due to their transfer, and this is accomplished through the utilization of what is known as the *balance-sheet approach*. According to Reynolds,[13] "the balance-sheet approach to international compensation is a system designed to equalize the purchasing power of employees at comparable position levels living overseas and in the home country, and to provide incentives to offset qualitative differences between assignment locations." A typical balance sheet is shown in Figure 6-1. There are five major categories of outlays that cover all the types of expenses incurred by expatriate families:

1. *Goods and services*—home-country outlays for items such as food, personal care, clothing, household furnishings, recreation, transportation, and medical care.

2. *Housing*—the major costs associated with the employees' principal residence.

3. *Income taxes*—payments to federal and local governments for personal income taxes.

4. *Reserve*—contributions to savings, payments for benefits, pension contributions, investments, education expenses, social security taxes, etc.

5. *Shipment and storage*—the major costs associated with shipping and storing personal and household effects.

Thus, MNEs seek to develop international packages that are competitive in all of the following aspects of compensation:

Salary
- home rate/home currency
- local rate/local currency
- salary adjustments or promotions—home or local standard
- bonus—home or local currency, home or local standard
- stock options
- inducement payment/hardship premium—percent of salary or lump sum payment, home or local currency

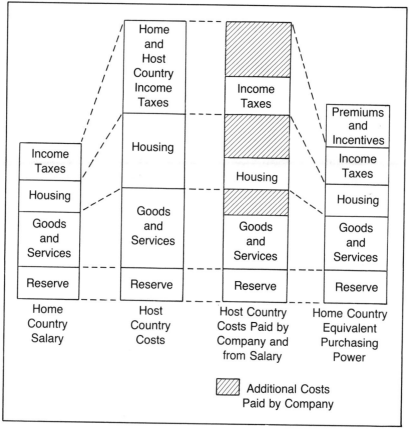

FIGURE 6-1   The Balance Sheet

Source: C. Reynolds, "Compensation of Overseas Personnel," in *Handbook of Human Resource Administration* (2nd ed.), ed. J. J. Famularo (New York: McGraw-Hill, 1986), p. 51. Reprinted with permission.

- currency protection—discretion of split basis
- global salary and performance structures

Taxation
- tax protection
- tax equalization
- other services

Benefits
- home-country program
- local program
- social security program

Allowances
- cost-of-living allowances
- housing standard
- education
- relocation
- perquisites
- home leave
- shipping and storages

Although some of these aspects of international compensation may not apply to TCNs or HCNs, all do apply to expatriates. They may not, however, apply *equally* to all because there is a tendency for multinationals to differentiate among types of expatriates. Separate types of policies may be established that are based on the length of assignment (temporary transfer, permanent transfer, or continual relocation) or on the type of employee. Cash remuneration, special allowances, benefits, and pensions are determined in part by such classifications. Short-term expatriates (for example, whose two- or three-year tours of duty abroad are interspersed with long periods at home) may be treated differently from career expatriates who spend most of their time working in various locations abroad. Both of these groups are different from TCNs, who often move from country to country in the employ of one multinational (or several) headquartered in a country other than their own (for example, a Swiss banker may be in charge of a German branch of a British bank). In effect, these are the real global employees, the ones who can weave together the far-flung parts of a multinational. As the global company increases in importance, it is likely that TCN employees will become more valuable and thus be able to command levels of compensation equivalent to expatriates.

THE COMPENSATION PACKAGE

The various aspects of international compensation are now discussed in detail.

Base Salary

The term *base salary* acquires a somewhat different meaning when employees go abroad. At home, base salary denotes the amount of cash compensation that serves as a benchmark for other compensation elements (for example, bonuses and benefits). For expatriates, it is the primary component of a package of allowances, many of which are directly related to base salary (foreign service premium, cost-of-living allowances, housing allowances, and tax protection, for example) as well as the basis for in-service benefits and pension contributions. When applied to TCNs, base salary may mean the prevailing rate paid for a specific skill in the employee's home country. In the Schuler and Dowling survey,[14] all of the respondents indicated that their companies used local compensation levels as guidelines when developing HCN compensation policies. Conditions that force compensation policies to differ from those in the United States include: inflation/cost of living, housing, security, school costs, and taxation. For example, it is far less costly to recruit a construction engineer from Spain or Taiwan to work in the Middle East than to recruit one from the United Kingdom or the United States. As a 1987 study[15] found, more than half the American companies surveyed linked their base salaries to the home countries of the TCN they employed rather than to U.S. or host-country salary structures. The primary objective was to reduce cost, since base levels of most other countries were below those of the United States.

The base salary of an expatriate is usually paid either in the home currency at the home rate or in the local currency at a rate equivalent to the rate paid locally for the same job. Similarly, salary adjustments and promotional practices may be fashioned according to either home-country or local standards. In some select cases, global salary and performance structures have been implemented.

Bonus Payments

If the MNE utilizes any type of incentive bonus system, a policy is usually established. Bonuses may be in accordance with either home- or host-country policies. Actual payments can be made in either local or foreign currency and may often be a combination of the two or at the choice of the recipient. For example, the overall policy of a majority of U.S. financial services companies bases compensation for PCNs on the U.S. salary structure (this includes bonus programs and salary increase practices). Most often, this compensation is paid partly in U.S. dollars and partly in the local currency. While the local currency portion is generally pegged to pay ordinary living expenses, bonuses are typically paid in U.S. dollars. Salary practices for TCNs tend to vary more widely and may be based on the home structure, a U.S. structure, or the host-country structure.

Questions that multinationals generally have to address when planning for their incentive bonuses include:

- What techniques can be used to provide management incentives abroad?
- Can the incentive bonuses that help many companies achieve their objectives at home be used effectively in subsidiary operations?[16]

Of course, it depends on whether the MNE is applying incentive bonuses to all categories of employees. Bishko considers that, given the current preference for incentive compensation, "it will not be surprising to see companies exporting such plans overseas to cover their U.S. and non-U.S. expatriates, as well as their local nationals."[17] He identifies three approaches:

a. exporting U.S. incentive bonus plans overseas

b. modifying U.S. incentive bonus plans to accommodate applicable local rules

c. implementing local incentive bonus plans

The first approach implies an attitude that "what works at home will work here" and does not take into consideration the fact that host-country laws might radically affect the intended results of the incentive plan.[18] Therefore, the techniques used to provide management incentives abroad need to consider local laws and practices in order to effect the same outcome as that achieved at home.

When evaluating whether to modify its own incentive bonus plans or to implement a local approach, Bishko[19] argues that the American multinational needs to consider which of its employee groups are to be covered, for he believes that the goals of the incentive plan for the local national employee will differ significantly from the goals of the plan for the American expatriate and the TCN. As you will see from Exhibit 6-1, the goal of the incentive bonus for the local national is to deliver, at no increased cost to the employer, as much as possible to the local national. For the U.S. expatriate and the TCN, as Exhibit 6-2 shows, U.S.-tax effectiveness is the goal. To illustrate his point, Bishko assumes that expa-

E X H I B I T   6 - 1   Incentive Plans Compared: The Goal (Broadly Stated)

Payout/Reward When Targets/Vesting Achieved	
Local National	*U.S. Expatriate and TCN*
Locally tax-effective to the employee	U.S. tax-effective to the employee
No increase in employer cost	Locally tax-effective to minimize employer tax reimbursement cost

E X H I B I T   6 - 2   Incentive Plans Compared: Cash Bonus in 60% Tax Rate Country

Local National		*U.S. Expatriate and TCN*	
Net to employee:		*Net to employee:*	
Bonus	100	Bonus	100
Local tax	(60)	U.S. hypothetical tax	(28)
Net	40	Net	72
Employer cost:		*Employer cost:*	
Bonus	100	Net payment	72
		Gross-up	108
		Total	180

triates and TCNs are covered by a plan of tax equalization (which we will discuss later) against a U.S. hypothetical tax, thus enabling these two groups of employees to be considered together for the purpose of designing effective incentive bonuses. Bishko[20] explains the difference this way:

> Let us assume the employer wants to pay a cash bonus of 100 (units of the local currency) in a country where the applicable tax rate is 60%. When a local national receives this amount, it is subject to a tax of 60, resulting in a net to the employee of 40. The cost to the employer company would be 100, subject to any applicable corporate tax deduction benefit. For the U.S. expatriate and the TCN, however, the figures are very different. Assuming that both of these groups of employees would

be tax equalized to the United States—that is, their tax burden would be limited to the same tax that would apply had they been subject to tax only in the United States (the U.S. hypothetical tax)—the net guaranteed to the employee is 72, the figure equal to the gross bonus of 100 less the tax applicable in the United States, currently 28%. The resulting gross cost to the employer is 180, which represents the original net of 72 plus the tax gross-up of 108. (Thus, the total gross payment of 180 would be subject to local tax at 60%, or 108, resulting in an actual net payment to the employee of 72.)

A multinational may defer the payment of bonuses until the expatriate returns to his or her home country if its tax rate is lower. Another approach is to pay the bonus as a benefit-in-kind. Alternatively, stock options can be used as a form of bonus payment. In fact, American multinationals frequently link stock opportunities to executive performance. Recent tax law changes in a number of Western countries make stock ownership even more feasible than in the past,[21] though a recent survey of European pay practices revealed that "employee share options are a minority practice everywhere apart from the U.K. where they are used by over half of all employers."[22] It would appear that European and Asian multinationals are less likely to offer stock options to local nationals. For example, a recent Hay Group survey[23] showed that only 38 percent of foreign subsidiaries in the United States offered local staff incentives such as stock options or annual bonuses, although intense competition for senior executives may affect that. The reason is cultural. Europeans receive social welfare benefits that are not available to U.S. nationals, such as free medical care, and Japanese MNEs traditionally do not offer incentives.

With all these incentive schemes, though, it is important that the multinational take into consideration taxation implications, host-country legislation, local competitors' practices, and equity implications affecting the various employee groups.

Inducement/Hardship Premium

Parent-country nationals often receive a salary premium as an inducement to accept a foreign assignment or as compensation for any hardship caused by the transfer. Under such circumstances, the definition of hardship, eligibility for the premium, and amount and timing of payment must be addressed. In cases in which hardship is determined, U.S. companies often refer to the U.S. Department of State's Hardship Post Differentials Guidelines to determine an appropriate level of payment. As Ruff and Jackson[24] have noted, however, making international comparisons of the cost of living is problematic. It is important to note that TCNs do not receive these payments as often as expatriates. Foreign service inducements, if used, are most commonly made in the form of a percentage of salary, usually 5 to 40 percent of base pay. Such payments vary, depending upon the assignment, actual hardship, tax consequences, and length of assignment. In addition, differentials may be considered; for example, a host country's work week may be longer than that of the home country, and a differential payment may be made in lieu of overtime, which is not normally paid to PCNs or TCNs.

Currency Protection

Currency protection is also an issue affecting compensation and may be extended in several ways. Employees may have discretion over the currency used in payments, or a standard split basis for all expatriates may be used. A split basis may be applied case-by-case, depending upon the particular country assignment. When payments are made in local currency, a policy of exchange-rate adjustments is necessary to ensure that all employees are being treated fairly.

Taxation

This aspect of international compensation is probably the one that causes the most concern to practitioners and expatriates (both PCNs and TCNs), as taxation generally evokes emotional responses. No one likes paying taxes! To illustrate the potential problems, for the U.S. expatriate an assignment abroad can mean being double-taxed—in the country of assignment and in the United States. This tax cost, combined with all of the other expatriate costs, makes U.S. multinationals think twice about making use of expatriates. In fact, many U.S. companies could not afford to use expatriates if it were not for Section 911 of the Internal Revenue Service code, which contains the provisions permitting a $70,000 deduction on foreign-earned income.

The multinational is anxious to preserve expatriate entitlements so that they remain both an effective incentive to foreign assignments and a reward for performance. There are two major approaches to handling taxation:

a. Tax equalization—Companies withhold an amount equal to the home-country tax obligation of the PCN, and they pay all taxes in the host country.

b. Tax protection—The employee pays up to the amount of taxes he or she would pay on compensation in the home country. In such a situation, the employee is entitled to any windfall received if total taxes are less in the foreign country than in the home country.

In her review of global compensation, Stuart[25] adds two other approaches: (1) ad hoc (each expatriate is handled differently, depending upon the individual package agreed to with the company); and (2) laissez-faire (employees are "on their own" in conforming to host-country and home-country taxation laws and practices). However, we shall focus on tax equalization and tax protection, as these are the most common approaches.

Addressing tax protection and/or tax equalization can be extremely expensive as well as challenging for MNEs. According to the Schuler and Dowling survey,[26]

> For PCNs (and TCNs) in high tax countries the greatest challenge is tax effective compensation and reduction/avoidance of the pyramid effect of tax equalization. A senior executive earning $100,000 in Belgium, for example, could cost a company close to $1.0 million on taxes over a 5–7 year period.

Tax equalization is by far the more common taxation policy used by MNEs. For example, two U.S. surveys[27] in 1990 (one by Organization Resource Counsellors Inc., the other by Price Waterhouse) showed 86.7 percent and 80 percent of respondents (respectively) used tax equalization. Thus, for a U.S. expatriate, tax payments equal to the liability of a U.S. taxpayer with same income and family status are imposed on the employee's salary and bonus. Any additional premiums or allowances are typically paid by the company, tax-free to the employee. This seemingly straightforward policy actually illustrates the tremendous complexity in international compensation. In granting premiums or allowances, the multinational needs to determine the expatriate's tax status in the home country and in the host country and then decide which to pay. Because the decision can be costly to the individual, organizations can gain a competitive advantage in attracting employees through their compensation policies. This competitive advantage depends on the definition of income covered by equalization, the type of hypothetical taxes to which the policy is applied, and the level of tax deductions allowed. Most MNEs consider both state and federal taxes of both the home country and the host country when designing their policies, but not all of them include a spouse's income under the policy.

Other tax considerations in forming either protection or equalization policies involve state and local tax payments, tax return preparation, and the definition of an employee's total income on which the company is basing its calculations. (For example, does total income include stock options or spouse's income?)

As MNEs operate in more and more countries, they are subject to widely discrepant tax rates. A sample of this diversity is illustrated in Exhibit 6-3. Many multinationals have responded to this complexity and diversity across countries by retaining the services of an international accounting firm to provide advice. Many firms also use internal and external accountants to prepare host-country and home-country tax returns for their expatriates.

Wage levels also vary greatly across nations. When companies plan compensation packages, they need to consider how specific practices can be modified in each country to provide the most tax-effective, appropriate rewards for PCNs, HCNs, and TCNs within the framework of overall company policy.

The policies discussed in this section usually pertain to expatriates. In the case of TCNs, many different approaches have been used. Although a detailed analysis of each different approach is beyond the scope of this chapter, the major approaches include a U.S. balance sheet, a non-U.S./home-country balance sheet, a host-country package, a host-country package including extras, a U.S. salary including local benefits, or a U.S. package less tax equalization.[28]

Benefits

As one international HRM manager noted, the difficulties in international compensation "are not compensation so much as benefits." Pension plans are very difficult to deal with country to country, as cultural practices vary endlessly. Transportability of pension plans, medical coverage, and social security benefits are very difficult to normalize.[29] Therefore, companies need to address many issues when considering benefits, including:

EXHIBIT 6-3   Maximum Marginal Federal Tax Rates*

Country	1985 Maximum Marginal Rate	1988 Maximum Marginal Rate	Income Level at Which Reached	
			In Local Currency	In U.S. Dollars**
Argentina	45%	38.25%	A416,500	$119,000
Australia	49	49	A$35,001	25,984
Belgium	72	70.8	BFr4,202,000	121,235
Brazil	60	50	Cz$2,784,600	38,536
Canada	34	29.87	Can$55,000	44,571
France	65	56.8	FFr720,000	128,251
Germany	56	56	DM260,000	157,100
Hong Kong	17.5	16.5	HK$300,000	38,462
Italy	65	62	Lit600,000,000	488,599
Japan	70	60	¥50,000,000	403,714
Korea	55	55	W60,000,000	79,915
Mexico	55	50	Ps45,063,804	20,484
Netherlands	72	72	Fi229,625	123,521
Singapore	40	33	S$400,000	200,100
Spain	66	56	Pta8,000,000	72,483
Sweden	50	45	SKr190,000	32,418
Switzerland	13.75	11.5	SFr423,600	310,557
United Kingdom	60	40	£19,300	36,415
United States	50	33	US$71,900	71,900
Venezuela	45	45	Bs8,000,000	271,647

*Maximum marginal rates are those applicable to resident citizens as of January 1, 1988, with one exception: the rate for the U.K. reflects April 1988 changes. Where different rates apply to married and single employees, the married employee rate is shown. Social security taxes are excluded.

**Based on April 1, 1988 exchange rates, adjusted for high inflation countries.

Source: TPF&C, 1987. Adapted with permission.

- Whether or not to maintain expatriates in home-country programs, particularly if the company does not receive a tax deduction for it.
- Whether companies have the option of enrolling expatriates in host-country benefit programs and/or making up any difference in coverage.

- Whether host-country legislation regarding termination affects benefit entitlement.

- Whether expatriates should receive home-country or host-country social security benefits.

- Whether benefits should be maintained on a home-country or host-country basis, who is responsible for the cost, whether other benefits should be used to offset any shortfall in coverage, and whether home-country benefit programs should be exported to local nationals in foreign countries.

Most U.S. PCNs typically remain under their home country's benefit plan. For example, U.S. financial companies typically include expatriates in U.S. retirement/capital accumulation programs, medical/death/disability programs, and social security programs. With regard to social security, a Towers, Perrin, Forster & Crosby (TPF&C) survey[30] found:

> Totalization agreements between the U.S. and Belgium, Canada, Italy, Norway, Switzerland, the U.K. and West Germany effectively eliminate dual social security coverage of citizens of one country working temporarily in another. Each agreement defines which country's coverage applies under specific employment situations. However, U.S. citizens can elect to be covered only by U.S. social security if they work for foreign subsidiaries of U.S. companies.

In some countries, expatriates cannot opt out of local social security programs. In such circumstances, the company normally pays for these additional costs. European PCNs and TCNs enjoy portable social security benefits within the European Community. Laws governing private benefit practices differ from country to country, and company practices also vary. Multinationals have generally done a good job of planning for the private retirement needs of their expatriate employees, but this is less the case for TCNs.[31] There are many reasons for this: TCNs may have little or no home-country social security coverage; they may have spent many years in countries that do not permit currency transfers of accrued benefit payments; or they may spend their final year or two of employment in a country where final average salary is in a currency that relates unfavorably to their home-country currency. How their benefits are calculated and what type of retirement plan applies to them may make the difference between a comfortable retirement in a country of their choice and a forced penurious retirement elsewhere.

As Figure 6-2 shows, parent-company plans rarely cover TCNs. American MNEs generally provide either host-country or umbrella plans,

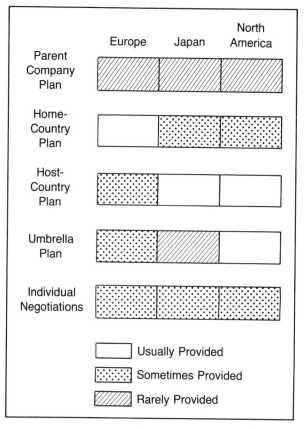

F I G U R E 6 - 2   Sources of TCN Retirement Income (by location of corporate headquarters)

Source: TPF&C, 1987. Adapted with permission.

Japanese firms prefer host-country plans, and European firms often rely on home-country plans. Many companies believe that an umbrella plan is most compatible with their benefit philosophy. Such a plan may include a formal contract stipulating certain pension guarantees based on the final three years' average earnings of the TCN, offset by certain social security and statutory benefit entitlements and any local private plan benefits to which an employee may be entitled. When such plans are used, it is important to find a formula for calculating the benefits in more than one currency if the TCN moves to another country during the final period, as many do. Similarly, allowance must be made for currency conversions, indexation, if required, and many other factors, not least of which is determining what percentage of final average salary represents an equitable retirement benefit for a once-invaluable employee.

In addition to the already discussed benefits, multinationals also provide vacations and special leave. Included as part of the employee's regular vacation, annual home leave usually provides airfares for families to return to their home countries. Rest and rehabilitation leave, based on the conditions of the host country, also provides the employee's family with free airfares to a more comfortable location near the host country. In addition to rest and rehabilitation leave, emergency provisions are available in case of a death or illness in the family. Employees in hardship locations often receive additional leave expense payments and rest and rehabilitation periods.

Because of the complexities, challenges, and costs of providing benefits to international employees, companies need to address several questions when planning to do business abroad.

- With millions of dollars invested in benefit plans abroad, and with the costs of these plans steadily increasing, how can the MNE measure, control, and contain costs while keeping benefit promises to employees?
- Should benefit promises be reevaluated?
- Can benefits be reduced?
- Can better funding vehicles be found for pension investments?
- Can companies ensure that a proper charge to income is made for benefit plans abroad?

Allowances

Issues concerning allowances can be very challenging to a firm establishing an overall compensation policy, partly because of the various forms of allowances that exist. The *cost-of-living allowance* (COLA), which typically receives the most attention, involves a payment to compensate for differences in expenditures between the home country and the foreign country (to account for inflation differentials, for example). Often this allowance is difficult to determine, so companies may use the services of organizations such as Organization Resource Counselors, Inc. (a U.S.-based firm) or Employment Conditions Abroad (based in Britain). These firms specialize in providing COLA information on a global basis, regularly updated, to their clients. The COLA may also include payments for housing and utilities, personal income tax, or discretionary items.[32] Some companies, however, are turning away from a local or national cost-of-living index. Instead, they use an efficiency price index, which recognizes the reality that, as individuals get to know an area better, they know where to shop for bargains.

The provision of a *housing allowance* implies that employees should be entitled to maintain their home-country living standards (or, in some cases, receive accommodation that is equivalent to that provided for similar foreign employees and peers). Such allowances are often paid on either an assessed or an actual basis. Other alternatives include company-provided housing, either mandatory or optional; a fixed housing allowance; or assessment of a portion of income, out of which actual housing costs are paid. Housing issues are often addressed on a case-by-case basis, but as globalization grows, formal policies become more necessary and efficient. Financial assistance and/or protection in connection with the sale or leasing of an expatriate's former residence is offered by almost all MNEs, although those in the finance industry tend to be the most generous, offering assistance in sale or leasing, payment of closing costs, payment of leasing management fees, rent protection, and equity protection. Third-country nationals receive these benefits much less frequently.

There is also a provision for *home leave allowances.* Many employers cover the expense of one or more trips back to the home country each year. The purpose of paying for such trips is to give expatriates the opportunity to renew family and business ties, thereby helping them to avoid adjustment problems when they are repatriated. Although firms traditionally have restricted the use of leave allowances to travel home, a growing number of organizations are giving expatriates the option of applying the allowances to foreign travel. Allowances that cover foreign travel may be particularly important in situations where the expatriate's spouse is not able to work abroad as a result of visa restrictions or the lack of suitable employment.[33]

Education allowances for expatriates' children are also an integral part of any international compensation policy. Allowances for education can cover items such as tuition, language class tuition, enrollment fees, books and supplies, transportation, room and board, and uniforms. (Outside of the United States, it is quite common for high school students to wear uniforms.) The level of education provided for, the adequacy of local schools, and transportation of dependents who are being educated in other locations may present problems for multinational companies. Parent-country nationals and TCNs usually receive the same treatment concerning educational expenses. The cost of local or boarding school for dependent children is typically covered by the employer, although there may be restrictions, depending on the availability of good local schools and on their fees. Attendance at postsecondary schools may also be provided for when deemed necessary.

In the past, Japanese firms rarely sent an executive's family abroad, even when the assignment lasted several years, but this practice is changing. Now, when the family accompanies the executive abroad, an allowance is customarily made of approximately 30 percent of base salary for the spouse and 5 percent for each child. When the family remains in Japan, an allowance equal to about 80 percent of the executive's base salary is paid.[34]

Relocation allowances usually cover moving, shipping, and storage charges; temporary living expenses; subsidies regarding appliance or car purchases (or sales); and down payments or lease-related charges. Allowances regarding perquisites (cars, club memberships, servants, and so on) may also need to be considered (usually for higher-management positions). These allowances are often contingent upon tax-equalization policies and practices in both the home and the host countries. A trend here is for firms to offer expatriates lump sum payments to cover moving expenses, rather than expense reimbursements. This practice may save the company money, as full reimbursement does not provide workers with an incentive to minimize costs.[35]

Increasingly, MNEs are also offering *spouse assistance* to help guard against or offset income lost by an expatriate's spouse as a result of relocating abroad. Although some companies may pay an allowance to make up for a spouse's lost income, U.S. firms are beginning to focus on providing spouses with employment opportunities abroad, either by offering job-search assistance or employment in the firm's foreign office. This practice, though, raises other issues. For example, while tax equalization is a standard part of an expatriate's compensation package, there is not yet consensus among firms as to whether "trailing spouses" should be provided the same treatment.[36]

To summarize all of this, multinationals generally pay allowances in order to encourage employees to take international assignments and to keep employees "whole" relative to home standards. In terms of housing, companies usually pay a tax-equalized housing allowance in order to discourage the purchase of housing and/or to compensate for higher housing costs. This allowance is adjusted periodically based on estimates of both local and foreign housing costs. For example, MNEs in the finance industry are beginning to purchase or lease company housing, which is provided directly through a lease or rent-back arrangement.

Third-country nationals most often receive housing aid in the form of a fixed subsidy or a subsidized loan program. Similarly, almost all financial services companies compensate for differences in the cost of living between the expatriate's home and host countries. This payment is usually assessed by an independent organization and is in the form of cash. Very infrequently, a negative adjustment is made when the cost of living is lower in the foreign location. Normally, TCNs do not receive any type of cost-of-living allowance. Most financial companies pay a lump sum relocation allowance (typically equivalent to one month's base salary) for expenses associated with moving. For both PCNs and TCNs, most organizations pay shipping and storage costs as well as transportation to and from the foreign location, in accordance with typical business travel standards. Cars are usually not shipped abroad, although some companies will provide sale protection.

MNEs in the automobile industry generally pay cost-of-living allowances based on the host country's inflation index and exchange rate fluctuation. Housing and schooling allowances are also provided. Both Ford and General Motors either fully cover or substantially underwrite the costs of both housing and offspring education. Policies with regard to home-country housing, however, differ between the two companies. General Motors tries to encourage employees to retain ownership of their home-country housing. The company will pay all rental management fees and will reimburse the employee for up to six months' rent if the house remains unoccupied. If the employee decides to sell his or her home, the company will reimburse the selling costs. Ford provides its employees with three options: a program similar to GM's, with certain maximums on fees to be covered; a guaranteed house-purchase offer; and a lease-termination procedure. Both companies cover most moving and storage costs incurred by the employee.[37]

STRATEGIC IMPERATIVES

International compensation is complex and costly yet vital to the success of the global corporation. Consequently, we find several strategic imperatives in this area.

Linking to the Business

To succeed in an ever-changing international environment, firms must look beyond next year's goals and develop clear but flexible long-term compensation strategies. As Pucik[38] has noted,

An effective managerial reward system should be linked to long-term corporate strategy and should anticipate changes in employee valence for different organizational rewards. On the one hand, multinational settings make the complex task of developing such a system even more difficult; on the other hand, the fact that the corporation operates in many different environments permits the establishment of unique reward programs, unavailable in more conventional environments.

In addition, MNEs need to match their compensation policies with their staffing policies and general HRM philosophies. If, for example, a firm has an ethnocentric staffing policy, its compensation policy should be one of keeping the expatriate whole (that is, maintaining relativity to PCN colleagues plus compensating for the costs of international service). If, however, the staffing policy follows a geocentric approach (that is, staffing a position with the "best person," regardless of nationality), there may be no clear "home" for the TCN, and the MNE will need to consider establishing a system of international base pay for key managers paid in a major reserve currency such as the U.S. dollar or the Deutsche Mark. This system allows MNEs to deal with considerable variations in base salaries for managers.

A successful compensation package should also be in line with the specific type of business and its unique international needs. As Reynolds[39] points out,

> Most successful and effective international compensation plans are designed to support basic corporate staffing objectives and still more fundamental business plans. For example, high-tech companies are often anxious to send employees abroad for short-term assignments and bring them home very quickly. The main objective is technology transfer. These companies want to avoid keeping an expatriate out of the domestic mainstream, which inevitably creates rapid skill erosion. For these companies, compensation practices that encourage expatriation and easy reintegration to the domestic salary structure are clearly desirable. Different salary levels for expatriates of different nationalities is usually not a problem, since each perceives his or her peers as those "back home."
>
> International banks, on the other hand, typically want to keep their employees overseas for a longer period of time. Mobility between countries is important, but repatriation is far less of an issue for banks than for high-tech companies. When many expatriates of different nationalities work side by side, nationality discrimination in terms of pay can become a major problem. For these reasons, banks tend to have international compensation programs that provide equal pay for equal work to employees of all nationalities.

A related issue is the link between management philosophy, international strategy, and compensation. An argument put forward by Gomez-Mejia[40] is pertinent here. He claims that the reward system of an organization affects the extent to which the organization's culture has a global or domestic orientation. In other words, a firm that has a conscious global strategy, the achievement of which relies on developing an international team of managers, will foster a global "mindset" as part of the global strategy by placing great emphasis on international experience as a criterion for career advancement. The compensation package will be designed to encourage staff transfers to all areas of the firm's global operations and to attract high-caliber staff for international assignments. Thus, as Reynolds[41] stresses, "It is important to recognize that there are different ways to design international compensation plans and that the design should facilitate and support the basic staffing and business plans."

Cost Containment

Containing the costs of international compensation is becoming a major strategic imperative. Companies are going about this by reducing expatriate staff, developing tax plans, and by taking several other smaller steps.[42]

Reduction of Expatriate Staff

The most effective and popular cost-containment approach is to reduce the number of expatriates. For example, there are 25 percent fewer American expatriates today than there were three years ago.[43] But no matter how much a company reduces the excesses of its international compensation policy, expatriates will remain expensive (two to six times salary, depending on the country of assignment). This situation, however, appears to have some important exceptions. Anderson[44] refers to a recent Ernst & Young study which demonstrated that, due to the impact of Social Security totalization agreements now in effect and various tax-planning techniques, expatriates in certain countries can be less expensive than local staff. In other countries the gap in costs often can be reduced to make the three categories (that is, TCNs, PCNs, and HCNs) of employees competitive, allowing the company to make its selection of the international executive on the basis of qualification rather than cost. According to Anderson:[45]

France, for example, now has the following elements in its new formula for U.S. expatriates:

- A headquarters ruling (obtained from the French government) for companies with an office coordinating their European operations to eliminate French individual taxation of the expatriate's tax reimbursement, schooling, and excess housing allowances.

- Treaty provisions to eliminate the taxation in France of income the expatriate derives from U.S. source dividends, interest, royalties, and capital gains.

- A totalization agreement to eliminate French Social Security taxation.

- International rules and treaty provisions to eliminate French taxation for work performed outside of France while a French resident.

- Internal rules and planning techniques to substantially reduce or eliminate French taxation of stock option income.

Tax Planning

Another cost-containment device is tax planning, described above in the discussion of bonuses. Various deferral techniques, such as one-year rollovers and loan bonus arrangements, which are also used to mitigate a quite substantial foreign tax burden, have great potential in certain countries. Providing payments in kind rather than in cash can be cost-effective, particularly in several countries in Asia. Dual contracts (when expatriates have responsibilities in more than one country and travel frequently) can also provide savings under certain conditions.

Other Cost-Saving Measures

Although reducing the number of expatriates and tax planning present the greatest opportunities for savings, a number of U.S. companies recently have reported implementing other money-saving measures. Some of these measures are summarized below.[46]

- The percentage of companies *not paying* premiums of any kind or paying them only selectively has increased from 5 percent to 9 percent.

- Although most companies have made no changes since 1982, more companies have decreased (6 percent) than increased (3 percent) their expatriate premiums.

- Some companies have found mobility premiums (lump-sum payments at the beginning and end of assignments) preferable to ongoing premiums paid with each paycheck. The percentage of companies paying ongoing premiums has dropped from 70 percent to 65 percent.

- Twenty-eight percent of companies (up from 20 percent in 1983) now insist that expatriates live in furnished quarters rather than ship their furniture overseas.

- Twenty-nine percent of companies (up from 23 percent in 1983) now decline to pay housing allowances to expatriates who buy housing instead of renting it while on assignment.

- Seventy-four percent of companies (up from 64 percent 1983) now insist that expatriates use company-designated tax preparers.

- Twenty-one percent of companies make use of negative indexes in countries less expensive than the home country to avoid providing a windfall to expatriates in those locations. Thus, companies are beginning to adjust income both up *and* down, according to the relative cost of living in the foreign country.

- Although the majority still ignore state hypothetical tax deductions (which employees would pay if they worked in their home states), the trend is clearly toward deducting for state taxes.

- More companies are using customized compensation data to reflect more closely their own reimbursement and support policies rather than using generalized indexes only.

Another suggestion for cost containment is to switch to regional-based compensation plans. Simply paying expatriates their domestic pay plus a flat percentage of salary (the amount of which would depend upon the assignment location) is another option.[47]

However, MNEs should be careful that the quest for cost containment does not have negative consequences. The results of a 1992 U.S. survey[48] sounds a note of caution. While the expatriates surveyed reported that the financial benefits provided by their respective companies were "basically sufficient," respondents indicated that an early return from the overseas assignment is likely if the manager perceives a lack of financial support. More significantly, respondents were less satisfied with nonfinancial support (such as education assistance), and the study concludes that the manager is more likely to leave the company if there is a perceived lack of personal or family support. Reducing benefits must be handled in such a way that the objectives of compensation packages are still realized.

Termination Liabilities

Multinationals need to consider the strategic consequences of a decision to terminate overseas operations. In most countries, some traditional or legally required practices come into play in the event of a plant shut-down or a substantial reduction in the local workforce.[49] In general, these practices place more extensive and costlier obligations on the employer than do the "marketplace" layoffs in the United States and Canada. One of the most costly obligations is the payment of cash indemnities, which are in addition to the individual termination payments that may be required by law, collective bargaining agreement, or individual contracts. These indemnities can range from as high as two years' pay in Mexico to a flat amount, adjusted for increases in the cost of living, in Belgium. In some countries, these costs are spelled out in collective agreements that may stipulate termination payments greater than those required by law. In other countries, the employer may have to negotiate the amounts with employees, unions, and often the government. An example of the estimated costs of these payments is shown in Figure 6-3.

In many countries, a company that wishes to close down or curtail operations also must develop a social plan or its equivalent, typically in concert with unions and other interested parties. The plan may cover continuation of pay, benefit-plan coverage, retraining allowances, relocation expenses, and supplementation of statutory unemployment compensation. Frequently, a company planning a partial or total plant shut-down must present its case to a government agency. Authorities in the Netherlands, for example, may deny permission for a substantial reduction in workforce unless management is able to demonstrate that the cutback is absolutely necessary for economic reasons and that the company has an approved social plan.

Compensation Practices in Other Countries

Pay schedules vary greatly from country to country, as do rates of inflation and currency valuations. Evidence of the disparity between management compensation across countries is shown in Exhibit 6-4, which compares (in British pounds) gross salary and cost-of-living figures across nine countries.

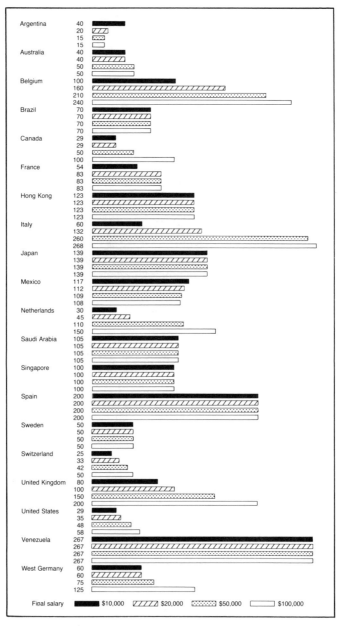

FIGURE 6-3 Typical Payments for Involuntary Termination as a % of Annual Cash Remuneration in U.S. Dollars. (Payments include both severance pay and pay in lieu of notice. All employees are married, age 40, with children and 15 years of service.)

Source: TPF&C, 1987. Adapted with permission.

EXHIBIT 6-4   Cost of Keeping Up Home-Country Pattern of Spending on Consumer Goods in Nine Countries

Nationality of Mid-rank Manager*	Gross Salary in Homeland £	United Kingdom £	United States £	Switzer- land £	Nether- lands £	Germany £	France £	Australia £	Singa- pore £	Hong Kong £
Swiss	74,248	13,779	14,180	19,721	15,630	17,893	17,921	12,908	16,690	16,778
Hong Kong	52,822	19,308	20,295	31,016	22,094	24,643	25,390	17,750	19,355	17,717
German	68,888	13,067	13,459	20,204	14,819	15,804	17,023	12,246	15,836	15,913
French	52,744	13,162	13,495	20,496	14,968	16,575	15,537	12,187	15,138	15,511
Singaporean	47,480	17,276	17,183	26,198	19,751	21,674	22,103	15,403	13,939	18,126
American	57,026	16,189	13,793	24,187	18,892	20,396	20,682	14,163	17,444	18,441
British	36,600	11,232	13,174	20,425	14,637	16,827	16,958	11,962	15,042	15,004
Dutch	47,711	9,234	9,797	14,883	9,788	12,197	12,312	8,780	11,437	11,268
Australian	32,561	11,288	11,061	17,132	12,758	14,111	14,241	9,216	13,316	13,171

*Responsible for function such as marketing in medium-sized company.

Source: Financial Times (London), January 5, 1993, p. 24. Reprinted with permission.

Cash is, of course, the basis of compensation everywhere, but "pay" often includes additional noncash elements. In France, for example, subsidized transportation services and company restaurant lunches or luncheon vouchers are common. Workers in the Philippines often receive a measure of rice, with better-quality rice provided to skilled workers. In many countries, flour, grain, or potatoes are provided as pay supplements. Consumer product companies may offer their employees a choice of cash or the cash equivalent of their pay in company products at a discounted price. Employees are free to resell these products at a profit, thereby increasing their actual earnings. Voluntary noncash or "in-kind" payments are made because they are tax-effective. In some countries they may come to be regarded as acquired rights—payments to which employees are legally entitled.

In addition to pay practices that vary from country to country, multinationals must deal with salary management systems that differ radically from West to East. European and North American MNEs usually base compensation on the type of work individual employees or classes of employees perform and the skill required for each defined job position. In Hong Kong and Singapore, individual performance and skill can dramatically affect compensation. Japanese companies tend to base compensation on the age and seniority of employees as well as the performance of their group or company; little or no pay differential is offered for individual performance or exceptional skills. Latin American firms, which do pay differentials for individual performance or exceptional skills, also often continue to pay aging, nonproductive workers as much as they do young, vigorous ones because they cannot force the older employees to retire without making additional payments on top of termination indemnities. Clearly, a company cannot ignore the compensation practices of the countries in which it operates. Even comparisons between the United States and Europe reveal significant differences with respect to the "company car." IHR in the News in Exhibit 6-5 illustrates that ignorance of local custom invites disaster; knowledge of laws, practices, and employer obligations should form the basis for all international compensation.

SUMMARY

A host of complexities arises when companies move from compensation at the domestic level to compensation in an international context. Compensation policy becomes, in the process, "an art rather than a science."[50] In addition to considering parent-country financial, legal, and customary practices, foreign standards and practices must also be taken into account.[51] Many varying viewpoints—parent- and host-country companies, host governments, PCN/TCN employees and their families, and HCNs—must be considered in the development of a firm's compensation agenda and goals. Consequently, international compensation becomes harder to control and communicate. All these conditions make it important to be responsive and flexible, yet fair. Clearly, there is an emerging trend toward more flexibility, away from applying fixed formulas. Another trend is toward cost containment, particularly where expatriates are concerned.

In this chapter we have noted how these concerns may affect salary, taxation, benefits, and allowances, and we have looked at the issues that must be confronted in these areas. Also, we have argued that all of the components of international compensation should be combined and positioned within the long-term strategic goals of the firm. Rather than being an auxiliary corporate concern, compensation programs should be used to further the international competitive standing of the global corporation.

EXHIBIT 6-5   IHR in the News

For European Executives, Company Car Is Routine

By Charles Goldsmith
International Herald Tribune

Brussels—While the middle manager in the United States would be horribly brazen to ask for a company car, his European counterpart might feel he was taken for a ride if he did not receive some shiny wheels the very first day on the job.

The company car, a rarity in America but entrenched in Britain for two decades, is now regarded as a God-given right for managers throughout much of Europe.

"The United Kingdom led, and other countries in Europe followed," said Daniel Morgan, public affairs director of Monsanto Europe SA, the subsidiary of the U.S. chemical giant.

Britain still leads the pack, with company cars, including those bought by self-employed people, accounting for 22 percent of all vehicles, says the Society of Motor Manufacturers and Traders in

(continued)

EXHIBIT 6-5 *(continued)*

London, though fresh changes in British tax laws will make company cars less attractive in the future.

In Belgium, company cars account for 9 percent of the 3.8 million vehicles on the road.

"We've got to respond to the competitive situation, and we're going to look at Belgium compared to Greece compared to Austria," said Don Gorman, director of human resources for Europe at SmithKline Beecham Corp., an Anglo-American pharmaceuticals company. "If in Austria only the general manager would get a car, we would respond to that market lead. If it goes lower to other employees, we've got to track that as well."

The U.S. tax system entices American employees to prefer cash over cars, but the tax structure in much of Europe makes a car a lucrative part of many compensation packages.

"If somebody is paid in cash, there's no question about what's subject to social security and tax," said Germain Van Tieghem of the Arthur Andersen & Co. accounting firm in Brussels. "If a company car is supplied, the amount added to an employee's taxable income is less than the actual benefit the employee gets."

The significance of the corporate vehicle in Europe, experts say, goes far beyond mere pocketbook issues. "It's important to realize how sensitive an issue the company car is to European employees in terms of status," said Henk Van Ursel of Continental Benefit Consultants, a Brussels-based management consulting firm.

"To me, having a company vehicle means the company feels I'm worth having, because you don't lease a car for someone unless you want them around," said Clive Grafton-Reed, European applications specialist for Lumonics Ltd., a Canadian-based industrial and scientific laser firm.

The experts' advice: when in Rome, do as the Romans do, because multinational companies ignore local practice only at their own peril.

"We have some U.S. firms say to us, 'We don't want to include a company car in our remuneration package in Europe because we do not do it in the United States.' We advise them that this might cause difficulties in terms of attracting and keeping good people," said Mr. Van Ursel.

(continued)

To provide a roadmap for international managers, Continental Benefit Consultants surveyed 72 companies, mostly multinationals and more than half with American parents, whose fleets totaled 3,376 automobiles.

Half the companies have written policies, covering recipient guidelines, a description of models allowed or the maximum cost, and a list of the employee's rights and obligations in using the vehicle.

Only 31 percent of those surveyed provide a car to "all" managers: most make a distinction based on job level or content, with the dividing line often falling between middle management and white-collar support staff.

Not surprisingly, freedom of model choice varies with rank on the corporate ladder.

"We allow a fairly free choice subject to a cost limit and environmental performance, but we do not encourage people to take two-seater sports cars or other racy models," said Mr. Morgan of Monsanto. "We use the word 'appropriate,' and we all realize what an appropriate car is."

Employees find expensive German-made performance sedans appropriate indeed, the survey found: of all cars granted to managers, 24 percent were Audis, 13 percent Mercedes and 10 percent BMWs.

Marketing managers are twice as likely to get a Renault rather than a Mercedes, while sales representatives are most likely to wind up with an Opel, usually the Kadett model.

Long-term leasing is the financing formula chosen by about 75 percent of the companies surveyed.

"One of the nice things about having a leased company car is that you don't have to worry about breakdowns and the cost of repairing the car," said Mr. Grafton-Reed, the laser company specialist.

Good thing for him: He woke up on the May Day holiday to find that someone had stolen the left rear wheel of his leased Volkswagen Jetta.

Source: International Herald Tribune, May 2, 1991, pp. 9, 13. Reprinted with permission.

QUESTIONS

1. What should be the main objectives of international compensation policies?

2. Describe the issues associated with home-based, host-based, and regional compensation plans.

3. Are there differences in salary compensation consideration for PCNs and TCNs? Cite reasons either for such differences or for the absence of differences.

4. What are the main points firms must consider when deciding how to provide benefits?

5. Why is it important for MNEs to understand the compensation practices of other countries?

FURTHER READING

1. National Foreign Trade Council, International Compensation Committee, *Expatriate Compensation Manual.* New York: National Foreign Trade Council, Inc., 1987.

2. J. M. Kadet and R. J. Gaughan, Jr., "Manage Expatriate Expenses for Capital Returns," *Personnel Journal,* February, 1987, pp. 66–76.

3. B. A. Murdock and B. Ramamurthy, "Containing Benefits Costs for Multinational Corporations," *Personnel Journal,* March, 1986, pp. 80–84.

4. M. O'Reilly, "Total Remuneration: The International View," *Compensation and Benefits Review,* Vol. 20, Sept.–Oct., 1988, pp. 68–71.

5. J. M. Putti and K. C. Wong, "Flexible Wage Systems in Newly Industrialized Countries," *Compensation and Benefits Review,* November–December 1988, pp. 46–55.

6. J. Rayman and B. Twinn, *Expatriate Compensation and Benefits: An Employer's Handbook* (London: Kogan Page, 1983).

7. A. M. Townsend, K. D. Scott, and S. E. Markham, "An Examination of Country and Culture-based Differences in Compensation Practices," *Journal of International Business Studies,* Vol. 21, No. 4 (1990) pp. 667–678.

8. B. J. Springer, "1992: The Impact on Compensation and Benefits in the European Community," *Compensation and Benefits Review,* July–August 1989, pp. 20–27.

NOTES

1. R. S. Schuler and P. J. Dowling, "Survey of SHRM/I Members" (New York: Stern School of Business, New York University, 1988).

2. *Worldwide Total Remuneration* (New York: Towers, Perrin, Forster & Crosby, 1987).

3. C. Reynolds, "Cost-Effective Compensation of Expatriates," *Topics in Total Compensation*, Vol. 2, No. 4 (1988) pp. 319–326.

4. C. Reynolds, "High Motivation and Low Cost Through Innovative International Compensation," in *Proceedings of ASPA's Fortieth National Conference*, Boston (1989).

5. J. B. Anderson, "Compensating Your Overseas Executives, Part 2: Europe in 1992," *Compensation and Benefits Review*, July–August 1990, p. 29.

6. Ibid.

7. C. Reynolds, "Cost-Effective Compensation," p. 320.

8. L. P. Crandall and M. I. Phelps, "Pay for a Global Work Force," *Personnel Journal*, February, 1991, pp. 28–33.

9. Anderson, "Compensating Your Overseas Executives," pp. 29–30.

10. Ibid.

11. This discussion of the regional-based plan is adapted from C. Reynolds, "Cost-Effective Compensation," pp. 320–321. Used with permission of the author.

12. See B. W. Teague, *Compensating Key Personnel Overseas* (New York: The Conference Board, 1972), for a discussion of the concept of keeping the expatriate "whole."

13. This discussion of the "balance-sheet" approach is based on C. Reynolds, "Compensation of Overseas Personnel," in *Handbook of Human Resources Administration* (2nd ed.), ed. J. J. Famularo (New York: McGraw-Hill, 1986). Used with permission.

14. Schuler and Dowling, "Survey of SHRM/I Members."

15. *HR Reporter Update*, Vol. 3, No. 2 (1987) p. 2.

16. *Worldwide Total Remuneration*.

17. M. J. Bishko, "Compensating Your Overseas Executives, Part 1: Strategies for the 1990s," *Compensation and Benefits Review*, May–June 1990, pp. 37–38.

18. Ibid., p. 38.

19. Ibid.

20. Ibid.

21. For a review of the issues involved in providing incentives for expatriate managers, see B. J. Brooks, "Long-term Incentives for the Foreign-Based Executive," *Compensation and Benefits Review*, Vol. 19, No. 3 (1985) pp. 46–53; Bishko, "Compensating Your Overseas Executives, Part 1"; and R. B. Klein, "Compensating Your Overseas Executives, Part 3: Exporting

U.S. Stock Option Plans to Expatriates," *Compensation and Benefits Review*, September–October 1990, pp. 27–38.

22. *The Price Waterhouse Cranfield Project on International Strategic Human Resource Management* (1991), Cranfield School of Management, p. 34.

23. Klein, "Compensating Your Overseas Executives."

24. H. J. Ruff and G. I. Jackson, "Methodological Problems in International Comparisons of the Cost of Living," *Journal of International Business Studies*, Vol. 5, No. 2 (1974) pp. 57–67.

25. P. Stuart, "Global Payroll—A Taxing Problem," *Personnel Journal*, October, 1991, pp. 80–90.

26. Schuler and Dowling, "Survey of SHRM/I Members," p. 3c.

27. P. Stuart, "Global Payroll."

28. For further information, see C. Reynolds, "Compensation of Overseas Personnel."

29. Schuler and Dowling, "Survey of SHRM/I Members."

30. *Worldwide Total Remuneration*, p. 12.

31. Ibid.

32. See Ruff and Jackson, "Methodological Problems."

33. "Trends in Expatriate Compensation," *Bulletin to Management*, October 18, 1990, p. 336.

34. *Worldwide Total Remuneration*.

35. "Trends in Expatriate Compensation."

36. Ibid.

37. This information is from MBA student projects done at the University of Michigan.

38. V. Pucik, "Strategic HRM in Multinational Corporations," in *Strategic Management of Multinational Corporations*, ed. H. V. Wortzel and L. H. Wortzel (New York: John Wiley, 1985) p. 430.

39. Reynolds, "Cost-Effective Compensation," pp. 319–320.

40. L. R. Gomez-Mejia, "The Role of Human Resources Strategy in Export Performance: A Longitudinal Study," *Strategic Management Journal*, Vol. 9 (1988) pp. 493–505.

41. Reynolds, "Cost-Effective Compensation."

42. This section on cost containment is adapted from C. Reynolds, "Cost-Effective Compensation," pp. 321–322. Used with permission.

43. The reduction in the numbers of U.S. expatriates is the result of many interrelated factors; compensation cost containment is one such factor.

44. Anderson, "Compensating Your Overseas Executives."

45. Ibid., pp. 26–27.

46. Reynolds, p. 322.

47. Ibid.

48. "1992 SHRM/CCH Survey," Commerce Clearing House, Inc., July 8, 1992, p. 11.

49. Part of this section is adapted from R. L. Foltz and R. G. Foltz, "International Human Resource Management," in *Readings in Personnel and Human Resource Management* (3rd ed.), ed. R. S. Schuler, S. A. Youngblood, and V. L. Huber (St. Paul, Minn.: West Publishing Co., 1988).

50. Flavio Carvalho, Vice President, Human Resources, World Banking Group, Bank of America, from a presentation at the International Chapter of the Society for Human Resource Management, National Conference, San Francisco, March 12, 1991.

51. L. R. Gomez-Mejia and T. Welbourne, "Compensation Strategies in Global Context," *Human Resource Planning,* Spring 1991, pp. 29–42.

Chapter S E V E N

International Labor Relations

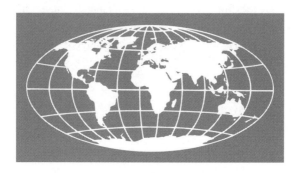

Before we examine the key issues in international labor relations as they relate to MNEs, we need to consider some general points about the field of international labor relations.[1] First, it is important to realize that it is difficult to compare industrial relations systems and behavior across national boundaries; a labor relations concept may change considerably when translated from one industrial relations context to another.[2] The concept of collective bargaining, for example, in the United States is understood to mean negotiations between a labor union local and management; in Sweden and Germany the term refers to negotiations between an employers' organization and a trade union at the industry level. Cross-national differences also emerge as to the objectives of the collective bargaining process and the enforceability of collective agreements. Many European unions view the collective bargaining process as an ongoing class struggle between labor and capital, whereas in the United States union leaders tend toward a pragmatic economic view of collective bargaining rather than an ideological view.

Second, it is generally recognized in the international labor relations field that no industrial relations system can be understood without an appreciation of its historical origin.[3] As Schregle[4] has observed,

> A comparative study of industrial relations shows that industrial relations phenomena are a very faithful expression of the society in which they operate, of its characteristic features and of the power relationships between different interest groups. Industrial relations cannot be understood without an understanding of the way in which rules are established and implemented and decisions are made in the society concerned.

An interesting example of the effect of historical differences may be seen in the structure of trade unions in various countries. Poole[5] has identified several factors that may underlie these historical differences:

- the mode of technology and industrial organization at critical stages of union development
- methods of union regulation by government
- ideological divisions within the trade union movement
- the influence of religious organizations on trade union development
- managerial strategies for labor relations in large corporations

As Exhibit 7-1 shows, union structures differ considerably among Western countries. These include industrial unions, which represent all grades of employees in an industry; craft unions, which are based on skilled occupational groupings across industries; conglomerate unions, which represent members in more than one industry; and general unions, which are open to almost all employees in a given country. These differences in union structures have had a major influence on the collective bargaining process in Western countries.

The less one knows about how a structure came to develop in a distinctive way, the less likely one is to understand it. As Prahalad and Doz[6] note, the lack of familiarity of MNE managers with local industrial and political conditions has sometimes needlessly worsened a conflict that a local firm would have been likely to resolve.[7] Increasingly, MNEs are recognizing this shortcoming and admitting that industrial relations policies must be flexible enough to adapt to local requirements. This

EXHIBIT 7-1   Trade Union Structure in Leading Western Industrial Societies

Australia	general, craft, industrial, white-collar
Belgium	industrial, professional, religious, public sector
Canada	industrial, craft, conglomerate
Denmark	general, craft, white-collar
Finland	industrial, white-collar, professional and technical
Great Britain	general, craft, industrial, white-collar, public sector
Japan	enterprise
The Netherlands	religious, conglomerate, white-collar
Norway	industrial, craft
Sweden	industrial, craft, white-collar and professional
Switzerland	industrial, craft, religious, white-collar
United States	industrial, craft, conglomerate, white-collar
West Germany	industrial, white-collar

Source: M. Poole, *Industrial Relations: Origins and Patterns of National Diversity* (London: Routledge & Kegan Paul, 1986), p. 79. Reprinted with permission.

change is occurring even in multinationals that follow a nonunion industrial relations strategy where possible, as IHR in the News in Exhibit 7-2 points out.

KEY ISSUES IN INTERNATIONAL LABOR RELATIONS

The focus of this chapter is the labor relations strategies adopted by MNEs rather than the more general topic of comparative labor relations.[8] The central question for labor relations in an international context is that of the orientation of MNEs to organized labor. Because national differences in economic, political, and legal systems produce markedly different labor relations systems across countries, multinational firms generally delegate the management of labor relations to their foreign subsidiaries. However, a policy of decentralization does not keep corporate headquarters from exercising some coordination over labor relations strategy. Generally, corporate headquarters will become involved in or oversee labor agreements made by foreign subsidiaries because these agreements may affect the international plans of the corporation and/or create precedents for negotiations in other countries. Robock and Simmonds[9] note that labor relations throughout a system become of direct importance to corporate headquarters when transnational sourcing patterns have been developed, that is, when a subsidiary in one country relies on another foreign subsidiary as a source of components or as a user of its output. In this context, a coordinated labor relations policy is one of the key factors in a successful global production strategy.[10]

EXHIBIT 7-2   IHR in the News

Advice for Companies Going Global

The key to successfully expanding overseas is to become one with the culture of the location, even if it means unionization of employees, Michael R. Quinlan, chairman and chief executive officer of McDonald's Corp., tells conferees at a meeting of the Human Resources Management Association of Chicago.

After opening fast-food restaurants in 53 nations, McDonald's has learned that it must follow the established practices of a foreign country to succeed there, Quinlan says. For example, a number of European countries and Australia have very strict unionization standards, and operations there are unionized as a condition of doing business. Acknowledging that McDonald's has had some "horrible union fights around the world," Quinlan advises employers considering expansion into other nations to "do it their way, not your way."

The main implication of dealing with unions is the increased cost of wages and benefits, according to Quinlan. Still, he adds that he does not feel unionization has interfered with employees' loyalty to McDonald's, or to the company's philosophy of service and employee motivation. Declaring that unions do not "bring much to the equation" of the employee/employer relationship, Quinlan says McDonald's is "basically a nonunion company" and intends to stay that way.

Another source of difficulty for McDonald's in its expansion overseas lies in the fact that fast-food restaurants are unfamiliar in most nations. Opening the first McDonald's inside the Communist-bloc, in Yugoslavia, took 12 years, Quinlan notes. He also points out that the company's policy is to staff its restaurants, from crew through management, only with nationals—for the 3,300 foreign outlets, the corporation employs only 35 expatriate U.S. citizens, and its goal is to have 100 percent local employees within five years.

Source: The Bureau of National Affairs, *Bulletin to Management*, March 7, 1991, pp. 66–67 (P.O. Box 40949, Washington D.C., 20016–0949). Copyright 1991 by The Bureau of National Affairs, Inc. Reprinted with permission.

There is also evidence of differences between European and U.S. MNEs in terms of headquarters involvement in labor relations. A number of studies by Hamill have revealed that U.S. MNEs exercise greater centralized control over labor relations than do British companies.[11]

Bean[12] cites three factors that may explain the greater degree of centralized control over labor relations exercised by U.S. MNEs:

- A number of studies[13] have shown that, compared to European MNEs, U.S. firms tend to concentrate authority at corporate headquarters, with greater emphasis on formal management controls and a close reporting system (particularly within the area of financial control) to ensure that planning targets are met.

- European MNEs have tended to deal with labor unions at industry level (frequently via employer associations) rather than at company level. The opposite is more typical for U.S. firms. In the United States, employer associations have not played a key role in the industrial relations system, and company-based labor relations policies are the norm.[14]

- A final factor is the extent of the home product market. If domestic sales are large relative to overseas operations (as is the case with many U.S. companies), it is more likely that overseas operations will be regarded by the parent company as an extension of domestic operations. This is not the case for many European MNEs, whose international operations represent the major part of their business. Bean cites as an example the two leading Swiss MNEs whose domestic sales represent less than 4 percent of their output. Lack of a large home market is a strong incentive to adapt to host-country institutions and norms.

An additional important factor is that of management attitudes or ideology concerning unions.[15] Knowledge of management attitudes concerning unions may provide a more complete explanation of MNE labor relations behavior than could be obtained by relying solely on a rational economic model. Thus, management attitudes should also be considered in any explanation of managerial behavior along with such factors as market forces and strategic choices. This is of particular relevance to U.S. MNEs, since union avoidance appears to be deeply rooted in the value systems of American managers.[16] As Exhibit 7-3 shows, the United States has one of the lowest union-density rates (the percentage of wage and salary employees who are union members) in the Western world. Hence, U.S. managers are less likely to have extensive experience with unions than managers in many other countries.

Although there are several problems inherent in data collection for a cross-national comparison of union-density rates, several theories have been suggested to explain the variations among countries. Such theories

EXHIBIT 7 - 3   Aggregate Union-Density Rates for Selected Countries, 1970–1988

	Union Density					Change in Density		OECD Rank Order*	
	1970	1975	1980	1985	1988	1970–80	1980–8	1970	1988
Australia	52[h]	51[a]	49[b]	46[c]	42	NA	−14[f]	NA	11
Canada[d]	31[e]	34	35	36	35	13	−1.4	16	14
France	22	23	19	16	12	−15	−37	19	24
Germany	33	37	37	37	34	12	−8.6	15	15
Italy	36	47	49	42	40	36	−20	13	13
Japan[d]	35	34	31	30	27	−11	−14	14	17
Sweden	68	74	80	84	85	18	6.6	1	1
UK	45	48	51	46	42	13	−18	11	12
USA	NA	23	23	18	16[g]	NA	−29	NA	22

Notes

a. 1976; b. 1982; c. 1986; d. recorded membership; e. 1971; f. 1982–8; g. 1989; h. BLS unpublished series January 1991.

*Rank order of 20 OECD countries in 1970, but 24 in 1988.

Source: G. J. Bamber and G. Whitehouse, "International Data on Economic, Employment and Human Resource Issues," *International Journal of Human Resource Management*, Vol. 3, No. 2 (1992) p. 364. Reprinted with permission.

consider economic factors such as wages, prices, and unemployment levels; social factors such as public support for unions; and political factors. In addition, studies indicate that the strategies utilized by labor, management, and governments are particularly important.[17]

Labor Relations Practices of MNEs

Much of the literature on the labor relations practices of MNEs tends to be at a more cross-national or comparative level and there is a dearth of research on labor relations practices at the enterprise level. An exception to this pattern is the work of Hamill.[18] In a series of studies, Hamill surveyed U.S.-owned and British-owned MNEs operating in Britain to compare their labor relations practices, their decision-making practices with regard to labor relations, and their labor relations performance. First, he surveyed eighty-four U.S.-owned and fifty British-owned MNEs operating in three British industries to compare their labor relations practices with regard to the following factors:

- union recognition
- employer association membership
- management organization for labor relations purposes
- the state of their negotiating arrangements
- the level and nature of collective agreements
- grievance procedures
- wage-payment systems
- level of wages and employee fringe benefits

According to this study, the U.S. MNEs were less likely than their British counterparts to recognize trade unions, preferred not to join employer associations, had more highly developed and specialized personnel departments at plant level, and tended to pay higher wages and offer more generous employee fringe benefits than local firms.

A second study focused on MNEs' decision making regarding labor relations.[19] Hamill conducted a series of interviews, usually with personnel directors, in the British subsidiaries of thirty companies operating in Britain. His basic conclusion was that the labor relations function within the MNE is far from being either wholly decentralized or wholly centralized. The extent of corporate involvement in the subsidiary's labor relations was influenced by the following factors:

- The degree of intersubsidiary production integration. A high degree of integration was found to be the most important factor leading to the centralization of the labor relations function within the MNEs studied.

- Whether the subsidiary was U.S.-owned or European-owned. The former were found to be much more centralized in labor relations decision making than the latter. Hamill attributed this difference in management procedures to the more integrated nature of U.S. MNEs, the greater divergence between British and U.S. labor relations systems than between British and other European systems, and the more ethnocentric managerial style of U.S. MNEs.

- Whether subsidiaries were well-established indigenous firms that were acquired by a MNE or greenfield sites set up by a MNE. The former tended to be given much more autonomy over labor relations than the latter.

- Whether subsidiaries were performing well or poorly. Poor performance tended to be accompanied by increased corporate involvement in labor relations. Where poor performance was due to labor relations problems, the MNE tended to attempt to introduce parent-country labor relations practices aimed at reducing industrial unrest or increasing productivity.

- Whether the MNE was a significant source of operating or investment funds for the subsidiary. If this was the case, there was increased corporate involvement in labor relations.

The third study by Hamill[20] examined strike-proneness of MNE subsidiaries and indigenous firms in Britain across three industries. Strike-proneness was measured via three variables—strike frequency, strike size, and strike duration. There was no difference across the two groups of firms with regard to strike frequency, but MNE subsidiaries did experience larger and longer strikes than local firms. Hamill suggests that this difference indicates that foreign-owned firms may be under less financial pressure to settle a strike quickly than local firms—possibly because they can switch production out of the country.

Commenting on the overall results of his research, Hamill[21] concludes that

> general statements cannot be applied to the organization of the labor relations function within MNCs. Rather, different MNCs adopt different labor relations strategies in relation to the environmental factors

peculiar to each firm. In other words, it is the type of multinational under consideration which is important rather than multinationality itself.

STRATEGIC ASPECTS OF INTERNATIONAL LABOR RELATIONS

Labor unions may limit the strategic choices of MNEs in three ways: (1) by influencing wage levels to the extent that cost structures may become uncompetitive; (2) by constraining the ability of MNEs to vary employment levels at will; and (3) by hindering or preventing global integration of the operations of MNEs.[22] We shall briefly examine each of these potential constraints.

Influencing Wage Levels

Although the importance of labor costs relative to other costs is decreasing, labor costs still play an important part in determining cost competitiveness in most industries. The influence of unions on wage levels is, therefore, important. MNEs that fail to successfully manage their wage levels will suffer labor cost disadvantages that may narrow their strategic options.

Constraining the Ability of MNEs to Vary Employment Levels at Will

For many MNEs operating in Western Europe, Japan, and Australia, the inability to vary employment levels at will may be a more serious problem than wage levels. Many countries now have legislation that limits considerably the ability of firms to carry out redundancy or layoff programs unless it can be shown that structural conditions make these employment losses unavoidable. Frequently, the process of showing the need for redundancy programs is a long and drawn-out process. Redundancy legislation in many countries also frequently specifies that firms must compensate redundant employees through specified formulas such as one week's pay for each year of service. In many countries, payments for involuntary terminations are rather substantial, especially in comparison to those in the United States. Exhibit 7-4 indicates the wide variations in compensation paid to manufacturing workers across eleven countries.

E X H I B I T 7 - 4   Hourly Compensation in U.S. Dollars for Workers in Manufacturing

	1975	1980	1985	1991
Britain	$3.32	$7.83	$6.19	$19.42
China	$0.17	$0.30	$0.24	$0.26[3]
Germany*	$6.35	$12.33	$9.57	$22.17
India	$0.19	$0.44	$0.35	$0.39[2]
Ireland	$3.03	$5.95	$5.92	$11.90
Jamaica[1]	N.A.	N.A.	$1.44	$1.61[3]
Japan	$3.05	$5.61	$6.43	$14.41
Mexico	N.A.	N.A.	$1.60	$2.17
Singapore	$0.84	$1.49	$2.47	$4.38
Thailand	N.A.	N.A.	$0.53	$0.68[3]
U.S.	$6.36	$9.87	$13.01	$15.45

*East & West Germany combined for 1991.
[1]ILO data. [2]1986. [3]1990.
Source: Bureau of Labor Statistics data in *Fortune*, December 14, 1992, p. 58. © 1992
Time Inc. All rights reserved. Reprinted with permission.

Labor unions may influence this process in two ways: by lobbying their
own national governments to introduce redundancy legislation; and by
encouraging regulation of MNEs by international organizations such as
the Organization for Economic Cooperation and Development. (Later in
this chapter we describe the *Badger* case, which forced Raytheon to finally accept responsibility for severance payments to employees made
redundant by the closing down of its Belgian subsidiary.) MNE managers who do not take these restrictions into account in their strategic planning may well find their options severely limited. In fact, recent evidence
shows that multinationals are beginning to consider the ability to dismiss
employees one of the priorities when making investment location decisions. Exhibit 7-5, IHR in the News, illustrates this point.

Hindering or Preventing Global Integration
of the Operations of MNEs

In recognition of these constraints, many MNEs make a conscious decision not to integrate and rationalize their operations to the most efficient
degree, because to do so could cause industrial and political problems.
Prahalad and Doz[23] cite General Motors as an example of this "suboptimization of integration." GM was alleged in the early 1980s to have

EXHIBIT 7 - 5   IHR in the News

Ground Rules for the Firing Squad

**Recent large-scale layoffs have highlighted the
ways European countries protect workers.
FT writers explain the variations.**

The French government's reaction to the decision by Hoover to shift some of its production from France to Scotland was to proclaim a further tightening of the rules governing redundancies and plant closures.

This was an understandable response from a government facing a national election, but it is not necessarily in the long-term interests of French workers and appears to be running against the European tide.

David Rees, investment location expert at Ernst & Young, says that multinational companies, especially American ones, are starting to add ease of "exit", or at least rationalisation, to the list of priorities when making investment location decisions.

Within the European Community that should favour the UK, Ireland and Denmark, the three most *laissez-faire* countries when it comes to closures and sackings. It will count against the southern European economies—Portugal, Spain, Italy and Greece—which are restrictive and costly, probably one reason why the EC's poorer outer rim has not attracted more investment.

There are many other factors in an investment location decision besides ease of exit, and Rees says it is still only an influence "at the margin". Nevertheless, with the barrier-free single market encouraging companies to concentrate production on one site, as opposed to scattering it around the EC's national markets, such advantages could become increasingly important.

There is, currently, little new multinational investment into the EC, so the extent to which the UK's devalued currency, relatively low wage costs, and "hire and fire" industrial culture will suck in a disproportionate amount of investment should not be overstated.

Nevertheless, the debate about whether the UK is winning a legitimate competitive advantage or is undercutting workers' rights across the EC through "social dumping" looks likely to intensify.

(continued)

Opponents of the UK can take heart from the fact that its advantages are likely to be limited to certain sectors.

Most analysts believe the UK will have a competitive advantage in semi-skilled manufacturing, if it is not undercut by eastern Europe, but the continuing weakness of its education system will cause it to lose out in higher skill or R&D-based investment.

In the longer run the current restructuring of the welfare state is likely to shift more cost on to employers and thus undermine the UK's advantage of low non-wage labor costs.

In the short-term, the UK is likely to lose more jobs than it gains from multinational re-structuring within Europe precisely because of the ease with which workers can be dismissed.

Hoover decided to move to Scotland despite the fact that shedding jobs in France is considerably more costly and complex, a measure of the cost advantage from much lower UK non-wage labour costs.

The French government seems convinced that, at least at this stage in the economic cycle, "locking in" jobs through raising the cost of closure is the most suitable response to multinational restructuring. The new French redundancy law returns the situation to something close to the time prior to 1986 when official approval was still required for large-scale redundancies.

The new law requires official approval of the "social plan" for the workers who are losing their jobs. France thus rejoins that large group of EC countries—including Spain, Portugal, Greece, Italy, the Netherlands and Germany—which give government or workers an effective veto over redundances. A veto which can only be circumvented with time and money.

There are, however, indications that several countries, most notably Italy and Spain, are starting to recognise that the sky-high cost of dismissal is both a disincentive to international capital and to domestic restructuring. This trend is still weak but will gather momentum when EC growth picks up.

The trend might be strengthened by the introduction of common EC rules on large redundancies which could provide political cover for countries like Spain.

(continued)

EXHIBIT 7-5   *(continued)*

A spate of Hoover-type, beggar-my-neighbour, rows over jobs and investment is just what EC officials have for years been fearing. The Social Charter and its latest manifestation, the Social Chapter, were, in part, meant to soften the process of industrial restructuring within the EC. But as they, quite properly, do not address the question of relative labor costs, they have had no impact on companies like Hoover.

The one EC-wide redundancy rule already in operation requires worker representatives to be given 90 days' notice and proper consultation over larger redundancies. After Hoover there is also a move to breathe life back into the idea of European works councils—forums for companies operating in more than one EC country where employee representatives must be informed of major corporate plans.

European union leaders say that such councils would have prevented Hoover playing off the workers in two different countries against each other.

It is debatable whether a works council would have made much difference in the Hoover case. But it is certain that if compulsory works councils are introduced under the Social Chapter—from which the UK has opted-out—many US multinationals will be horrified and will be even more likely to concentrate their EC investment in the UK.

David Goodhart

Source: Financial Times (London) February 15, 1993, p. 8. Reprinted with permission.

---

undertaken substantial investments in Germany (matching its new investments in Austria and Spain) at the demand of the German metalworkers' union (one of the largest industrial unions in the Western world) in order to foster good labor relations in Germany. One observer of the world auto industry suggested that car manufacturers were suboptimizing their manufacturing networks partly to placate trade unions and partly to provide redundancy in sources to prevent localized social strife from paralyzing their network. This suboptimization led to unit manufacturing costs in Europe that were 15 percent higher, on average, than an economically optimal network would have achieved. Prahalad and Doz draw the following conclusion from this example:[24]

> Union influence thus not only delays the rationalization and integration of MNCs' manufacturing networks and increases the cost of such adjustments (not so much in the visible severance payments and 'golden handshake' provisions as through the economic losses incurred in the meantime), but also, at least in such industries as automobiles, permanently reduces the efficiency of the integrated MNC network. Therefore, treating labor relations as incidental and relegating them to the specialists in the various countries is inappropriate. In the same way as government policies need to be integrated into strategic choices, so do labor relations.

THE RESPONSE OF LABOR UNIONS TO MNEs

Labor union leaders have long seen the growth of MNEs as a threat to the bargaining power of labor because of the considerable power and influence of large MNEs. Kennedy[25] has identified the following seven characteristics of MNEs as the source of labor unions' concern about MNEs:

- Formidable financial resources. This includes the ability to absorb losses in a particular foreign subsidiary that is in dispute with a national union and still show an overall profit on worldwide operations.
- Alternative sources of supply. This may take the form of an explicit "dual sourcing" policy to reduce the vulnerability of the corporation to a strike by any national union.
- The ability to move production facilities to other countries.
- Superior knowledge and expertise in labor relations.
- A remote locus of authority (i.e., the corporate head office management of a MNE).
- Production facilities in many industries. As Vernon[26] has noted, most MNEs operate in many product lines.
- The capacity to stage an "investment strike," whereby the multinational refuses to invest any additional funds in a plant, thus ensuring that the plant will become obsolete and economically noncompetitive.

The response of labor unions has been threefold: to form international trade secretariats (ITSs); to lobby for restrictive national legislation; and finally, to try and achieve regulation of MNEs by international organizations. The function of an ITS is to provide worldwide links for the national unions in a particular trade or industry (e.g., metals, transport, and chemicals).[27] The long-term goal of each ITS is to achieve transnational bargaining with each of the MNEs in its industry. According to Willatt,[28] each ITS is following a similar program to achieve the goal of transnational bargaining. The elements of this program are (1) research and information, (2) calling company conferences, (3) establishing company councils, (4) companywide union-management discussions, and (5) coordinated bargaining. To date, the ITSs have met with limited success, the reasons for which Northrup[29] attributes to (1) the generally good wages and working conditions offered by MNEs, (2) strong resistance from multinational managements, (3) conflicts within the labor movement, and (4) differing laws and customs in the labor relations area.

A further difficulty for unions when dealing with MNEs is conflicting national economic interests. In times of economic downturn, this factor may become an insurmountable barrier for trade union officials. Blake[30] gives an example of such a situation. In the early 1970s the Ford Motor Company indicated that the labor climate in Britain was a disincentive to further investment in that country. In response, a group of Dutch businesspeople urged Ford to consider The Netherlands for future investment. Despite strong criticism of Ford by British unions, the leadership of the Dutch trade unions did not object to these suggestions that investment funds be transferred to their country.

On a political level, labor unions have lobbied for restrictive national legislation in the United States and Europe and the regulation of MNEs by international organizations. The motivation for labor unions to pursue restrictive national legislation is based on a desire to prevent the export of jobs via multinational investment policies. For example, in the United States, the AFL-CIO has lobbied strongly in this area.[31] To date, these attempts have been largely unsuccessful, and, with the increasing internationalization of business, it is difficult to see how governments will be persuaded to legislate in this area.

Attempts by labor unions to exert influence over MNEs via international organizations have met with some success. Through trade union federations such as the European Trade Union Confederation (ETUC) and the International Confederation of Free Trade Unions (ICFTU), the labor movement has been able to lobby the International Labor Organization (ILO), the United Nations Centre on Transnational Corporations (UNCTC), the Organization for Economic Cooperation and Development (OECD), and the European Community (EC). In 1977 the ILO adopted a code of conduct for MNEs (Tripartite Declaration of Principles Concerning MNEs and Social Policy) while the UNCTC has to date been concerned with more technical aspects of international business.[32] The ILO code of conduct, which was originally proposed in 1975, was influential in the drafting of the OECD guidelines for MNEs, which were approved in 1976. These voluntary guidelines cover disclosure of information, competition, financing, taxation, employment and industrial relations, and science and technology.[33]

A key section of these guidelines is the *umbrella* or *chapeau clause* (the latter is the more common term in the literature) that precedes the guidelines themselves. This clause states that MNEs should adhere to the guidelines "within the framework of law, regulations and prevailing labor relations and employment practices, in each of the countries in which they operate." Campbell and Rowan[34] state that employers have understood the chapeau clause to mean compliance with local law supersedes the guidelines while labor unions have interpreted this clause to mean that the guidelines are a "supplement" to national law. The implication of this latter interpretation is significant: a company could still be in violation of the OECD guidelines even though its activities have complied with national law and practice. Given the ambiguity of the chapeau clause and the fact that the OECD guidelines are voluntary, it is likely that this issue will remain controversial.

There is also some controversy in the literature as to the effectiveness of the OECD guidelines in regulating multinational behavior.[35] This lack of agreement centers on assessments of the various challenges to the guidelines. The best-known of these challenges is the *Badger* case. The Badger Company is a subsidiary of Raytheon, a U.S.-based MNE. In 1976 the Badger Company decided to close its Belgian subsidiary, and a dispute arose concerning termination payments.[36] Since Badger (Belgium) NV had filed for bankruptcy, the Belgian labor unions argued that Raytheon should assume the subsidiary's financial obligations. Raytheon refused, and the case was brought before the OECD by the Belgian government and the International Federation of Commercial, Clerical, Professional and Technical Employees (FIET), an international trade secretariat. The Committee on International Investments and MNEs (CIIME) of the OECD indicated that paragraph six of the guidelines (concerned with plant closures) implied a "shared responsibility" by the subsidiary and the parent in the event of a plant closing. Following this clarification by the CIIME and a scaling down of initial demands, Badger executives and Belgian government officials negotiated a settlement of this case.

Blanpain[37] concludes that the *Badger* case made clear the responsibility of the parent company for the financial liability of its subsidiary, but that this responsibility is not unqualified. As to whether the *Badger* case proved the "effectiveness" of the OECD guidelines, Jain[38] and Campbell and Rowan[39] point out that the Belgian unions devoted considerable resources to make this a test case and had assistance from both American unions (which, through the AFL-CIO, lobbied the U.S. Department of State) and the Belgian government in their negotiations with the OECD and Badger executives. Liebhaberg[40] is more specific in his assessment:

> Despite an outcome which those in favor of supervision consider to be positive, the Badger Case is a clear demonstration of one of the weaknesses in the OECD's instrument, namely that it does not represent any sort of formal undertaking on the part of the twenty-four member states which are signatories to it. The social forces of each separate country must apply pressure on their respective governments if they want the guidelines applied.

Recognizing the limitations of voluntary codes of conduct, European labor unions have also lobbied the Commission of the European Community (EC) to regulate the activities of MNEs. As Latta and Bellace[41] point out, unlike the OECD, the Commission of the EC can translate guidelines into law, and through its directorates of company law and social affairs has developed a number of proposals concerning disclosure of information to make MNEs more "transparent." Exhibit 7-6 summarizes the various directives from the EC concerning information disclosure. Of these directives, the most contentious has been the Vredeling directive (associated with Henk Vredeling, a former Dutch member of the EC Commission).[42] The Seventh (Vredeling) Directive's requirement of disclosure of company information to unions faced strong opposition led by the British government and employer representatives. They argued that employee involvement in consultation and decision making should be voluntary. At the signing of the Treaty on European Union in Maastricht in February 1992, Britain was allowed to opt out of the social policy agreements. The other eleven member states were party to a protocol (The Social Policy Protocol), which allows them to agree their own directives without Britain's participation.[43]

E X H I B I T 7 - 6   European Community Directives on Disclosure of Company
Information to Unions

Company Law	
Fifth Directive	On employee participation on company boards
Seventh Directive	On group accounts for European subsidiaries
Ninth Directive	On the formation and operation of groups of companies
Social Affairs	
Collective Redundancies	On employee representatives' rights to information and consultation in the event of lay-offs or closure
Acquired Rights of Workers on Transfers of Undertakings	On the safeguarding of employees in the event of a change of ownership of all or part of a business
"Vredeling" directive	On the rights of employees in large, complex companies to information and consultation on certain issues

Source: Adapted from G. W. Latta and J. R. Bellace, "Making the Corporation Transparent: Prelude to Multinational Bargaining," *Columbia Journal of World Business,* Vol. 18, No. 2 (1983) p. 76. Used with permission.

Implications of the Single European Market

In the Treaty of Rome (1957), some consideration was given to social policy issues related to the creation of the European Community. The Social Charter of the Council of Europe came into effect in 1965, and the directives listed in Exhibit 7-6 demonstrate attempts by the EC Commission to take social policy issues into consideration. The major objective of the Single European Act, which came into force in 1987 and established the Single European Market (SEM) on December 31, 1992, was to enhance the free movement of goods, money, and people within the SEM. In fact, the Single European Act "was widely considered to add a caring, social dimension to the single market. The Social Dimension is now described by the European Commission as one of its 'flanking policies,' alongside the single market programme."[44]

The Social Dimension aims to achieve a large labor market by bringing down the barriers that restrict the freedom of movement and the right of domicile within the SEM and is guided by the European Community Charter of the Fundamental Social Rights of Workers (referred to simply as the Social Charter). The major areas to be addressed by the Social Charter are: freedom of movement; employment and remuneration; improvement of living and working conditions; freedom of association and collective bargaining; equal treatment for men and women; health protection and safety in the workplace; vocational training; and information, consultation, and participation for workers. It also covers protection of children and adolescents, elderly and disabled persons, and social protection. The Social Charter, then, establishes a broad framework for a social dimension of the SEM but requires implementation by member states "in accordance with national practices, notably through legislative measures or collective agreements."[45] The general objectives of the Social Charter are translated into EC policy via the Social Action Programme. Naturally, the Social Charter has been the subject of much debate: Proponents defend the social dimension as a means of achieving social justice and equal treatment for EC citizens, while critics see it as a kind of social engineering.[46]

At this time, it is too early to predict whether the Social Charter will have a significant impact on companies operating within the SEM. Obviously all companies will need to become familiar with EC directives and keep abreast of changes. As Briscoe[47] points out, "the HR manager will need to understand the labor markets of all countries involved within the expanded trade zone" and realize, as well, that each member state has its own peculiarities, such as demographic shifts. While harmonization of labor laws can be seen as the ultimate objective, Michon[48] argues that the notion of a European social community does not mean a unification of all social conditions and benefits, or, for that matter, of all social systems. However, the SEM does aim to establish minimal standards for social conditions that will safeguard the fundamental rights of workers.

Social "Dumping"

One of the concerns related to the formation of the SEM was its impact on jobs. There was alarm that those member states that have relatively low social security costs would have a competitive edge and that firms would locate in those member states that have lower labor costs. The counter-alarm was that states with low-cost labor would have to increase their labor costs, to the detriment of their competitiveness.[49]

There are two industrial relations issues here: the movement of work from one region to another, and its effect on employment levels; and the need for trade union solidarity to prevent workers in one region from accepting pay cuts to attract investment, at the expense of workers in another region. As you will recall from Exhibit 7-5, these issues were highlighted at the end of January 1993 when Hoover, the American manufacturing company, decided to close its factory at Dijon, in eastern France (with the loss of six hundred French jobs) and transfer production to its Cambuslang plant near Glasgow, Scotland (which gained four hundred jobs). The French government saw this as another example of "job poaching" or "social dumping" within the SEM and lodged a formal complaint to the Commission of the EC. The president of the European Commission, Jacques Delors, led calls for a relaunch of the EC social policy. The French trade union leader, Marc Blondel, admitted in a newspaper interview,[50] that, had union leaders established a relationship with their colleagues in Scotland, they could have explained what the company was doing and jointly called upon the European Trade Union Confederation (ETUC) to intervene. The absence, however, of such a relationship resulted in the Scottish workers' acceptance of an agreement that involved one-off (once-only) payments in return for the end of restrictive practices and demarcation lines.

Some analysts suggest that the British opt-out of the Maastricht social policy agreement was a factor in this situation, along with the relative freedom of Britain's "hire-and-fire" workplace culture and relatively lower labor costs. Hoover management admits that nonwage labor costs were a factor in its decision to shift production, but it was also influenced by the fact that the Scottish plant had spare capacity, and an intensive review of its manufacturing operations indicated that plant rationalization and product harmonization were correct strategic responses to the SEM.[51] Nevertheless, the Hoover case illustrates the real concerns of social dumping—the result of luring investors with low wage costs, weak labor laws, and minimal government intervention—and the apparent failure of European labor unions to obtain uniform EC regulations to replace disparate national labor and social systems.[52]

The Implications of the North America Free Trade Agreement (NAFTA)

Another important regional economic integration involves the formation of a free trade zone between the United States, Canada, and Mexico. The Canada–United States Free Trade Agreement (FTA) went into effect on

January 1, 1989, and a draft accord to create NAFTA, which brought Mexico into the trading bloc, was announced in August, 1992. It is important to stress here that the NAFTA differs from the Single European Market in that it is a free trade zone and *not* a common market. The NAFTA deals only with the flow of goods, services, and investments among the three trading partners. It does not address labor mobility or other common policies of the SEM.[53]

There are, however, significant HR implications in NAFTA that must be considered by HR managers in North American firms. While the NAFTA does not include workplace laws and their enforcement, as was discussed in the context of the SEM, the country with the least restrictive workplace laws will have a competitive advantage. A comparison of these labor laws in the three NAFTA nations appears in Exhibit 7-7.

According to Daniels and Radebaugh,[54] the low wage rates in Mexico pose a threat to low-skill unions in Canada and the United States: "Organized labor in both Canada and the United States will suffer as low-paying jobs disappear and downward pressure is put on wages." In other words, the concern about social dumping is similar to the concern at the formation of the SEM, but there is a difference. In the case of NAFTA, "jobs will be able to cross borders, but workers will not."[55]

SUMMARY

The literature reviewed in this chapter and the discussion surrounding the formation of regional economic zones such as the Single European Market and the North American Free Trade Agreement, supports the conclusion that transnational collective bargaining has yet to be attained by labor unions. As Enderwick[56] has stated:

> The international operations of MNCs do create considerable impediments in effectively segmenting labor groups by national boundaries and stratifying groups within and between nations. Combining recognition of the overt segmentation effects of international business with an understanding of the dynamics of direct investment yields the conclusion that general multinational collective bargaining is likely to remain a remote possibility.

Enderwick argues that labor unions should opt for less ambitious strategies in dealing with MNEs, such as (1) strengthening national union involvement in plant-based and company-based bargaining; (2) supporting research on the vulnerability of selective MNEs; and (3) consolidating the activities of company-based ITSs. Despite setbacks, especially with

EXHIBIT 7-7   Comparisons of Private-Sector Labor Law among NAFTA Nations*

	U.S.	Canada	Mexico
Minimum wage (US$)	$4.25/hr.	$3.51/hr.	$0.46/hr. (avg.)
Maximum work week	40 hrs. (8×5)	varies with province	48 hrs. (8×6)
Pensions	optional	required contribution	optional
Social security (old age)	required contribution	required contribution	required contribution
Social security (disability)	required contribution	no provision	required contribution
Health care benefits	optional	required contribution	required contribution
Unemployment insurance	required contribution	required contribution	no provision
Workers' compensation insurance	required	yes, varies with province	no provision
Pay equity/ comparable worth	no provision	yes in Ontario	no provision
Plant-closing notification	60 days	yes, varies with province	yes
Severance pay	optional	varies with province	90 days pay
Housing assistance	optional	optional	5% base salary
Profit sharing	optional	optional	10% net profits
Christmas bonus	optional	optional	15 days pay
Holiday leave	optional	3+ paid holidays	7 paid holidays
Vacation leave	optional	10 paid days	6+ paid days
Sick leave	optional	paid by gov't. after 3 wks.	paid by gov't.
Maternity leave	optional	17 weeks+24 weeks	12 weeks
Gender discrimination	prohibited	prohibited	prohibited
Race/color discrimination	prohibited	prohibited	prohibited
Religious discrimination	prohibited	prohibited	prohibited
National origin discrimination	prohibited	prohibited	no provision
Age discrimination	prohibited	prohibited	no provision
Disability discrimination	prohibited	prohibited	no provision
Marital status discrimination	no provision	prohibited	no provision

*In all NAFTA countries, states and provinces also have jurisdiction over labor law and may set additional standards.

Source: Institute of International Human Resources, Society for Human Resource Management, *Briefing Paper on the North American Free Trade Agreement,* January 1993.

the regional economic integration issues discussed in this chapter, it is likely that labor unions and the ILO will pursue these strategies and continue to lobby for the regulation of MNEs via the European Commission and the United Nations.

Further research is needed on how multinationals view developments in international labor relations and whether these developments will influence the overall business strategy of the enterprise. Research is also needed on how global firms implement labor relations policy in various countries. The work by Hamill[57] on the labor relations policy of a number of MNEs operating in Britain provides an excellent example of research that has sought to overcome some of the generalities and methodological flaws evident in much of the previous research on international labor relations.

QUESTIONS

1. Why is it important to understand the historical origins of national industrial relations systems?

2. In what ways can labor unions constrain the strategic choices of MNEs?

3. Identify four characteristics of MNEs that give labor unions cause for concern.

4. How have labor unions responded to MNEs? Have these responses been successful?

5. What is "social dumping," and why should unions be concerned about it?

FURTHER READING

1. *World Labour Report 1992*, International Labour Office, Geneva, 1992.

2. P. Marginson, "European Integration and Transnational Management-Union Relations in the Enterprise," *British Journal of Industrial Relations*, Vol. 30, No. 4 (1992) pp. 529–545.

3. T. A. Kochan, R. Batt, and L. Dyer. "International Human Resource Studies: A Framework for Future Research" in *Research Frontiers in Industrial Relations and Human Resources*, ed. D. Lewin, O. S. Mitchell, and P. D. Sherer (Madison, Wisc.: Industrial Relations Research Association, 1992).

4. M. Poole, "Managerial Strategies and 'Styles' in Industrial Relations: A Comparative Analysis," *Journal of General Management*, Vol. 12, No. 1 (1986) pp. 40–53.

5. F. Bournois and J-H. Chauchat, "Managing Managers in Europe" *European Management Journal*, Vol. 8, No. 1 (1990) pp. 56–71.

NOTES

1. These introductory comments are drawn from J. Schregle, "Comparative Industrial Relations: Pitfalls and Potential," *International Labour Review,* Vol. 120, No. 1 (1981) pp. 15–30.

2. This point is also referred to as the *emic-etic* problem. See Chapter 1 for a detailed discussion of this point.

3. O. Kahn-Freund, *Labor Relations: Heritage and Adjustment* (Oxford: Oxford University Press, 1979).

4. J. Schregle, "Comparative Industrial Relations," p. 28.

5. M. Poole, *Industrial Relations: Origins and Patterns of National Diversity* (London: Routledge, 1986).

6. C. K. Prahalad and Y. L. Doz, *The Multinational Mission: Balancing Local Demands and Global Vision* (New York: The Free Press, 1987).

7. We noted in Chapter 3 that many U.S. MNEs are reducing the number of expatriates on overseas assignment (see S. J. Kobrin, "Expatriate Reduction and Strategic Control in American Multinational Corporations," *Human Resource Management,* Vol. 27, No. 1 [1988] pp. 63–75). With regard to labor relations, this reduction has the effect of reducing the opportunities of U.S. managers to gain firsthand experience of labor relations in various countries.

8. For general reviews of the comparative labor relations literature, see T. Kennedy, *European Labor Relations* (Lexington, Mass.: Lexington Books 1980); R. Bean, *Comparative Industrial Relations: An Introduction to Cross-National Perspectives* (New York: St. Martin's Press, 1985); Poole, *Industrial Relations; International and Comparative Industrial Relations,* G. J. Bamber and R. D. Lansbury, ed. (Sydney: Allen & Unwin, 1987).

9. S. H. Robock and K. Simmonds, *International Business and Multinational Enterprises,* 4th ed. (Homewood, Ill.: Irwin, 1989).

10. See also D. F. Hefler, "Global Sourcing: Offshore Investment Strategy for the 1980's," *Journal of Business Strategy,* Vol. 2, No. 1 (1981) pp. 7–12.

11. B. C. Roberts and J. May, "The Response of Multinational Enterprises to International Trade Union Pressures," *British Journal of Industrial Relations,* Vol. 12 (1974) pp. 403–416; J. Hamill, "The Labor Relations Practices of Foreign-owned and Indigenous Firms," *Employee Relations,* Vol. 5, No. 1 (1983) pp. 14–16; J. Hamill. "Multinational Corporations and Industrial Relations in the U.K.," *Employee Relations,* Vol. 6, No. 5 (1984) pp. 12–16.

12. Bean, *Comparative Industrial Relations.*

13. See J. La Palombara and S. Blank, *Multinational Corporations and National Elites: A Study of Tensions* (New York: The Conference Board, 1976); A. B. Sim, "Decentralized Management of Subsidiaries and Their

Performance: A Comparative Study of American, British and Japanese Subsidiaries in Malaysia," *Management International Review*, Vol. 17, No. 2 (1977) pp. 45–51; and Y. K. Shetty, "Managing the Multinational Corporation: European and American Styles," *Management International Review*, Vol. 19, No. 3 (1979) pp. 39–48.

14. See D. Bok, "Reflections on the Distinctive Character of American Labor Law," *Harvard Law Review*, Vol. 84 (1971) pp. 1394–1463; and *Employers Associations and Industrial Relations: A Comparative Study*, J. P. Windmuller and A. Gladstone, ed. (Oxford: Clarendon Press, 1984).

15. For a lucid discussion of the importance of understanding ideology, see G. C. Lodge, "Ideological Implications of Changes in Human Resource Management," in *HRM Trends and Challenges*, ed. R. E. Walton and P. R. Lawrence (Boston: Harvard Business School Press, 1985).

16. T. A. Kochan, R. B. McKersie, and P. Cappelli, "Strategic Choice and Industrial Relations Theory," *Industrial Relations*, Vol. 23, No. 1 (1984) pp. 16–39.

17. See Bean, *Comparative Industrial Relations*; Poole, *Industrial Relations*; and J. Visser, "Trade Unionism in Western Europe: Present Situation and Prospects," *Labour and Society*, Vol. 13, No. 2 (1988) pp. 125–182.

18. Hamill, "The Labor Relations Practices" and "Multinational Corporations"; and J. Hamill, "Labor Relations Decision-making Within Multinational Corporations," *Industrial Relations Journal*, Vol. 15, No. 2 (1984) pp. 30–34.

19. Hamill, "Labor Relations Decision-making."

20. Hamill, "Multinational Corporations."

21. Hamill, "Labor Relations Decision-making," p. 34.

22. This section is based in part on Chapter 5, "The Impact of Organized Labor," in Prahalad and Doz, *The Multinational Mission*.

23. Ibid.

24. Ibid., p. 102.

25. Kennedy, *European Labor Relations*.

26. R. Vernon, *Storm Over the Multinationals: The Real Issues* (Cambridge, Mass.: Harvard University Press, 1977).

27. For a detailed analysis of ITSs, see R. Neuhaus, *International Trade Secretariats: Objectives, Organization, Activities*, 2nd ed. (Bonn: Friedrich-Ebert-Stiftung, 1982).

28. N. Willatt, *Multinational Unions* (London: Financial Times, 1974).

29. H. R. Northrup, "Why Multinational Bargaining Neither Exists Nor Is Desirable," *Labor Law Journal*, Vol. 29, No. 6 (1978) pp. 330–342.

30. D. Blake, "Corporate Structure and International Unionism," *Columbia Journal of World Business*, Vol. 7, No. 2 (1972) pp. 19–26.

31. See Kennedy, *European Labor Relations*; and R. B. Helfgott, "American Unions and Multinational Enterprises: A Case of Misplaced Emphasis," *Columbia Journal of World Business*, Vol. 18, No. 2 (1983) pp. 81–86.

32. For example, see the following UNCTC reports: *Transborder Data Flows: Transnational Corporations and Remote-sensing Data* (New York, 1984); and *Transnational Corporations and International Trade: Selected Issues* (New York, 1985).

33. For a detailed description and analysis of the OECD Guidelines for Multinational Enterprises, see D. C. Campbell and R. L. Rowan, *Multinational Enterprises and the OECD Industrial Relations Guidelines.* Industrial Research Unit (Philadelphia: The Wharton School, University of Pennsylvania, 1983); and R. Blanpain, *The OECD Guidelines for Multinational Enterprises and Labour Relations, 1982–1984: Experiences and Review* (Deventer, The Netherlands: Kluwer, 1985).

34. Campbell and Rowan, *Multinational Enterprises and OECD.*

35. J. Rojot, "The 1984 Revision of the OECD Guidelines for Multinational Enterprises," *British Journal of Industrial Relations*, Vol. 23, No. 3 (1985) pp. 379–397.

36. For a detailed account of this case see R. Blanpain, *The Badger Case and the OECD Guidelines for Multinational Enterprises* (Deventer, The Netherlands: Kluwer, 1977).

37. R. Blanpain, *The OECD Guidelines for Multinational Enterprises and Labour Relations, 1976–1979: Experience and Review* (Deventer, The Netherlands: Kluwer, 1979).

38. H. C. Jain, "Disinvestment and the Multinational Employer—a Case History from Belgium," *Personnel Journal*, Vol. 59, No. 3 (1980) pp. 201–205.

39. Campbell and Rowan, *Multinational Enterprises and OECD.*

40. B. Liebhaberg, *Industrial Relations and Multinational Corporations in Europe* (London: Gower, 1980) p. 85.

41. G. W. Latta and J. R. Bellace, "Making the Corporation Transparent: Prelude to Multinational Bargaining," *Columbia Journal of World Business*, Vol. 18, No. 2 (1983) pp. 73–80.

42. For a detailed analysis of the Vredeling Directive, see D. Van Den Bulcke, "Decision Making in Multinational Enterprises and the Information and Consultation of Employees: The Proposed Vredeling Directive of the EC Commission," *International Studies of Management and Organization*, Vol. 14, No. 1 (1984) pp. 36–60.

43. J. Pickard, "Maastricht Deal Worries the Multinationals," *PM Plus*, January 1992, p. 4; and B. Fitzpatrick, "Community Social Law after Maastricht," *Industrial Law Journal*, Vol. 21, No. 3 (1992) pp. 199–213.

44. H. De Cieri and P. J. Dowling, "An Examination of the Implications of the Social Dimension for Entry of Australian Firms to the Single European

Market." Paper presented at the 17th Annual Meeting of the European International Business Association, Copenhagen, December 15–17, 1991, p. 2.

45. Commission of the European Communities, *Community Charter of the Fundamental Social Rights of Workers* (Luxembourg: Office for Official Publications of the European Communities, 1990) p. 20.

46. See, for example, J. Lodge, "Social Europe: Fostering a People's Europe?" in *European Community and the Challenge of the Future*, ed. J. Lodge (London: Pinter, 1989); and J. Addison and S. Siebert, "The Social Charter of the European Community: Evolution and Controversies," *Industrial and Labor Relations Review*, Vol. 44, No. 4 (1991) pp. 597–625.

47. D. R. Briscoe, "Coping with the Human Resource Implications of EC 1992," in *Proceedings of the Third Conference on International Personnel and HRM*, Vol. 1, ed. P. S. Kirkbride and B. Shaw, Ashridge (July, 1992).

48. F. Michon, "The 'European Social Community': A Common Model and Its National Variations? Segmentation Effects, Societal Effects," *Labour and Society*, Vol. 15, No. 2 (1990) pp. 215–236.

49. W. Nicoll and T. C. Salmon, *Understanding the European Community*, (Hertfordshire, U.K.: Philip Allan, 1990) p. 191.

50. "We Can Prevent Another Hoover," *The European*, February 4–7, 1993, p. 35.

51. "Hoover Has French Fuming at Vacuum," *The Times* (London) January 28, 1993, p. 27; "Hoover Workers Get Lump Sum For Deal," *Financial Times* (London) February 3, 1993, p. 9; and "Social Dumping: Hardly an Open and Shut Case," *Financial Times* (London) February 4, 1993, p. 2.

52. S. J. Silvia, "The Social Charter of the European Community: A Defeat for European Labor," *Industrial and Labor Relations Review*, Vol. 44, No. 4 (1991) pp. 626–643.

53. Society for Human Resource Management, *Briefing Paper on the North American Free Trade Agreement*, International Division, Institute of International Human Resources, Washington, D.C., January, 1993, p. 1.

54. J. D. Daniels and L. H. Radebaugh, *International Business: Environments and Operations*, 6th ed. (Reading, Mass.: Addison-Wesley, 1992) p. 426.

55. Society for Human Resource Management, *Briefing Paper*, p. 6.

56. P. Enderwick, "The Labor Utilization Practices of Multinationals and Obstacles to Multinational Collective Bargaining," *Journal of Industrial Relations*, Vol. 26, No. 3 (1984) p. 357.

57. Hamill, "The Labor Relations Practices"; "Multinational Corporations"; and "Labor Relations Decision-making."

Chapter E I G H T

Future Directions and Theoretical Developments in IHRM

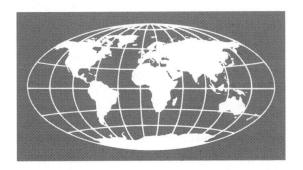

The aim of this book has been to explore the international dimensions of HRM through an examination of the human resource choices that confront multinational firms, the major factors to consider when making those choices, and the practices adopted as a consequence. In the process, we have examined the similarities and differences between domestic and international HRM and given attention to the major activities of recruitment and selection, training and development, performance appraisal, compensation, and labor relations. In this concluding chapter, we try to identify emerging trends and issues in IHRM that may help to shape the nature and direction of IHRM activities in the coming decade. We also discuss theoretical developments and requirements as the field of IHRM matures.

211

TRENDS AND FUTURE ISSUES IN IHRM

Continued Growth in the Recognition of the Importance of IHRM

Given that IHRM has only recently emerged as a field of inquiry within the HRM discipline, the progress made in the past decade reflects a growing recognition of the importance of HRM issues and practices as a critical success factor in the global arena. Accompanying this growing awareness has been a greater understanding of the international dimensions of HRM. For example, some of the major factors affecting staff availability, cultural adjustment and expatriate failure, and repatriation are now well documented. More companies are recognizing the implications of moving staff into other cultural settings, and helping to prepare the employee and family members for the international assignment has increasingly become an important activity for HR departments in international firms. However, there remains a need for further work in other areas, such as designing equitable performance appraisal criteria that take into account the variables that influence expatriate performance.

The size of the various chapters in this edition, therefore, reflects the degree of attention given both by companies and academics to the various areas of IHRM. However, the current imbalance in focus and attention is likely to shift as the field of IHRM grows, both as an area of academic study and as a strategically important area within international companies. As globalization forces continue to push more and more firms out into the international arena and competition accelerates, the emphasis on the HR function will continue to grow.

There are also encouraging signs that international HRM is beginning to come of age. As we noted in the epilogue to the first edition, the International Chapter of the Society for Human Resource Management (SHRM/I) and the Human Resource Planning Society are gaining recognition as key sources of expertise in the field, and the activities of the World Federation of Personnel Management Associations (WFPMA) continue to attract interest. In addition, the increasing number of international conferences and symposiums either entirely devoted to IHRM issues or as sessions within meetings of international professional associations such as the Academy of International Business, attest to the growing recognition being given to this area by professionals, scholars, and researchers alike.

Perhaps the most significant indicator of the growing recognition of the importance of IHRM is occurring in the workplace itself. Recent surveys of practitioners reveal that an organization's human resource capability is increasingly regarded by top management as a critical success factor. For example, the Korn Ferry International/Columbia University Graduate School of Business 1989 Global Survey[1] found that HRM skills and ability was ranked second (after strategy formulation) as an area of critical expertise required by the chief executive officer of the twenty-first century. A similar finding was noted in the 1990 Ashridge/Economist Intelligence Unit survey of U.S., Japanese, and European multinationals. One conclusion of this survey was that[2]

> the development of a transnational capability will depend greatly on a company's approach to international human resource management (HRM). Certainly, among the companies surveyed, international HRM issues, including management development, vie with customers, partnerships and organisation design as top priorities for the future.

Likewise, in a worldwide survey of human resource management conducted in 1992, IBM/Towers Perrin found that "65 percent of CEOs and 75 percent of HR executives see HR as critical to the success of business today and going up to 85 percent and 90 percent respectively by the year 2000."[3] Discussing the implications of the survey, Schuler points out the following:[4]

> The importance and centrality of the HR function in organizations has changed dramatically over the years. Most recently, it has gained in significance due to the rapid changes in the external environment. Changes in demographics and workforce characteristics, global economic and business conditions, legal and regulatory events, and technological developments have brought forth important challenges for many organizations. Because these challenges directly influence a firm's human resources and the organization's need to survive and be competitive, the HR function has become more important than ever.

Schuler concludes that, for worldwide competitiveness, firms will need world-class HR departments, characterized as:

- responsive to a highly competitive marketplace amid global business structures
- closely linked to business strategic plans
- jointly conceived and implemented by line and HR managers
- focused on quality, customer service, productivity, employee involvement, teamwork, and workforce flexibility

Such an approach requires the HR department to work more closely with line management. In some firms, some HR activities are being devolved, with line managers retaking control of the HR function as they realize that many people, events, and concerns are really business issues. In other firms, HR managers are becoming important members of the management team.

A concurrent and related trend is that the concept of strategic HRM appears to have gained momentum, in both the domestic and the international arenas.[5] As part of a response to the dynamic environment, some organizations are involving the HRM function at the corporate strategy level in recognition that human-related considerations can be critically important to organizational success. Proponents of strategic HRM advocate the inclusion of HRM implications at the policy-formulation stage, a compelling proposal in relation to expatriate management. As was discussed in Chapter 2, the literature links HRM issues with the growth of the international firm. As a multinational evolves from simple foreign operations (such as exporting) to foreign direct investment and the establishment of worldwide subsidiaries, its staffing requirements change. In other words, a shift in strategic direction requires HRM responses, and these will be proactive and effective only if IHRM implications are included in the strategy-formulation stage.[6]

The Need to Develop an International Perspective

In Chapter 1, we included "attitudes of senior management to international operations" as an important variable with respect to the development of international HR skills and capability in a firm. Given that the globalization trend is likely to continue, the challenge will be for firms to develop outward-looking executives at all levels of the organization, so that decisions are based on information with as wide a perspective as possible. Carrott[7] argues that, to succeed, global businesses and alliances require management with a different mindset, and this applies to the board of directors as well as the chief executive officer (CEO) and the senior executive team. This wider point of view is necessary if management is to expand the policy-making perspective of the corporation. Carrott points out that, presently, the composition of most boards of directors of MNEs, particularly those headquartered in the United States, remains parochial. To counter this, some companies have attempted to widen the perspective of their boards by attracting former U.S. cabinet officers to serve on their boards or have established regional advisory boards.

Given the importance of the key decision maker in formulating corporate policy, organizations that are driven by internationally focused CEOs are most likely to succeed. However, there is a risk associated with the creation of a global mindset at the top only, or among a select group of people.[8] The broad international outlook is required at all levels of the global organization. Policy needs to be converted into action. The business and functional levels tend to be where strategic choices are implemented, so it is important that the organization also develop internationally aware managers at these strategic levels. According to Spivey and Thomas,[9] to survive in the current competitive environment the firm itself, including operations management, must "globalize":

> Financial management, marketing, management and product development, quality management and its fuller integration into operations at all levels, and many other functional activities which previously had been approached with a domestic mindset, must now reflect these competitive influences and be absorbed into what is called a global mindset.

As Bartlett and Ghoshal[10] contend, in order to achieve global integration yet maintain local flexibility, it is necessary to have an appreciation of the entire global network of affiliates as well as headquarters operations. They point out that one effective way of ensuring such a global appreciation is to transfer staff throughout the global network. Kobrin supports this view. In his discussion of an identified trend among U.S. multinationals to reduce their use of expatriates, Kobrin[11] argues the dangers of such a policy—reduced identification with the global difficulties, and the lack of opportunities for Americans to gain international experience through overseas assignments. However, as we highlighted in the first chapter of this book, it is possible to identify organizations, such as AT&T Europe, Colgate-Palmolive, IBM, Rank Xerox, and Dow Chemical, that are attempting to achieve this international perspective among their staffs.[12] A recent study of sixty-nine European MNEs by Oddou and Derr[13] examined the strategies adopted by respondent firms for the internationalization of their managers. A variety of methods were identified by the authors of the study. The most common were expatriation, international seminars, and travel (which was not clearly defined, but implies brief visits to foreign operations). The organization's capacity and commitment to enhancing managerial mobility is a key factor for success, and its approach to HRM activities will reflect this.[14] The challenge here is to align staffing practices with the overall strategic direction of the firm. This applies equally to small- and medium-sized firms as well as to emerging transnationals.

The IHRM Implications of the Changing Global Marketplace

Recent political and economic events have significant implications for international business, and the way that organizations seek to cope with these changes will affect the HR function. In fact, these changes add another dimension to IHRM.

1. Emerging Democracies of Eastern Europe and the Former Soviet Union

The rapid collapse of communism in the past two years is a dramatic reminder of the volatility and complexity of the global marketplace in which firms have to compete.[15] The emerging democracies of Eastern Europe and the former Soviet Union require assistance from the industrialized nations as they move from state-run enterprises to privately owned companies. There has already been great demand on management skills, and firms entering these new markets are beginning to recognize the management challenges involved, especially the deficiency of trained managers who possess a capitalistic mode of thinking.

Western firms entering these countries have quickly recognized that the HRM systems we are familiar with do not exist in these countries, since, in a command economy HR issues are essentially *political* issues. People who have not visited a communist country often have difficulty comprehending the level of intrusion of the political process into the functioning of all types of organizations in a command economy. Perhaps one of the best depictions of this level of intrusion can be found in Tom Clancy's novel *The Hunt for Red October.* The opening chapter describes the start of the first cruise of the submarine *Red October,* as Captain First Rank Marko Ramius of the Soviet Navy opens his sealed orders in the required presence of Captain Second Rank Ivan Putin, the submarine's political officer, whose primary role is to monitor the political loyalty of Ramius and the rest of the crew. Needless to say, Putin is despised by most of the crew, who, when Putin is killed, readily accept the explanation offered by Ramius that Putin broke his neck by slipping on a wet floor!

This form of dual control by line managers and political masters operates throughout a command economy and is perhaps the major reason why, even at a local or enterprise level, there is little opportunity or reward for managers to take the initiative on even minor issues. Managers who have been conditioned by this system often find it difficult to think beyond the parameters of their limited experience. Thus, the shortage of trained managers in these emerging democracies reflects more than simply a skills shortage. There is a shortage of managers who have had the opportunity to exercise managerial prerogatives and discretion. Consequently, management and management development, are seen in very narrow terms, and the effective management of people is rather low on the agenda compared to areas such as production management, finance, and marketing. Naturally, this narrow focus on the most basic aspects of a market economy reflects, in part, the urgent need to begin a process of privatization. Only when this process is well under way will any attention be given to the issues that have dominated management thought in the West for the last decade: how to increase productivity and quality by more effective management of the physical, financial, and human resources within organizations.

Staffing new ventures in these transforming economies will be a challenge for U.S., western European, Scandinavian, and Japanese multinationals and place special demands on the skills of those expatriates selected to oversee such ventures. Some Western companies are already coming to terms with these challenges. A case in point is the General Electric (GE)–Tungsram venture.[16] In 1989, GE purchased a 75-percent equity in Tungsram, a Hungarian light bulb producer. Staffing played a key role in developing the venture. GE assigned its own manager (who was Hungarian-born, emigrated to the United States in 1956, and spent his working life with GE) to install Western management systems and the GE corporate culture. As well, key executives from the United States were transferred on short-term assignments, and local staff were trained in Western management techniques. This strategy was complemented with visits of Hungarian managers to GE plants in the United States, exposing them to the GE work environment and corporate culture as well as life in a Western country.

Selecting and training local staff can be a time-consuming and expensive task, but it is an issue that MNEs must resolve if they wish to be successful. As the IHR in the News item in Exhibit 8-1 shows, compensation and retention of key local staff are ongoing issues for MNEs.

2. The Single European Market

According to Bournois and Chauchat "human resources will be of paramount importance in helping companies reduce some of the major uncertainties brought about by the Single Market."[17] In 1990, these authors conducted more than forty interviews with human resource directors and managing directors of large European companies and found that the

E X H I B I T   8 - 1   IHR in the News

Ex-pats and Poles Apart

Three years after the collapse of communism in Poland, managers recruited locally by foreign companies are experiencing the frustrations of reporting to expatriate superiors.

There are at least 1,000 locally-recruited Polish managers working for foreign companies. By offering high salaries (by local standards) the foreign companies were able to cream off the best of the experienced managerial talent as well as attract young graduates.

But one expatriate management consultant says: "The younger staff are beginning to get bored now that they have learned the jobs that they were taken on to do."

Marius Bialek, from H Neumann, an Austrian management consulting company, says: "I know there is something wrong when good people I recruited a year ago come to me looking for another job."

He believes some frustration will be alleviated by sending the more talented managers to run new offices elsewhere in eastern Europe. As for those who leave, few are likely to seek jobs with Polish-owned companies. Instead they will look to other multinationals.

One reason is pay. A senior executive working for a Polish company earns about $12,000 (£7,900) a year although top salaries can go as high as $80,000. Foreign companies pay between $28,000 and $72,000 to locally-recruited senior executives. That contrasts, however, with the $60,000 to $200,000 a year their expatriate colleagues and superiors are earning.

But the era of the expatriate manager in Poland may be limited. Gaspol, for example, is a joint venture between a number of Polish liquified petroleum gas distributors and the UK's Calor group, Primagaz of France and SHV from Holland.

Bob West, the managing director, says "The four expatriates in place should be out of here in three years. After all, I shall never know the market, the language and the country as well as the local people."

Christopher Bobinski

Source: Financial Times (London), December 7, 1992, p. 13. Reprinted with permission.

human dimension was not overlooked. On the contrary, the management of human resources was assigned a significant role in the strategic process (the finance function was cited half as often as the HR function).[18]

As discussed in Chapter 7, the 1990 Charter of Fundamental Social Rights places specific demands on organizations operating within the Single European Market (SEM), especially with regard to employee involvement in consultation and decision making, freedom of association and collective bargaining, and health and safety standards. While Britain has been exempted from some aspects of the Social Charter, the likely inclusion of Sweden and Finland (with their long history of social welfare) as members of the SEM is likely to strengthen support for the Social Charter. Therefore, organizations that have not encouraged worker participation programs will find it necessary to develop management styles that foster such participation. For some U.S. firms operating in Europe, this change will pose a major challenge, while those that have been implementing changes in their workplace to empower workers will find conforming to the European directives an easy transition.

The Single European Market, with the removal of work permit requirements, should permit freer movement of staff throughout the member states. However, HRM practices will still retain local variation in areas such as selection and promotion. Outplacement (firing) procedures will need to conform to local laws regarding severance pay, for example. There will also be pressure for multinationals to generate HR information systems, as Briscoe notes:[19]

> It will be difficult to generate meaningful, comparable data across national borders when procedures for reporting new hires or terminations, the approval process for hiring or promotions, or the process for sending personnel files when an employee transfers from one location to another vary so much (and when there is still a lack of agreement between EC countries on what data can be freely transmitted from one country to another).

The full ramifications of all the proposed changes will not appear for some time, but it is apparent even now that there are definite implications for the HR department as well as for the multinational, whether it is European-based or not. In the short term, firms may take a regiocentric approach to staffing and develop "Euromanagers," but there is a danger that limiting staff transfers to European operations may result in a pool of talent capable of appreciating things European but not available for transfer to operations outside of that region.[20] As we have previously discussed, organizations need to develop international operators so that there is the required depth of managerial skills to support the globalization of international operations, especially to capitalize on the growth occurring in Southeast Asia.

3. The Growth of the Asia-Pacific Region

The rise of Japan as a leading player in the world economy, and the reasons for the success of Japanese firms in the international marketplace, are now well documented. One could argue that the influence Japan has had upon Western (especially U.S.) approaches to management has been greatest in the area of production techniques such as quality circles, just-in-time inventory, and robotics—all of which have had HR implications for firms that have attempted to implement such techniques in their own enterprise workplace. The companies that have been successful in transplanting Japanese approaches appear to be those prepared to invest the necessary time and resources into changing managerial-worker relationships from an adversarial to a cooperative one and to adapt Japanese techniques to suit the specific and unique characteristics of the organization. In these cases, HR practices have been aligned to support these changes.[21]

Japanese corporations have had their IHRM challenges too. For example, in our discussion of expatriation management, we have seen that the challenges facing Japanese corporations in the movement of staff throughout the global enterprise have been similar to those encountered by U.S. and European multinationals, especially in the areas of cross-cultural adjustment and repatriation. Though Japanese companies have been successful in transplanting their approaches to production and procurement (e.g., "just-in-time"), it has been more difficult for these companies to transfer some of their personnel approaches. The HR function tends to conform to local responsiveness. For example, Kumar[22] found that recruitment and selection of German personnel to work in Japanese subsidiaries follows, by and large, German practices, and that the Japanese expatriates often experience difficulties performing HR activities such as conducting employment interviews, due to differing expectations. Industrial relations is another area where the Japanese have encountered implementation difficulties. Kumar points out that Japanese managers view many German rules and regulations as barriers to effective human resource management.

Japanese multinationals also have expanded their operations into neighboring newly industrialized countries (NICs), such as Singapore and Indonesia, as well as into the developing economies of China and Vietnam. As has been the case with U.S. and European multinationals, lower wage rates have been a primary reason for Japanese firms to establish production facilities in these countries.[23] The *World Labour Report 1992* notes that, in contrast to MNEs (multinational enterprises) from the other advanced economies, Japanese MNEs have a majority of their employees (62 percent) in developing countries.[24]

For Western multinationals operating in Asia, the cultural differences can be profound, especially where HR practices are concerned. For example, one Australian multinational hired a Malay who had studied in Australia to be personnel manager of its first production facility in Malaysia. The company assumed that he would be more appropriate than an Australian, given his knowledge of local customs regarding hiring staff. While the Malay handled that aspect of his job adequately, there were repeated complaints regarding the food in the staff canteen, which was also under the control of the personnel manager. Puzzled by the personnel manager's apparent reluctance to dismiss the canteen manager, the managing director investigated and discovered that, in line with local custom, the personnel manager had taken the canteen manager as his second wife.[25]

Daniels and Radebaugh[26] also warn of the social constraints that Western firms can encounter when operating subsidiaries in Southeast Asian countries, and cite the example of a U.S. firm that set up a plant in Taiwan without realizing that the class structure, built largely on the military hierarchy, would affect their hiring practices. "The U.S. managers hired the person they considered most qualified to head the organization. In practice, however, this individual consistently deferred to a subordinate who had outranked him during their military experience."

These simple examples demonstrate the critical importance of adequate cultural awareness training (which includes language skills) before assigning Western staff to Asian-Pacific countries.

4. IHRM as a Critical Success Factor in Interfirm Linkages

As we briefly discussed in Chapter 2, there are distinct HRM implications arising from the trend toward various forms of interfirm linkages, and we pointed out that these implications vary, depending upon the type of alliance involved. As it is likely that this trend will continue, it is important to examine the HRM implications in more depth. To do this, we have elected to explore the international joint venture (IJV). This form is perhaps the most challenging interfirm linkage to manage, as it involves greater interaction among people from the collaborating companies, with equity partly owned by another firm, usually from the relevant host country. At the same time, an examination of the IJV illustrates the general HR challenges arising from interfirm linkages.[27]

The major force behind the growing use of international joint ventures appears to be the quest for improving a firm's competitive advantage in the face of increasing global competition. The motives for entering into such an arrangement are many and varied, but a major reason is to spread the risks. However, as many firms soon discover, forming an IJV creates a risk in itself, and it is perhaps not surprising to find a high failure rate—some U.S. studies, for example, record 50 percent of IJVs failing, while others put the figure as high as 70 percent.[28] Consequently, writers in this area stress the importance of building up a relationship between the partners that will encourage cooperation and trust.

Success seems to come down to an ability to balance "the desire and need to control the venture on the one hand, and the need to maintain harmonious relations with the partner(s) on the other hand."[29] Likewise, the factors attributed to the failure of a joint venture are most frequently human-related—poor judgments, actual human behavioral errors, or unanticipated staffing events.[30] It would appear from this brief review of the literature that the very nature of the joint venture contributes to its failure, but it is not the form itself that is to blame. The failure may be the result of poor timing or poor planning; or forming a joint venture may not have been the best thing for the partners to do; or, simply, the wrong partner may have been selected.[31] That is, success depends on recognizing the difficulty and complexity in managing this form of enterprise and in handling these obstacles with skill and sensitivity. There are three major areas that may become obstacles if not addressed appropriately.

Control   Some firms fail to realize that equity is only one aspect of control. Often, the actual control of the operation depends on who is responsible for its day-to-day management. Harrigan[32] argues that ownership of distribution matters less than how the operating control and the various parties' participation in decision making is apportioned. Control can be obtained through the use of managers who are loyal to the parent company and its organizational ethos. However, questions of loyalty may still arise. "The ability to appoint the joint venture general manager increases the chances that the parents' interests will be observed, but it is no guarantee that the joint venture general manager will always accommodate that parent's preferences."[33] Also, top managers can face considerable role conflicts, and this may impede their ability to perform effectively.

Business and Cultural Differences   To be successful, working relationships must be established on mutual trust and respect, as control is easiest and most effective if a good working relationship prevails.[34] Managers must work to create this atmosphere if the joint venture is to be successful, yet this may be difficult to achieve if business and cultural differences are not appreciated. Datta[35] feels that many of the problems and misunderstandings in IJVs have their roots in cultural differences. For example, one party may favor a participative managerial style while the other believes in a more autocratic style of management. Another area is acceptance of risk taking. The MNE parent may be prepared to take more risks than the smaller, local partner. These differences often make the process of decision making slow and frustrating. The resulting conflict can be dysfunctional, if not destructive.

Differing Goals   In order to operate in some markets, many firms are forced to accept joint ownership, despite their preference for complete control.[36] Each of the parents, and the resultant "child," has its unique goals and operation mode, anchored in different national or cultural environments. An incongruence of interest may be the result, particularly when one of the parents is the host government and the foreign firm is forced into the IJV by necessity. The local partner, for example, may be concerned only with local strategies, where lower standards may suffice, while the foreign multinational parent may be concerned with global strategies that maintain its global image and reputation.[37] As Datta[38] states,

> Impediments to implementation and management can also arise out of the incongruencies in the goals of the venture partners or differences in perceptions regarding the strategic importance of the joint venture partner. The commitment of each partner is a function of the importance that the partner attaches to the project and, when such commitments differ significantly, management of the joint venture can be fraught with problems.

Thus, the level of commitment by the parties to the IJV is a contributing factor to either success or failure and, because of this, the selection of the joint venture partner is crucial.[39] As Lei and Slocum[40] point out:

One of the most difficult things for managers to remember is that joint ventures actually represent another form of competition: Venture partners are simultaneously competitors and collaborators. Many Japanese firms enter into joint ventures with partners they intend to compete fully with in other products and services.

HRM Issues   From our discussion of the management challenges for IJVs, it is evident that selecting the right key people is critical to success. As Shenkar and Zeira[41] point out, "Not all management and human resource problems in IJVs described in the literature are unique to that type of enterprise. Many occur also in other types of international settings." What differs is the *intensity* and *frequency* of these problems. Reviewing the available literature, Shenkar and Zeira identified staffing, promotion, loyalty, delegation, decision making, unfamiliarity, communication, information, and compensation as key areas of concern in joint ventures, but these authors also commented on the scant attention given to human resource issues in the joint venture literature. Although studies that address HR implications are relatively sparse, some writers do address human resource implications. For example, Lorange[42] includes performance evaluation and career and benefits planning in his list of success factors, and concludes that the IJV must have its own, strong, full-fledged human resource management function that has clear methods of working closely with each parent, particularly in the early years. Two major roles are assigned by Lorange to this function: (a) to assign and motivate people (via job skills, compatibility of styles, communication compatibility); and (b) to manage human resources strategically, so that the IJV is seen as a vehicle to produce not only financial rewards, but also managerial capabilities that can be used later in other strategic settings.

In their discussion of HRM issues, Lei and Slocum[43] consider three key aspects:

a. Training and developing managers in negotiation and conflict-resolution skills. It is important that managers learn how to effectively resolve the unexpected issues and problems inherent in the joint venture arrangement. Third-party consultation and integrative negotiation are two techniques suggested to defuse conflict-laden situations.

b. Managers also need to become acculturated to working with a foreign partner. For instance, American managers need to understand the role of "implicit communication" when dealing with counterparts from countries where this style is part of the culture.

c. The harmonization of management styles is essential. The joint venture ideally should be staffed with managers who are flexible in terms of different management styles and philosophies. This requirement adds an additional and somewhat crucial dimension to the issue of staff selection, particularly for expatriate staff.

Lei and Slocum add that careering-pathing managers through the IJV is one way managers and technical personnel can learn and share new skills.

Perhaps the most recent specific treatment in this emerging area of international business and HRM is that offered by Cascio and Serapio.[44] Their research recounts the results of a three-year study of four international alliances in the United States and the monitoring of several others. The authors not only address the usual HR issues of recruitment and staffing, performance appraisal, compensation and benefits, but add a discussion on job design and orientation and training of the alliance's new hires and current employees. Career issues and labor-management relations are also addressed.

Studies like those we have reviewed highlight the challenges in managing interfirm linkages, particularly the international joint venture. A focus on the HRM issues explored in this section is one way to enhance the probability of success.

5. Ethics and Social Responsibility Issues

Recently, there has been a "rediscovery" of business ethics, reflected in the inclusion of courses on this subject in business schools. It is not our intention to enter into the debate surrounding the teaching of business ethics. It is, rather, to draw out the implications of operating in different cultural and social environments and to stress the need to develop policies to assist staff who make decisions that have ethical and moral consequences.

Some MNEs neglect to issue policy and behavioral guidelines for expatriate, TCN, and local staff, opting consciously or by default to leave ethical considerations up to the individual. This policy not only may contribute to the pressures of operating in a foreign environment (and perhaps contribute to poor performance or early recall of the expatriate), but it also leads to internal inconsistencies that affect total global performance. More aware MNEs recognize that the onus is on the firm to develop ethical guidelines or codes of conduct, that assist all employees. For example, one Australian MNE that has subsidiary operations in Southeast Asia, Europe, and North America has a code of conduct that prohibits employees from engaging in bribery. This consistent policy is well advertised to staff and clients and is considered to lessen the possibilities of employees being placed in situations in which a bribe may be expected.

As mentioned in Chapter 4, the U.S. Foreign Corrupt Practices Act (FCPA) was amended in 1988. The FCPA addresses the problem of questionable foreign payments by MNEs and their managers.[45] Given the strong positions taken by governments on ethical behavior, it is important that all staff are fully briefed on their responsibilities in this regard. In this task, the HR function may play an important role.

The requirement that corporations behave in a socially responsible manner will continue as concern for the world environment grows. Pressure on governments from strong, vocal, lobby groups is increasing, and there has been much debate about the role of developed countries in helping the developing nations industrialize yet protect rain forests and other resources. One response has been sustainable development management: an attempt to balance environmental protection with economic growth. It places a requirement on corporate managers to include long-range environmental considerations in their strategic formulation and implementation activities. In fact, the United Nations Centre on Transnational Corporations (UNCTC) has produced a list of criteria to assist transnationals to contribute to environmentally sustainable development.[46] Three of these criteria have direct implications for the HR function: educating staff on this issue; linking rewards to the exposure of problems or discovery of new environmentally sound products and processes; and including progress in this area in the evaluation of subsidiary performance.

It would appear that ethics and social responsibility issues will continue to place pressure on companies operating internationally and will require appropriate policy responses.

THEORETICAL DEVELOPMENTS

As we pointed out at the beginning of this chapter, there is a greater understanding of the international dimensions of HRM. A contributing factor is that a theoretical base is beginning to emerge. The early studies into IHRM concentrated on the perspectives of HR managers and expatriates. This focus was a logical starting point for a scientific field in its infancy, and the studies were significant in that they identified the HRM activities involved in the effective management of expatriates: selection, training and development, compensation and repatriation. Recently developed theoretical models (such as the one proposed by Mendenhall, Dunbar, and Oddou discussed in Chapter 5) continue this valuable development of knowledge of these important activities, which help companies to formulate and implement effective HRM programs and policies.

Despite this progress, as Laurent[47] comments, many questions about the interrelationships between HRM and other aspects of international business remain. There is still a need for further research that extends beyond the HRM activities covered in this book to develop a well-grounded, holistic theory.[48] While third-country nationals may be included in the expatriate category, to date there has been little attention given to effective management of local national employees in the IHRM literature. Further work in this area should draw on the growing body of literature in the fields of cross-cultural and comparative management.

Another important point here is that, as we discussed in Chapter 2, HRM activities do not occur in a vacuum but are influenced by organizational and environmental factors. It would seem that the IHRM activities of selection, training and development, and compensation discussed in this book are related to the company's management-staffing philosophy, but what is not yet clear is what factors determine that staffing philosophy. Research studies that place IHRM activities in the context in which they occur are required so that interrelationships between the HR function and organizational and environmental factors can be more fully understood.

Work linking organizational life cycles and strategic IHRM is assisting this process, and further research that explores IHRM, the organization, and its environment will contribute to the development of a more holistic theoretical base. Recent papers by Kochan, Batt, and Dyer,[49] Welch,[50] and Schuler, Dowling, and De Cieri[51] use these broader concepts and represent the direction that future research is likely to take— thus moving IHRM as a field of scientific inquiry out of its infant state.

NOTES

1. This survey was reported in an article by L. B. Korn, "How the Next CEO Will Be Different," *Fortune*, May 22, 1989, pp. 111–113.

2. K. Barham and M. Devine, *The Quest for the International Manager: A Survey of Global Human Resource Strategies*, Ashridge Management Research

Group, Special Report #2098, The Economist Intelligence Unit, 1990, p. 8.

3. *A Twenty-first Century Vision: A Worldwide Human Resource Study*, (New York: Towers Perrin, 1992).

4. R. S. Schuler, "World Class HR Departments: Six Critical Issues" (New York: Stern School of Business, New York University, 1992).

5. R. S. Schuler, P. J. Dowling, and H. De Cieri, "An Integrative Framework of Strategic International Human Resource Management," *Yearly Review Journal of Management*, September, 1993.

6. See D. Welch, "The Personnel Variable in International Business Operations" (Doctoral thesis, Monash University, Melbourne, Australia, 1990).

7. G. T. Carrott, "The International Company and Its Parochial Board," *Focus* (Egon Zehnder International), Vol. 1 (1991) pp. 11–14.

8. Barham and Devine, *The Quest for the International Manager*.

9. W. A. Spivey and L. D. Thomas, "Global Management: Concepts, Themes, Problems and Research Issues." *Human Resource Management*, Vol. 29, No. 1 (1990), p. 89.

10. C. A. Bartlett and S. Ghoshal, "Managing Across Borders: New Strategic Requirements," *Sloan Management Review*, Summer, 1987, pp. 7–17; see also S. Ghoshal and C. A. Bartlett, "The Multinational Corporation as an Interorganizational Network," *Academy of Management Review*, Vol. 15, No. 4 (1990) pp. 603–625; and C. A. Bartlett and S. Ghoshal, "What Is a Global Manager?" *Harvard Business Review*, September–October, 1992, pp. 124–132.

11. S. Kobrin, "Expatriate Reduction and Strategic Control in American Multinational Corporations," *Human Resource Management*, Vol. 27, No. 1 (1988) pp. 63–75.

12. These examples are taken from *Developing Effective Global Managers for the 1990s* (New York: Business International, 1991).

13. G. Oddou and C. B. Derr, "European MNC Strategies for Internationalizing Managers: Current and Future Trends," in *Proceedings of the Third Conference on International Personnel and Human Resource Management*, Vol. 1, ed. P. S. Kirkbride and B. Shaw, Ashridge Management College, Britain (July, 1992).

14. D. Welch "Maintaining Globalization Momentum by Developing an Effective Geocentric Staffing Policy," in *An Enlarged Europe in the Global Economy: Proceedings of the Seventeenth Annual Conference of the European International Business Association*, ed. H. Vestugaard, Copenhagen (December, 1991) pp. 123–152.

15. This section of the chapter draws on material from P. J. Dowling, "Human Resource Management Systems in Eastern Europe," paper presented at symposium, *From a Command Economy to a Demand Economy: Emerging Issues in Operations and Human Resource Management in Eastern Europe*, Annual meeting of the Academy of Management, Miami, Florida (1991).

16. "Tungsram's Leading Light," *International Management*, December 1992, pp. 42–45.

17. F. Bournois and J-H. Chauchat, "Managing Managers in Europe," *European Management Journal*, Vol. 8, No. 1 (1990) pp. 3–18.

18. See also C. Brewster and H. Larsen, "HRM in Europe: Evidence from Ten Countries," *International Journal of Human Resource Management*, Vol. 3, No. 3 (1992) pp. 409–434.

19. D. R. Briscoe, "Coping with the Human Resource Implications of EC 1992," in *Proceedings of the Third Conference on International Personnel and Human Resource Management*, Vol. 1, ed. P. S. Kirkbride and B. Shaw (July, 1992) Ashridge Management College, Britain (No pagination given); see also R. B. Sambharya and A. Phatak, "The Effect of Transborder Data Flow Restrictions on American Multinational Corporations," M*anagement International Review*, Vol. 30, No. 3 (1990) pp. 267–289.

20. Welch, "Maintaining Globalization."

21. See, for example, J. R. Lincoln, "Employee Work Attitudes and Management Practice in the U.S. and Japan: Evidence from a Large Comparative Survey," *California Management Review*, Fall 1989, pp. 89–106; and N. Oliver and A. Davies, "Adopting Japanese-Style Manufacturing Methods: A Tale of Two (UK) Factories," *Journal of Management Studies*, Vol. 27, No. 5 (1990) pp. 555–570.

22. N. Kumar, "Japanese Direct Investments in Germany: Trends, Strategies and Management Problems," in J. Duran (ed.) *Proceedings of the Sixteenth Annual Conference of the European International Business Association*, ed. J. Duran, Madrid (December, 1990) (pages unnumbered).

23. R. Thompson, "Japanese Investors Forced to Watch Bottom Line," *Financial Times* (London), December 9, 1992, p. 6.

24. International Labour Office, *World Labour Report 1992* (Geneva) p. 49.

25. Personal interview with the managing director concerned. Local sensitivity and a confidentiality request prevents company identification.

26. J. D. Daniels and L. H. Radebaugh, *International Dimensions of Contemporary Business* (Boston: PWS-KENT, 1993).

27. This section is based on three articles by the authors and others:

P. J. Dowling, D. E. Welch, and H. De Cieri, "International Joint Ventures: A New Challenge for Human Resource Management," in *Proceedings of the Fifteenth Annual Conference of the European International Business Association*, Vol. 2, ed. R. Luostarinen, Helsinki (December, 1989) pp. 1196–1221.

R. S. Schuler, S. E. Jackson, P. J. Dowling, D. E. Welch, and H. De Cieri, "Formation of an International Joint Venture: Davidson Instrument Panel," *Human Resource Planning*, Vol. 14, No. 1 (1991) pp. 51–60.

R. S. Schuler, P. J. Dowling, and H. De Cieri. "The Formation of an International Joint Venture: Marley Automotive Components," *European Management Journal*, Vol. 10, No. 3 (1992) pp. 304–309.

28. M. A. Lyles, "Common Mistakes of Joint Venture Experienced Firms," *Columbia Journal of World Business*, Vol. 22, No. 2 (1987) pp. 79–85; K. R. Harrigan, *Managing for Joint Venture Success* (Boston: Lexington Books, 1986); J. B. Levine and J. A. Byrne, "Corporate Odd Couples," *Business Week*, July 21, 1986, pp. 100–105.

29. J-L Schaan, "How to Control a Joint Venture Even as a Minority Partner," *Journal of General Management*, Vol. 14, No. 1 (1988) p. 5. For a summary of the literature on success factors, see P. Lorange and G. J. B. Probst, "Joint Ventures as Self-organizing Systems: A Key to Successful Joint Venture Design and Implementation," *Columbia Journal of World Business*, Vol. 22, No. 2 (1987) pp. 71–77.

30. M. A. Lyles, "Common Mistakes of Joint Venture Experienced Firms," p. 80.

31. B. Gomaz-Casserres, "Joint Ventures in the Face of Global Competition," *Sloan Management Review*, Spring 1989, pp. 17–25. See also, D. Morris and M. Hergert, "Trends in International Collaborative Agreements," *Columbia Journal of World Business*, Vol. 22, No. 2, (1987) pp. 15–21.

32. K. R. Harrigan, *Managing for Joint Venture Success*.

33. J-L Schaan, "How to Control a Joint Venture," p. 14. See also O. Shenkar and Y. Zeira, "International Joint Ventures: Implications for Organization Development," *Personnel Review*, Vol. 16, No. 1 (1987) pp. 30–37.

34. J-L Schaan, "How to Control a Joint Venture"; see also N. M. Tichy, "Setting the Global Human Resource Agenda for the 1990's," *Human Resource Management*, Vol. 27, No. 1 (1988) pp. 1–18.

35. D. K. Datta, "International Joint Ventures: A Framework for Analysis," *Journal of General Management*, Vol. 14, No. 2 (1988) pp. 78–91.

36. O. Shenkar and Y. Zeira, "International Joint Ventures," p. 30.

37. B. Gomaz-Casserres, "Joint Ventures in the Face of Global Competition."

38. D. K. Datta, "International Joint Ventures: A Framework for Analysis," p. 88.

39. J. F. Bere, "Global Partnering: Making a Good Match," *Directors and Boards*, Vol. 11, No. 2 (1987) p. 16.

40. D. Lei and J. W. Slocum, "Global Strategic Alliances: Payoffs and Pitfalls," *Organizational Dynamics*, Winter 1991, pp. 44–62.

41. O. Shenkar and Y. Zeira, "International Joint Ventures," p. 32.

42. P. Lorange, "Human Resource Management in Multinational Cooperative Joint Ventures," *Human Resource Management*, Vol. 25, No. 10 (1986) pp. 133–148.

43. D. Lei and J. W. Slocum, "Global Strategic Alliances."

44. W. F. Cascio and M. G. Serapio, "Human Resource Systems in an International Alliance: The Undoing of a Done Deal?" *Organizational Dynamics*, Winter 1991, pp. 63–74.

45. For further analysis of the FCPA, see O. R. Gray, "The Foreign Corrupt Practices Act: Revisited and Amended," *Business and Society*, Spring 1990, pp. 11–17; and W. Bottiglieri, M. Marder, and E. S. Paderon, "The Foreign Corrupt Practices Act: Disclosure Requirements and Management Integrity," *SAM Advanced Management Journal*, Winter 1991, pp. 21–27.

46. United Nations Centre on Transnational Corporations, Environmental Unit, *Criteria for Sustainable Development* (New York, 1990).

47. A. Laurent, "The Cross-Cultural Puzzle of International Human Resource Management," *Human Resource Management*, Vol. 25, No. 1 (1986) pp. 91–102.

48. D. Welch, "Determinants of IHRM Approaches and Activities: A Suggested Framework," *Journal of Management Studies* (forthcoming).

49. T. A. Kochan, R. Batt, and L. Dyer, "International Human Resource Studies: A Framework for Future Research," in D. Lewin, O. Mitchell, and P. Sherer, *Research Frontiers in Industrial Relations and Human Resources*," (Madison: Industrial Relations Research Association, University of Wisconsin, 1992) pp. 309–337.

50. D. Welch, "Determinants of IHRM approaches and activities."

51. R. S. Schuler, P. J. Dowling, and H. De Cieri, "An Integrative Framework."

Appendix

Research Issues in International HRM

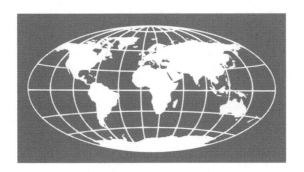

In this text we have frequently commented that there is a scarcity of international research (in HRM and the field of management generally) to assist managers and HRM practitioners. There are a number of reasons for this lack of international research. First, the field of international management has in the past been regarded as a marginal academic area by many management researchers. As Schollhammer[1] has noted, much of the field of international management has been criticized as (1) descriptive and lacking in analytical rigor, (2) ad hoc and expedient in research design and planning, (3) self-centered in the sense that the existing research literature is frequently ignored, and (4) lacking a sustained research effort to develop case material.

A second reason for the lack of international research is cost. International studies are invariably more expensive than domestic studies, and this is a liability for international researchers in a competitive research funding environment.[2] In addition, international research takes more time, involves more travel, and frequently requires the cooperation of host-country organizations, government officials, and researchers. Development of a stream of research is consequently much more difficult.

Third, there are major methodological problems involved in the area of international management. These problems greatly increase the complexity of doing international research and, as Adler[3] has noted, frequently are impossible to solve with the rigor usually required of within-culture studies by journal editors and reviewers. The major methodological problems in this area are (1) defining culture, (2) the emic-etic distinction, (3) static group comparisons, and (4) translation and stimulus equivalence. The problems of defining culture and the emic-etic distinction were discussed in Chapter 1. In this appendix we briefly explore the third and fourth of these problem areas.

STATIC GROUP COMPARISONS

An enduring issue in international research is that virtually all cross-cultural comparisons are based on "static group designs."[4] The difficulty with static group comparisons in international research is that subjects are not randomly assigned from a superordinate population to different levels of a treatment variable. In practice, it is impossible for cross-cultural researchers to avoid this methodological problem. This difficulty is further compounded by ill-defined notions of culture as an independent variable. As Malpass[5] has observed, "No matter what attribute of culture the investigator prefers to focus upon or to interpret as the causative variable, any other variable correlated with the alleged causative variable could potentially serve in an alternative explanation of a mean difference between two or more local populations." As a practical solution to this problem, Malpass recommends that investigators should attempt to obtain data on as many rival explanations as possible and then demonstrate that they are less plausible (by conducting post hoc statistical analyses, for example) than the investigator's favored interpretation.[6]

TRANSLATION AND STIMULUS EQUIVALENCE

Another issue in international research is that of translation and stimulus equivalence. Researchers need to be aware that problems may arise when translating concepts central to one culture into the language of another culture. Triandis and Brislin[7] note that the problem of translation has received a great deal of attention in the literature[8] and that translation problems should be "a starting point for research rather than a frustrating end to one's aspirations for data collection." Using methods such as the decentering technique,[9] which involves translating from the original to the target language and back again through several iterations, a researcher can test to see if there is any emic coloring of the concepts under investigation. If there are few differences between the original and target translation, then stimulus equivalence has been demonstrated.

Stimulus equivalence problems may also arise on a more subtle level when the researcher and target population speak the same language and national differences are less obvious (in the case, for example, of a U.S. researcher studying Australian managers). As with the emic-etic distinction, awareness of possible problems is a precondition for dealing with translation and stimulus equivalence problems.

SUMMARY

Despite the difficulties involved in international research, the need for research to assist managers and HRM practitioners remains. As Laurent[10] has pointed out:

> Many organizations are indeed confronted with the issues of managing human resources internationally. "Human Resource Managers" in such organizations are entitled to expect "Professors of HRM" to provide some useful insight on such processes. Yet these new international processes are so complex and so poorly defined and ill-understood at the moment that superficiality remains the mark of most treatments. . . . If the field of HRM is in a stage of adolescence, International HRM is still at the infancy stage.

These difficulties are not insurmountable, and as more managers and academics become aware of the many problems involved in international research, we should see progress in the field.

NOTES

1. H. Schollhammer, "Current Research in International and Comparative Management Issues," *Management International Review*, Vol. 15, No. 2–3 (1975) pp. 29–40.
2. See N. Adler, "Cross-Cultural Management Research: The Ostrich and the Trend," *Academy of Management Review*, Vol. 8 (1983) pp. 226–232.
3. Ibid.

4. See R. S. Bhagat and S. J. McQuaid, "Role of Subjective Culture in Organizations: A Review and Directions for Future Research," *Journal of Applied Psychology*, Vol. 67 (1982) pp. 653–685; D. T. Campbell and J. Stanley, *Experimental and Quasi-Experimental Design for Research* (Chicago: Rand-McNally, 1966); and R. S. Malpass, "Theory and Method in Cross-Cultural Psychology," *American Psychologist*, Vol. 32 (1977) pp. 1069–1079.

5. Malpass, "Theory and Method," p. 1071.

6. See L. Kelly and R. Worthley, "The Role of Culture in Comparative Management: A Cross-Cultural Perspective," *Academy of Management Journal*, Vol. 24 (1981) pp. 164–173; and P. J. Dowling and T. W. Nagel, "Nationality and Work Attitudes: A Study of Australian and American Business Majors," *Journal of Management*, Vol. 12 (1986) pp. 121–128 for further discussion on this point.

7. H. C. Triandis and R. W. Brislin, "Cross-Cultural Psychology," *American Psychologist*, Vol. 39 (1984) pp. 1006–1016.

8. See R. Brislin, *Translation: Applications and Research* (New York: Gardner Press, 1976) for a review of this literature.

9. O. Werner and D. Campbell, "Translating, Working Through Interpreters, and the Problem of Decentering," in *A Handbook of Method in Cultural Anthropology*, ed. R. Naroll and R. Cohen (New York: Natural History Press, 1970).

10. A. Laurent, "The Cross-Cultural Puzzle of International Human Resource Management," *Human Resource Management*, Vol. 25 (1986) pp. 91–102.

Glossary

As interest in international human resource management (IHRM) has grown, there are concepts and ideas that are new and different from traditional domestic HRM. A *lingua franca* or common language is developing to facilitate communication about these new and different ideas and concepts.

Unfortunately, it becomes increasingly difficult for HR professionals and academics new to the IHRM field to understand and/or participate in the dialogue. Also, if there is not precision and consistency in the terms and terminology, even those in the IHRM field can become confused.

This list of IHRM terms is neither exhaustive nor rigorously scientific. It does include, however, many more terms and concepts than were introduced in the chapters. As such it is a supplement as well as a glossary.

To avoid duplicative information, the definitions of the "terms" are grouped into major functional, subject areas as outlined in the following list:

This glossary was prepared by Patrick Morgan and is used here with his permission. According to the author:

"Three years ago I wrote down any term I heard or read that was unique to IHRM or relatively uncommon to traditional domestic HR operations. Approximately 250 terms were identified and a short definition and/or explanation for each term was developed.

"Additionally, a search was made for a print reference for each term. Approximately twenty personnel/HR/international management publications were reviewed to locate where more detail and perhaps additional reference material could be obtained on each term/subject. Print references for 75 percent of the terms have been located. References for most of the remaining terms exist, but frequently these are in publications or newsletters not widely available."

1. Planning

2. Recruitment and Selection

   a. Transfers/Repatriation

3. Training and Development

4. Labor Relations

5. Compensation and Benefits

   a. Administrative Issues

   b. Direct Compensation

   c. Indirect Compensation

   d. Benefit Plans

6. Travel

   a. Safety and Security

7. Operations

8. Government Relations

   a. Terms

   b. Visas

9. Dependent Relations

Planning

Assignment Status refers to whether an expatriate employee is accompanied by spouse and dependents on an international assignment. The types of assignment generally include:

Bachelor Status (see "Single Status")

Married Status the employee's spouse and dependent children are with the employee at the assignment location.

Family Status (as above)

Single Status the employee (married or not) does not have the spouse or dependents at the assignment location. Typically, only accommodation is provided.

Camp Status a special type of single status normally in remote locations, where employer provides messing, meals, laundry, etc., in a camp, in addition to accommodation.

Critical Path   a scheduling technique used to analyze a complex series of interconnected actions. The technique can be used to streamline
lengthy recruiting and processing activity for international assignments.
There are four broad employment approaches used internationally:

Ethnocentric   approach reflects home-country bias in selecting
candidates.

Geocentric   approach selects best candidates on a worldwide basis
without any bias to any particular country.

Polycentric   approach reflects a host-country bias in selecting
employees.

Regiocentric   approach selects best candidates on a regional basis
without bias to any particular country in that region.

Recruitment and Selection

Employee Categories   refers to the various types of employees. Some
of the examples of employee categories include:

Expatriate (Expat)   normally a professional/managerial employee
moved from one country to, and for employment in, another country.

Female Expatriate Manager   (as above)

Foreign Managers in the U.S.   an "expatriate" in the U.S. where
the U.S. is the host country and the manager's home country is
outside of the U.S.

Foreign National   frequently refers to the special case of a non-
U.S. citizen assigned to the United States as an expatriate.

Indigenous Employee   an alternate term for "local national/ national" not often used because of prejudice concerns.

Inpatriate   Foreign manager in the U.S. Can also be used for U.S.
expatriates returning to an assignment in the U.S.

International Staff   expatriate employees from home countries
other than the United States.

Local Hire   an employee hired in-country for work in that country.
Often has the special meaning that the employee is not a national of
that country, i.e., an American hired in country X for employment
in country X. However, the American's employment package is that
of a local national, not a U.S. expatriate.

Local National/National   an employee hired for employment in his or her own country.

PCN   Parent-country national.

HCN   Host-country national.

TCNs   Third-country nationals; often refers to expatriate employees who are not U.S. citizens, but citizens of a "third" country.

Cadre   (France) a categorization approach (similar to U.S. exempt/non-exempt) that is a major determinant on compensation and benefit programs.

Employment Agreement   (1) the written document defining the employer/employee relationship, (2) an arrangement for recruitment services with an external employment agency.

Employment Conditions   the compensation terms applicable to an assignment such as compensation uplifts, allowances, and paid absences.

Employment Contract   (see "Employment Agreement")

Host Country   The country in which the assignment/employment is performed.

International Selection   the process by which candidates for overseas assignments are identified and reviewed.

Zaibatsu   (Japan) family tradition of becoming an apprentice at a young age and learning from a master for a long period.

Transfers/Repatriation

Assignment   refers to the period of time an employee is an expatriate. Special types include:

Business Trip   normally for a short period, generally less than one month in duration.

Extended Business Trip   normally longer than one month and maybe up to two to three months' duration.

Foreign Assignment   additional emphasis that the assignment is at an overseas location rather than domestic.

Permanent Assignment in very few cases is an assignment truly "permanent." In most cases, an assignment of one or more years' duration is called "permanent."

Temporary Assignment refers to a shorter assignment period of longer than 2 to 3 months, but normally shorter than one year in duration.

Assignment Completion refers to the process of closing out an assignment and returning to the home country and/or point of origin.

Culture Shock the impact on employees and dependents when they arrive at a foreign location and begin to adjust and assimilate to the new location and its culture.

Expatriate Failure occurs when, for whatever reason, an expatriate fails to complete the anticipated assignment period.

Failure Rates turnover rate for employees.

Orientation the system of preparing employees and dependents for their overseas assignment.

Pre-departure Briefing or Counseling "Orientation" conducted prior to departure for an international assignment.

Processing all the activities necessary to arrange for an employee and dependents to depart and arrive at their assignment location. Included are such activities as passports, visas, household effects moving and storage, airline ticketing, vaccinations, etc.

Re-entry Shock the cultural readjustments necessary when a person returns to his or her home country.

Retrenchment a lay-off situation also referred to sometimes as redundancy.

Repatriation the process of return to the home country at completion of assignment.

Reverse Culture Shock (see "Re-entry Shock")

Safe Arrival Notification when employees/dependents have traveled to a remote assignment location, it is a common practice to advise family and friends in the home country of their safe arrival at the assignment location.

Training and Development

Cross-cultural Training process of sensitizing employees and dependents to the cultural differences between host- and home-country cultures.

Cultural Empathy an awareness of differences in culture and how those differences impact society and business.

Culturally-based Discrimination normally the result of a lack of cultural awareness and cultural empathy.

Cultural Assimilation training program to assist employees and dependents to live in a foreign culture.

Cultural Assimilator A programmed learning technique designed to expose members of one culture to some of the basic concepts, attitudes, role perceptions, customs, and values of another culture.

Cultural Orientation training program to familiarize employee and dependents on cultural issues.

Environmental Briefing training program on physical aspects of the location/country of assignment: climate, language, politics, etc.

Field Experience training program on living/working in a foreign environment.

Language Training preparation of expatriate employees and dependents for the host-country language.

Localization the process of replacing (normally higher cost) expatriates with local national employees.

Sensitivity Training training program to increase awareness of cultural issues.

Labor Relations

ACAS Advisory, Conciliation and Arbitration Service within the United Kingdom.

Arbitration a process whereby a neutral third party reviews employer and labor representative input on an item under dispute and renders a binding decision.

Conciliation a process whereby a neutral third party reviews employer and labor representative input on an item under dispute and attempts to have both parties agree to a compromise arrangement.

Labor Agreements terms and conditions agreed upon between an employer and unions that cover the company's operations.

Shunto spring wage offensive in Japan.

Taiso daily physical exercise routine practiced by many Japanese employers.

Pendulum Arbitration a process where an arbitrator has to choose between the last offer and the last claim by the parties. A compromise position is not permitted.

Tea Money (Australia) an allowance under a union agreement to provide money to allow the worker to buy refreshments (tea, etc.) for an approved rest break.

Compensation and Benefits

Administrative Issues

Balance-Sheet Approach is a compensation approach that identifies the gains and losses of a particular assignment due to taxes, cost-of-living, etc. and attempts to even out windfalls and shortfalls to achieve the desired incentive level.

Base Salary the salary the employee would receive for the same job in his or her own home country for a normal work week/month.

Base Work Week the length of a normal work week in the employee's home country, i.e., 5 days/40 hours, 6 days/48 hours, $4\frac{1}{2}$ days/$37\frac{1}{2}$ hours.

Bi-lateral Tax Agreement between the U.S. and a foreign government, which defines the personal income tax arrangements for U.S. expatriates assigned to that foreign country.

Bona-Fide Foreign Resident a term in the IRS tax code that relates to Section 911 and qualification for the Foreign Earned Income exclusion.

CPI Consumer Price Index.

Deferred Compensation   is earned but paid at a later date, through a variety of different arrangements, to reduce the income tax impact.

Devaluation   occurs when the value of a particular currency erodes against another currency.

Dual Employment Contracts   an employee resides and works in one country but travels to and works in another country. Two employment contracts cover this arrangement.

Exchange Rates   the value of a particular currency against another currency.

FIRP   the Foreign Income Information Returns Program is a system where the tax authorities of certain foreign nations agree to send IRS available information on the income earned in those nations by U.S. expatriates.

Foreign Earned Income Exclusion   provision of Section 911 of the IRS code allowing the deduction of certain income earned through employment overseas.

Foreign Housing Cost   when the employer pays or reimburses the housing costs for a U.S. expatriate, there is a tax implication.

Foreign Source Income   refers to income/compensation paid to an employee outside of the U.S.

Foreign Tax Credit   because U.S. citizens/residents are taxed on their worldwide income, expatriates often pay foreign tax and the U.S. government allows a credit against a U.S. tax liability.

Goods and Services   that portion of income that an employee spends on items such as food, medical, recreation, transportation.

Housing Exclusion   provisions of the IRS code relating to the manner in which housing costs are reported for tax purposes.

Hypothetical Tax   a theoretical income tax liability calculation based on assumptions on income, dependents, and deductions.

Incentives   the intended levels of additional compensation for undertaking an international assignment.

Market Basket   a selection of typical shopping items used to compare cost-of-living differences between host and home countries.

National Salary   for expatriates compensated in a host-country approach, often there is a need to develop a hypothetical home-country base salary for benefit plan purposes.

Overbase Compensation   additional payments over and above base salary to compensate for hardship, danger, extended work week, etc.

Physical Presence   relates to Section 911 of the IRS code and qualification for the foreign earned income exclusion.

Rest Day   in some countries, the compensation paid is for a 7-day period of which one or two days are paid rest days. In other countries, compensation is based on an "hours-worked" approach.

Section 401(K)   section of the IRS code that allows a salary reduction/deferred taxation arrangement.

Section 911   section of the IRS code that contains the foreign earned income provisions.

Spendable Income   that amount of net pay left after deductions for taxes and benefits.

Split Pay   where pay is delivered in a combination of host- and home-country currencies.

Split Payments   where compensation is delivered through a combination of delivery methods and/or currencies.

Split Payroll   where an employee is on two payrolls, with each paying only a portion of the salary, to reduce income taxes in the host country.

Tax Equalization   an expatriate is charged a hypothetical tax, and the employer then pays all other host- and home-country income taxes.

Tax Protection   employee pays host- and home-country taxes, and the employer reimburses excess taxes over agreed figure.

Thirteenth Month   compensation bonus-type arrangement where one month's extra salary is paid once a year.

U.S. Source Income   refers to income/compensation paid within the U.S.

VAT   (U.K., Europe) Value Added Tax, very similar to a sales tax.

Direct Compensation

Aguinaldo   (Mexico) a mandatory annual bonus of 15 to 30 days' pay, normally paid at Christmas time.

Antiquidates (Venezuela) a half a month bonus for service indemnity.

Cesantia (Venezuela) a half a month bonus for termination indemnity.

Completion Allowance additional compensation paid annually or at completion of assignment. Often used at remote hardship locations to encourage employees to remain for the full assignment period.

Convenios (Spain) annual salary increases.

Danger Pay at assignment locations where there is physical danger (war, etc.), often a special additional salary payment is made.

Expatriate Allowance payment to employee for undertaking an international assignment.

Expatriation Premium (as above)

Extended Workweek Premium to minimize the number of expatriate employees and their associated costs (i.e., instead of 3 expats working 40 hours a week, using 2 expats working 60 hours), often the normal scheduled workweek is increased and additional payment made.

Foreign Service Premium (see "Expatriate Allowance")

Hardship Allowance at locations that are less desirable and have more hardship, normally additional payment is made over and above the expatriation premium.

Salvencia (Venezuela) a 20-percent tax on temporary assignments.

Syndicato (Brazil) salary indexation tied to inflation rate.

Trienios (Spain) salary increases mandated by Spanish law at three-year intervals.

Uplifts payments often expressed as percents of base salary, to compensate employee for expatriation, hardship, danger, extended work week, and assignment completion.

Utilidates (Venezuela) two months' bonus.

Indirect Compensation

Assumed Shelter Cost in calculating a cost differential allowance often a hypothetical or assumed cost of housing in either or both the host and home country is used.

At-Post Education where dependent children can attend educational facilities at the assignment location.

Away-from-Post Education   when adequate schooling facilities are not available for dependent children at the assignment location, they frequently attend boarding schools in another country.

Cacabatro   (Algeria) vacation accrual plan.

Correspondence Allowance   where adequate schooling is not available at an assignment location, or a dependent child has special educational needs, correspondence courses are often used and reimbursed.

Cost Differential   a payment to compensate employee for differences in living costs (housing, goods, and services) between host and home countries.

Cost-of-Living Allowance   (see "Cost Differential")

Country of Origin   country from which employee originally departed and to which employee is returned at the end of assignment.

Education Allowance   payment to employee for increased education costs for dependent children.

Enroute Expenses   reimbursement for hotel, taxi, meals, porters, and other incidental costs associated with traveling between the home country and the assignment location.

Fringe Benefits   various forms of indirect compensation (also see "Perquisite").

Furnishing Allowance   reimbursement for cost of furnishing accommodations at the assignment location.

Home Leave   paid round-trip from assignment location to point and/or country of origin. Frequency often tied to degree of hardship at assignment location.

Household Effects   usually refers to home-country furniture which is usually stored in country of origin and a portion shipped to assignment location.

Housing Allowance   payment for accommodation costs at assignment location.

Living Allowance   (see "Cost Differential")

LVs   (U.K.) Luncheon Vouchers—has similarity to "food stamps" redeemable at restaurants.

Negative Differentials   situation where a calculation for an allowance such as a cost differential shows negative, i.e., costs of assignment location are less than home-country costs.

Per Diem Allowance   a flat daily allowance for travel expenses (see "Enroute Expenses").

Perqs   (see "Perquisite")

Perquisite   indirect compensation delivered in a form that has less income tax impact on employee and employer, i.e., company car.

Personal Effects   clothing and other personal items that are shipped, under a personal effects allowance, to the assignment location.

Point-of-Hire   location/city where the employee was hired.

Point-of-Origin   location to which employee is returned at end of assignment (see "Country of Origin").

R&R   at remote and hardship locations and/or where an employee is on an unaccompanied basis, provision is made to leave the assignment location for a short break.

Rest and Recreation Leave   (see "R&R")

Ramadan   one of the Hijrah calendar months in which Moslems fast from sunrise to sunset.

Relocation Allowance   paid to assist an employee relocate from home country to host country and also upon return.

Settling-In Allowance   reimbursement for living costs at the assignment location until the arrival of personal and household effects shipment and movement into permanent accommodation.

Severance Pay   in many countries at termination, a redundancy or final separation payment is required by law.

Travel Time   often a number of days' pay is allowed for travel to and from the assignment location from the home country.

Utilities Allowance   sometimes a payment, separate from the housing allowance, is made for local utility costs; water, power, sewage, telephone, gas.

Benefit Plans

Annuity Plan   a retirement plan that provides payment of normally a fixed amount on a monthly, quarterly, or annual basis.

Casoran   (Algeria) social insurance program.

Dirigenti   (Italy) a social insurance contribution for managers.

GOSI   (Saudi Arabia) a social insurance program.

Long Service Leave   (Australia) after a period of service with an employer (approximately 10 to 15 years), the employee is entitled to a paid leave of absence of approximately 3 to 6 months.

Provident Fund   a retirement savings type plan common to many countries.

Savings Plans   a retirement type plan where the employer withholds and "saves" a portion of the employee's pay.

Superannuation   a retirement type plan common to many countries.

Totalization Agreement   between the U.S. government and another foreign government covers arrangements on social security contributions and payments for their respective nationals in the other country.

War Risk Insurance   a special type of corporate insurance used when other insurance coverage lapses because of declared or undeclared war.

Travel

Airport Tax   some international airports impose an airport or departure tax for people departing the country.

ETA/ETD   estimated time of arrival; estimated time of departure.

Excess Baggage   that amount over and above the airline's "free" accompanied baggage allowance—often on weight basis.

FCU   Foreign Currency Unit system used by airlines to price tickets in different international currencies.

Health Certificate   used to record vaccinations against certain infectious diseases such as cholera, typhoid, smallpox.

Jet Lag   body clock disorientation caused by crossing time zones.

MCO   Miscellaneous Charges Order. These are credit notes issued by airlines.

Meet and Greet   for the first-time arrivals at foreign airports, often a company representative is available at the airport to assist in customs and immigration formalities.

NTSC   television transmission and reception format used in the U.S.

PAL   television transmission and reception format used in many European countries.

SECAM   television transmission and reception format used in some European countries.

Shot Book   (see "Health Certificate")

Transit Accommodations   where the assignment location is remote from a large urban area/international airport, it may be necessary to stay overnight, continuing travel the next day.

Vaccination Book   (see "Health Certificate")

Safety and Security

Contingency Plans   back-up plans of action in case of emergency.

Emergency Plans   usually cover protection of expatriate employees, dependents, and company property/records in case of civil disorder or national disaster.

Medivac   the evacuation of a sick employee and/or dependent from the assignment location to another location/country for emergency medical treatment.

Milton's   disinfectant solution used to treat fruit and vegetables of questionable origin and/or cleanliness.

Survival Kit   at the assignment location, pending the arrival of household and personal effects shipments, interim equipment is supplied.

Terrorism   includes concerns on travel and security at the assignment location.

Operations

Dating Systems   around the world, there are a variety of systems in use. Some countries use month/day/year, others use day/month/year. To avoid confusion as to whether 2/3/89 is February or March, many internationalists always use at least three alpha characters to eliminate confusion about the month, i.e., "3 FEB '89."

Global   a corporation offering uniform products worldwide because it's in a truly global industry. Also called a *transnational corporation.*

Gregorian Calendar   is the traditional 12-month, January through December, solar calendar.

Hijrah Calendar   an 11-month calendar used in the Middle East Islamic countries which is based on a lunar, rather than solar calendar; 1987 in the Gregorian calendar is approximately the year 1407 in the Hijrah calendar.

Joint Venture   an arrangement where a number of different companies associate to form a new legal entity to pursue or perform a specific objective. In addition to pooling resources, it allows the participating companies to spread the risk.

MNC or MNE   multinational corporation or multinational enterprise. A corporation operating facilities in several different countries of the world. Also called an *international firm.*

Government Relations

Terms

Consularization   process whereby a consular office endorses a document with a stamp attesting to the translation and/or validity of a document, i.e., college degree.

CONUS   the continental United States, i.e., the 48 contiguous states excluding Hawaii and Alaska.

Fiscal Clearance   prior to a foreign resident departing a host country, many countries require a document issued by the local Tax and/or Treasury department verifying that host-country income taxes have been paid.

Foreign Corrupt Practices Act   the U.S. Foreign Corrupt Practices Act of 1977 prohibits payments to foreign government officials.

International Driving Permit   Approximately 160 countries honor the 1949 United Nations Convention on Road Traffic and agree that a permit issued in the home country is valid to drive in the host country.

Labor Court   in some countries, there are special courts established to handle employee complaints on local labor law violations.

Labor Law   in some countries, the law applicable to employees has been codified into a consolidated labor law.

MOL   in many countries this is the Ministry of Labor (Labour).

Notarization   process whereby an authorized person attests to and confirms the validity of a document or signature.

Police Clearance   document required by many countries, prior to issuing the visa, that confirms employee does not have criminal record in the place of previous residence.

Quitas Fiscal   (Algeria) a clearance required to leave the country (see "Fiscal Clearance").

Visas

In *overseas* countries, there are a variety of *visa* types and formalities as follows:

Dependent Visa   permits a family to accompany or join employee in country of assignment.

Exit Visa   permits a foreign resident to leave the host country.

Exit/Re-entry Visa   permits a foreign resident to leave and then re-enter the host country.

Landed Immigrant   a permanent residence visa for Canada.

Multiple-Entry Visa   permits multiple entries to a country without the need to obtain a new visa each visit.

Residency Visa   permits entry and allows person to take up permanent residency in the country.

Single-Entry Visa   permits a one-time entry into a country. Another visa is required for any further visits.

Work Permit   authorizes paid employment in a country.

Work Visa   authorizes entry into a country to take up paid employment.

U.S. visa and immigration formalities involve a number of specialized terms as follows:

B-1 Visa   visitor on business visa.

F-1 Visa   student visa.

Green Card/Green Card Holder   U.S. resident alien.

H-1 Visa   temporary worker of distinguished merit and ability.

I-94 Form   record of entry into the U.S. issued at port of arrival and attached to the passport.

Immigrant Visa   a visa issued for entrance for permanent residence in the U.S.A.

INS   Immigration and Naturalization Service.

IRCA   Immigration Reform and Control Act of 1986.

J-1 Visa   exchange visitor.

L-1 Visa   intra-company transfer.

Non-Immigrant Visa   a visa issued for entrance and temporary residence in the U.S.

Resident Alien   an individual previously admitted on an immigrant visa and who is now a permanent resident of the U.S.

Visa Reference   six categories of priority for issuance of a U.S. immigrant visa.

White Book   issued to green card holders going outside the U.S. on an international assignment to document intent to return and remain as U.S. resident aliens.

Dependent Relations

Dependents   the spouse and children of the expatriate employee.

Pets   there are various regulations on the transportation and entry of pets into foreign countries.

Servants   household help at the assignment location.

Index